GREAT-POWER COMPETITION AND CONFLICT IN
AFRICA

MARTA KEPE | ELINA TREYGER | CHRISTIAN CURRIDEN

RAPHAEL S. COHEN | KURT KLEIN

ASHLEY L. RHOADES | ERIK SCHUH | NATHAN VEST

RAND
CORPORATION

For more information on this publication, visit **www.rand.org/t/RRA969-2**.

About RAND

The RAND Corporation is a research organization that develops solutions to public policy challenges to help make communities throughout the world safer and more secure, healthier and more prosperous. RAND is nonprofit, nonpartisan, and committed to the public interest. To learn more about RAND, visit www.rand.org.

Research Integrity

Our mission to help improve policy and decisionmaking through research and analysis is enabled through our core values of quality and objectivity and our unwavering commitment to the highest level of integrity and ethical behavior. To help ensure our research and analysis are rigorous, objective, and nonpartisan, we subject our research publications to a robust and exacting quality-assurance process; avoid both the appearance and reality of financial and other conflicts of interest through staff training, project screening, and a policy of mandatory disclosure; and pursue transparency in our research engagements through our commitment to the open publication of our research findings and recommendations, disclosure of the source of funding of published research, and policies to ensure intellectual independence. For more information, visit www.rand.org/about/research-integrity.

RAND's publications do not necessarily reflect the opinions of its research clients and sponsors.

Published by the RAND Corporation, Santa Monica, Calif.
© 2023 RAND Corporation
RAND® is a registered trademark.

Library of Congress Cataloging-in-Publication Data is available for this publication.

ISBN: 978-1-9774-1126-6

Cover: fonikum/DigitalVision Vectors; masterSergeant/iStock/Getty Images Plus.

Limited Print and Electronic Distribution Rights

About This Report

Although much of the U.S. Department of Defense's attention is focused on the two primary theaters of concern—the Indo-Pacific and, to a lesser extent, Europe—China and Russia are global powers, and the challenges they pose to international security are therefore global as well. This report is part of a series of reports that look at U.S.-China and U.S.-Russia competition outside those two primary theaters of concern; this report focuses on competition in Africa. The other reports in this series are as follows:

- Raphael S. Cohen, Elina Treyger, Irina A. Chindea, Christian Curriden, Kristen Gunness, Khrystyna Holynska, Marta Kepe, Kurt Klein, Ashley L. Rhoades, and Nathan Vest, *Great-Power Competition and Conflict in the 21st Century Outside the Indo-Pacific and Europe*, Santa Monica, Calif.: RAND Corporation, RR-A969-1, 2023
- Ashley L. Rhoades, Elina Treyger, Nathan Vest, Christian Curriden, Brad A. Bemish, Irina A. Chindea, Raphael S. Cohen, Jessica Giffin, and Kurt Klein, *Great Power Competition and Conflict in the Middle East*, Santa Monica, Calif.: RAND Corporation, RR-A969-3, 2023
- Irina A. Chindea, Elina Treyger, Raphael S. Cohen, Christian Curriden, Kurt Klein, Carlos Sanchez, Holly Gramkow, and Khrystyna Holynska, *Great-Power Competition and Conflict in Latin America*, Santa Monica, Calif.: RAND Corporation, RR-A969-4, 2023.

Note that these closely related volumes share some material, including descriptions, figures, and tables.

The authors of this report examine where and how the United States, China, and Russia are competing for influence; where and why competition might turn into conflict; what form conflict might take; and the implications for the U.S. government at large, the joint force, and the Department of the Air Force in particular. This research was completed in September 2021, just after the Taliban's takeover of Afghanistan and before the 2022 Russian invasion of Ukraine. The report has not been subsequently revised.

RAND is committed to ethical and respectful treatment of RAND research participants and complies with all applicable laws and regulations, including the Federal Policy for the Protection of Human Subjects, also known as the "Common Rule." The research described in this report was screened and, if necessary, reviewed by RAND's Human Subjects Protection Committee, which serves as RAND's institutional review board charged with ensuring the ethical treatment of individuals who are participants in RAND projects through observation, interaction, or use of data about them. RAND's Federalwide Assurance (FWA) for the Protection of Human Subjects (FWA00003425, effective until February 18, 2026) serves as our assurance of compliance with federal regulations. The views of the anonymous interviewees are solely their own and do not represent the official policy or position of the Department of Defense or the U.S. government.

The research reported here was commissioned by Headquarters Air Force A5S and conducted within the Strategy and Doctrine Program of RAND Project AIR FORCE as part of a fiscal year 2021 project, "Role of the Air Force in Regional Great Power Competition."

RAND Project AIR FORCE

RAND Project AIR FORCE (PAF), a division of the RAND Corporation, is the Department of the Air Force's (DAF's) federally funded research and development center for studies and analyses, supporting both the United States Air Force and the United States Space Force. PAF provides the DAF with independent analyses of policy alternatives affecting the development, employment, combat readiness, and support of current and future air, space, and cyber forces. Research is conducted in four programs: Strategy and Doctrine; Force Modernization and Employment; Resource Management; and Workforce, Development, and Health. The research reported here was prepared under contract FA7014-16-D-1000.

Additional information about PAF is available on our website:
www.rand.org/paf/

This report documents work originally shared with the DAF on October 14, 2021. The draft report, issued on October 28, 2021, was reviewed by formal peer reviewers and DAF subject-matter experts.

Acknowledgments

Like many projects, this series would not have been possible without the contributions of many individuals. First, we would like to thank Maj Gen Rodney Lewis, Brig Gen Mark Pye, LeeAnn Borman, Gerald Sohan, and the other members of Headquarters Air Force A5S and the Air Force Global Strike Command A5/8 for their support and guidance. We would also like to thank the Project AIR FORCE leadership, Stacie Pettyjohn, Bonny Lin, and Bryan Frederick for their feedback on earlier iterations of this work. In addition, we would like to acknowledge the experts who volunteered their time for interviews for this project. Although human subjects protections do not allow us to cite them by name, we found their insights invaluable. We also owe a special debt of gratitude to our U.S. Air Force fellows who worked on compiling some of the data that undergirded our competition analysis: Capt Erik Schuh, Col Brad Bemish, Maj Holly Gramkow, MSgt Carlos Sanchez, and Jessica Giffin. We would like to thank our peer reviewers, Adam Grissom and Michael Shurkin, for their thoughtful comments on a previous draft. Lastly, we would also like to thank our editor, Allison Kerns, for further refining the report.

Summary

Issue

The United States is in the midst of a shift in strategic focus from countering terrorism to countering China and Russia in the Indo-Pacific and Europe. Africa, a location for great-power competition not only during the Cold War but also in previous centuries, is yet again summoning more interest from the United States' great-power competitors—China and Russia. This report—part of a four-volume series—explores where and how the United States, China, and Russia are competing for influence in Africa; what kinds of interests they have in the continent; where and why competition might turn into conflict; what form that conflict might take; and what implications the findings have for the U.S. government at large, the joint force, and the Department of the Air Force in particular.[1]

Approach

The project team employed a multi-method approach. First, it developed a unique data set of 16 variables to measure diplomatic, informational, military, and economic potential for great-power competition in secondary theaters. Second, it combined the assessment of competition potential with measures of conflict potential to identify cases with the greatest theoretical chances for future great-power involvement in conflicts in Africa. Finally, it used qualitative methods—including interviews with subject-matter experts and analysis of primary and secondary source materials—to explore what conflict in Africa might look like and what the implications might be for the U.S. government at large, the joint force, and the Department of the Air Force in particular.

Key Findings

Although much of the United States' strategic focus has been on the Indo-Pacific and, to a lesser extent, Europe (as was the case during the Cold War), competition potential in secondary theaters, including Africa, is intensifying as well. During the Cold War, competition erupted into numerous proxy wars and interventions, with the United States and its allies backing one side and the Soviet Union and its allies backing the other. The analysis in this report suggests that even potentially intense competition in very conflict-prone countries is unlikely to inaugurate a return to Cold War–style proxy wars and military interventions but may present different challenges.

---

[1] Note that these closely related volumes share some material, including descriptions, figures, and tables.

The analysis yielded the following findings:

- Potential for competition in Africa is focused in the largest economies, countries with natural resources, and strategically important locations.
- The United States remains a dominant aid donor and military actor in Africa, but China's and Russia's influence-seeking there is growing.
- Great powers have limited motivations for involvement in military conflicts in Africa.
- Great-power competition in Africa may not be a zero-sum game.
- In some of the most-plausible conflict scenarios, the United States, China, and Russia are more likely to support the same actors rather than opposing sides.
- Conflicts with great-power involvement in Africa are likely to involve distinct challenges of deconfliction, harassment, and behind-the-scenes political contests.

Recommendations

In anticipation of the continuation and growth of the interests of the three great powers and other external actors in Africa, there are several ways that the United States can build a stronger position in the continent to be a viable competitor and position itself to be able to support effective military engagements, if necessary. This analysis yields several recommendations for the U.S. government, the joint force, and the Department of the Air Force in particular.

Recommendations for the U.S. Government

- Recognize that U.S. interests in Africa require a long-term vision for the region.
- Maintain long-term relations with key African partners.

Recommendations for the Joint Force

- Maintain and improve access to military and dual-use infrastructure.
- Maintain working relations with allies and partners.

Recommendations for the Department of the Air Force

- Prepare for increased and potentially shifting demand for U.S. Air Force assets. The U.S. Air Force may expect an increased demand for its airborne intelligence, surveillance, and reconnaissance assets; air mobility support capabilities; and air defense, aerial firepower, and precision strike capabilities—and in more locations across the continent.
- Prepare for multifaceted operational challenges, including deconfliction and harassment, in future conflicts that may involve China and Russia. The U.S. Air Force may

consider training airspace managers; helping develop airstrips; leveraging allied and partner resources in the region; and continuing to invest in its ability to ensure communications and data exchange with other U.S. military service representatives and local, regional, and European partners in Africa.

Contents

Figures and Tables

Figures

Tables

CHAPTER ONE

Introduction

At first glance, Africa does not hold a top position on the international security agendas of the United States, China, or Russia. However, all three competing powers have significant geostrategic, economic, or security interests in the continent. Historically, the convergence of great-power interests in Africa has often resulted in conflict. Although great-power interests and competition between the United States and its two near-peer rivals in Africa today may not be as intense as in Europe or the Indo-Pacific—or even as in Africa during the Cold War— the great powers might still become entangled in conflicts on the continent. In this report, we explore the potential for competition in Africa among the United States, China, and Russia, based on their influence-seeking activity across the diplomatic, informational, military, and economic domains, and the potential for the three countries to become involved in internal conflicts in the region. The report is part of a four-volume series examining the potential for competition and conflict among the great powers in secondary theaters (sometimes referred to as *regions* in this report).[1]

For the purposes of this report, we define the region of Africa as the boundaries of the area of responsibility for U.S. Africa Command (AFRICOM), excluding all island countries except for Madagascar (the largest one) and focusing our attention on mainland Africa.

This introductory chapter provides an overview of the interests and objectives of the three great powers in Africa; the past, present, and future prospects for great powers to become involved in internal conflicts on the continent; and our methodology to tackle the research questions addressed in this report.

---

[1] Note that these closely related volumes share some material, including descriptions, figures, and tables. See Raphael S. Cohen, Elina Treyger, Irina A. Chindea, Christian Curriden, Kristen Gunness, Khrystyna Holynska, Marta Kepe, Kurt Klein, Ashley L. Rhoades, and Nathan Vest, *Great-Power Competition and Conflict in the 21st Century Outside the Indo-Pacific and Europe*, Santa Monica, Calif.: RAND Corporation, RR-A969-1, 2023; Ashley L. Rhoades, Elina Treyger, Nathan Vest, Christian Curriden, Brad A. Bemish, Irina A. Chindea, Raphael S. Cohen, Jessica Giffin, and Kurt Klein, *Great-Power Competition and Conflict in the Middle East*, Santa Monica, Calif.: RAND Corporation, RR-A969-3, 2023; and Irina A. Chindea, Elina Treyger, Raphael S. Cohen, Christian Curriden, Kurt Klein, Carlos Sanchez, Holly Gramkow, and Khrystyna Holynska, *Great-Power Competition and Conflict in Latin America*, Santa Monica, Calif.: RAND Corporation, RR-A969-4, 2023.

Overview of the United States', China's, and Russia's Interests in Africa

U.S. objectives in Africa have been focused on countering terrorism, supporting stability, and providing aid and assistance.[2] More broadly, over the years, the United States has sought to support democracy, governance, and human rights; promote peace, security, and stability; maintain trade and commerce interests, particularly in the energy field; and support Africa's development.[3] U.S. economic interests in Africa are modest compared with such interests in other regions of the world. From a global perspective, U.S. trade volume with Africa is small and has been hovering between 1.5 and 2 percent of U.S. global trade since 2007.[4] In addition, U.S. energy imports from Africa are modest compared with those from other regions and have declined over time; for example, imports of crude oil and crude oil products dropped by one-third between 2006 and 2021, reflecting the overall fall in U.S. global crude oil imports.[5] Only 11 percent of U.S. mineral imports in 2019 came from Africa.[6] So, although the United States and U.S. companies are interested in African resources, the United States is not committing significant resources to promoting its enterprises in Africa, and U.S. businesses are underinvesting in the continent.[7]

The United States lacks a comprehensive vision for Africa and tends to approach it as a source of problems or a project that needs to be solved rather than as a prized strategic area of influence.[8] Although the United States has adopted several major policies toward the region over the years,[9] experts often point to a relative absence of a broader unified vision for U.S.-Africa relations.[10] That said, the United States does continue to be concerned about the instability in Africa potentially spilling over to a wider area and resulting in adverse effects

---

[2] Retired U.S. military officer previously stationed in Africa, interview with the authors, July 2021.

[3] Bureau of African Affairs, "Our Mission," webpage, U.S. Department of State, undated; and Joseph R. Biden, Jr., *Interim National Security Strategic Guidance*, Washington, D.C.: White House, March 2021.

[4] U.S. Census Bureau, "U.S. Trade in Goods by Country," webpage, undated, full data set for all countries from 2021.

[5] U.S. Energy Information Administration, "U.S. Total Crude Oil and Products Imports," webpage, last updated June 2021.

[6] South Africa was the only single African country among the top ten exporters of minerals to the United States that year (World Integrated Trade Solution, "United States Minerals Imports by Country and Region in US$ Thousand 2019," webpage, undated-c).

[7] Grant T. Harris, "Why Africa Matters to US National Security," Atlantic Council, May 25, 2017.

[8] Africa and special operations researcher, interview with the authors, July 2021.

[9] Such policies include the African Growth and Opportunity Act, the Millennium Challenge Corporation, the U.S.-African Leaders Summit, the U.S. International Development Finance Corporation, and the U.S.-Africa strategy adopted during the Trump administration.

[10] Former U.S. Department of State official, interview with the authors, July 2021.

on the global economy and security.[11] This is reflected by U.S. engagement in Africa, detailed in Chapter Two.

U.S. military engagement in Africa tends to be focused on emergencies, and U.S. forces often take the role of a fire brigade.[12] The United States' security and military interests in Africa have been dominated by counterterrorism, although the country also has been interested in helping reduce human-trafficking, transnational crime, and the illegal arms trade.[13] To advance these goals, the United States seeks to enhance partner nations' military capacities rather than opt for large-scale deployments.[14] There have been some fluctuations in the degree of U.S. engagement in Africa over the past several years. During President Donald Trump's administration, there was discussion of "optimization" of the U.S. forces in Africa, combined with a refocus from counterterrorism to great-power competition.[15] Most recently, there has been increased interest from the U.S. government, AFRICOM Commander Gen. Stephen Townsend, and the U.S. defense expert community in Africa as an area with increasing great-power competition.[16]

Meanwhile, China places great importance on Africa as a strategic long-term bet.[17] Over the next few decades, Beijing expects the continent to become one of the most economically dynamic places on earth and hopes to both facilitate and benefit from this rise.[18] Building the

---

[11] Retired U.S. military officer previously stationed in Africa, interview with the authors, July 2021; and Michael Shurkin, "The Good and Bad of the Trump Administration's New Africa Strategy," *The Hill*, December 20, 2018.

[12] Retired U.S. military officer previously stationed in Africa, interview with the authors, July 2021.

[13] U.S. Department of Defense (DoD), *Summary of the 2018 National Defense Strategy of the United States of America: Sharpening the American Military's Competitive Edge*, Washington, D.C., 2018a.

[14] In 2016, former AFRICOM Commander Gen. David M. Rodriguez said, "Relatively small but wise investments in African security institutions today offer disproportionate benefits to Africa, Europe, and the United States in the future, creating mutual opportunities and reducing the risks of destabilization, radicalization, and persistent conflict" (David M. Rodriguez, general, U.S. Army, "United States Africa Command 2016 Posture Statement," statement before the Senate Armed Services Committee, March 8, 2016).

[15] Marcus Hicks, Kyle Atwell, and Dan Collini, "Great-Power Competition Is Coming to Africa," *Foreign Affairs*, March 4, 2021.

[16] Jim Garamone, "Commander Says Africa Is Too Important for Americans to Ignore," *DoD News*, April 21, 2021; Associated Press, "China's Africa Outreach Poses Growing Threat, US General Warns," *Voice of America*, May 6, 2021; and Robbie Gramer, "U.S. Congress Moves to Restrain Pentagon over Africa Drawdown Plans," *Foreign Policy*, March 4, 2020.

[17] Zhao Chenguang [赵晨光], "America's 'New Africa Policy': Changes and Holdovers" ["美国'新非洲战略': 变与不变"], China Institute of International Studies [中国国际问题研究院], November 7, 2019.

[18] Ma Hanzhi [马汉智], "Africa Continental Free Trade Agreement Is Worth Looking Forward To" ["非洲自贸区故事值得期待"], China Institute of International Studies [中国国际问题研究院], December 29, 2020b; Wan Lingying [万玲英], "Changes and Prospects of Africa's International Position" ["非洲国际地位的变化及前景"], China Institute of International Studies [中国国际问题研究院], June 4, 2013; and Ruan Zongze [阮宗泽], "Winning the Next 10 Years: China's Multi-Strongpoint Diplomacy" ["赢得下一个十年: 中国塑造多支点外交"], China Institute of International Studies [中国国际问题研究院], July 23, 2013.

logistical and internet technology links that connect African nations to one another and to China provides an opportunity for China to productively employ its vast reserves of capital and industrial overcapacity, stimulates growth, and helps ensure that African nations are well disposed to Chinese firms and diplomats.[19] China seeks to further help its businesses benefit from Africa's rise by working with African governments to build a welcoming regulatory environment, especially in special economic zones designed for Chinese firms.[20]

Africa is also important to China as a source of natural resources. Such countries as Angola, Libya, and the Republic of the Congo are important energy exporters whose strategic significance is heightened by Beijing's desire to diversify its oil suppliers.[21] China also imports rare and strategically significant minerals predominantly from African states—for example, chromium from South Africa; titanium from Mozambique; cobalt from the Democratic Republic of the Congo (DRC); niobium, tantalum, and vanadium ore from Nigeria; and uranium from Namibia.[22]

In addition to the economic benefits that China hopes to reap from Africa, Beijing seeks to leverage the continent's many votes at the United Nations (UN) and other international forums with the aim of making the institutions of international governance more amenable to Beijing's interests.[23] China's investments in Africa, compared with those of the United States, often come with fewer political constraints, so China does not have the same limitations on investing in countries with poor human rights records. African partners often side with China on human rights issues at the UN and have sometimes supported China's attempts to dodge criticism for its human rights record and weaken international norms on human rights protections. For example, at the UN, several African governments have sided with China's policies toward its Uighur minority and have opposed the "practice of politicizing human rights issues."[24]

---

[19] Huang Yupei [黄玉沛], "Building a Sino-African 'Digital Silk Road': Opportunities, Challenges, and Options for Moving Forward" ["中非共建 '数字丝绸之路': 机遇、挑战与路径选择"], China Institute of International Studies [中国国际问题研究院], August 23, 2019; Ma, 2020b; and Jiayi Zhou, Karl Hallding, and Guoyi Han, "The Trouble with China's 'One Belt One Road' Strategy," *The Diplomat*, June 26, 2015.

[20] Huang Yupei [黄玉沛], "China-Africa Economic Cooperation Zones: Challenges and Means for Deepening Cooperation" ["中非经贸合作区建设: 挑战与深化路径"], China Institute of International Studies [中国国际问题研究院], July 25, 2018.

[21] Observatory of Economic Complexity, "China," webpage, undated-a; and Matthew T. Page, *The Intersection of China's Commercial Interests and Nigeria's Conflict Landscape*, Washington, D.C.: United States Institute of Peace, September 1, 2018, pp. 5–6.

[22] Observatory of Economic Complexity, undated-a.

[23] Zhang Ying [张颖], "China's Africa Diplomacy: Concepts and Practice" ["中国对非洲外交: 理念与实践"], China Institute of International Studies [中国国际问题研究院], January 22, 2018.

[24] Roie Yellinek and Elizabeth Chen, "The '22 vs. 50' Diplomatic Split Between the West and China over Xinjiang and Human Rights," *China Brief*, Vol. 19, No. 22, December 31, 2019.

China's grand plans to capitalize on Africa's rise are endangered by instability on the continent.[25] Conflict not only disrupts trade, endangers investments, and imperils Chinese citizens but also facilitates the growth of international terror organizations, such as the Islamic State. Such groups are of particular concern to Beijing because of their global ambitions and the possibility that their fighters or ideas could spread and destabilize countries on China's border, or even inside China's restive western regions.[26]

Finally, Russia's primary interests in Africa are geostrategic and economic. Africa is of increasing geopolitical importance for Russia as it seeks to extend its influence as a global power and diversify its international allies and partners following the souring of its relations with Europe and the United States, particularly since the beginning of the 2014 Russia-Ukraine conflict. This diversification of diplomatic and economic relations is a means of escaping future international isolation in international relations, including at the UN Security Council, and boosting Russia's trade relations in the face of international sanctions and falling oil prices. Russia is also interested in Africa because of its location relative to North Atlantic Treaty Organization (NATO) territory. Thus, Russia's strategic documents are more focused on stability in North Africa, a region that links Africa to Europe and the Middle East, as well as a region where access to infrastructure locations could help Russia influence security matters on NATO's southern border.[27] At the same time, Russia is increasingly interested in the South Atlantic and Indian oceans for ensuring access to sea lines of communication for its commercial shipping companies and as an opportunity to complicate the maritime freedom of movement of the United States and its allies and partners. Moreover, Africa is another region where Moscow seeks to undermine the Western international world order and the influence of the United States and its Western allies while portraying itself as a pragmatic, fair, and responsible strategic partner and power broker.[28] Russia does not attempt to sell a specific governance model as an alternative to that of the West. Instead, it seeks opportunities to undermine the governance and business models offered by the United States and the West as inequitable or morally corrupt.[29]

---

[25] Wang Hongyi [王洪一], "The Influence of New Security Challenges in Africa on Sino-African Cooperation" ["非洲安全新挑战及其对中非合作的影响"], China Institute of International Studies [中国国际问题研究院], July 25, 2018.

[26] Dong Manyuan [董漫远], "The Interregional Influence and Course of the Libyan Proxy War" ["利比亚代理人战争的跨地区影响及走向"], China Institute of International Studies [中国国际问题研究院], July 23, 2020; and Dong Manyuan [董漫远], "The Influence and Outlook for ISIS's Rise" ["'伊斯兰国'崛起的影响及前景"], China Institute of International Studies [中国国际问题研究院], October 14, 2014.

[27] Ministry of Foreign Affairs of the Russian Federation, "Foreign Policy Concept of the Russian Federation," Moscow, December 1, 2016.

[28] Raphael S. Cohen, Marta Kepe, Nathan Beauchamp-Mustafaga, Asha Clark, Kit Conn, Michelle Grisé, Roby Valiaveedu, and Nathan Vest, *Evaluating the Prospects for Great Power Cooperation in the Global Commons*, Santa Monica, Calif.: RAND Corporation, RR-A597-4, 2023.

[29] Joseph Siegle, "Russia's Strategic Goals in Africa," Africa Center for Strategic Studies, May 6, 2021.

Russia also has strong, yet underdeveloped, economic interests in the continent. Russia's strategic documents and Russian authors portray Africa as an area of future economic growth, second only to the Asia-Pacific region.[30] Russia's primary interest is to ensure Russian companies' access to and involvement in key economic sectors, such as energy (including nuclear power) and mineral resources, critical infrastructure, and space. Doing so also would help diversify Russia's trading partners and the clientele of Russia's government-linked large businesses. Meanwhile, its trade and economic relations have been traditionally more developed with countries in North and Southern Africa—Algeria, Morocco, Tunisia, and South Africa.[31]

The Past, Present, and Future of Great-Power Involvement in Conflicts in Africa: An Overview

During the Cold War, Africa was a particularly active area where the competition between the United States and the Soviet Union turned to conflict. The period of decolonization of African states and the emergence of competing independence movements and of political competition provided opportunities for external powers to apply various means of influence, including supporting local actors in conflicts.[32] The ideological underpinnings of the Cold War provided the motivation for the two rival powers to seize those ample opportunities. In the wars of national liberation in Africa, the Soviet Union saw opportunities to spread communist influence; in the words of Nikita Khrushchev, as Africa was getting rid of "imperialist" rule, there was "no force on earth now able to prevent the people of more and more countries from advancing to socialism."[33] As Soviet involvement in conflicts across the developing world, including Africa, grew, so did the U.S. view that the spread of Soviet influence and the political forces it supported must be stopped and rolled back.[34] Although the United States welcomed the break-up of European empires in Africa since the 1940s to some extent, it was also wary of the potential of the newly independent countries to gravitate toward communism—and thus was led to support political movements opposed to kin ideologies.[35]

[30] Anna Sysoeva and Ilya Kabanov, "Kak Rossii I EAES Obezpecit Svoyi Interesi V Afrike Odnim Klikom" ["How Russia and the EAEU Secure Their Interests in Africa with One Click"], Russian International Affairs Council, August 29, 2019.

[31] Kristina Miroshnichenko and Irina Mandrykina, "Rossiya–Afrika: Stariye Druzya I Perspektivniye Partneri" ["Russia–Africa: Old Friends and Promising Partners"], TASS, February 4, 2021.

[32] Seyom Brown, "Purposes and Pitfalls of War by Proxy: A Systemic Analysis," *Small Wars and Insurgencies*, Vol. 27, No. 2, 2016.

[33] Deborah Welch Larson, *Anatomy of Mistrust: U.S.-Soviet Relations During the Cold War*, Ithaca, N.Y.: Cornell University Press, 1997.

[34] See, for example, Roger E. Kanet, "The Superpower Quest for Empire: The Cold War and Soviet Support for 'Wars of National Liberation,'" *Cold War History*, Vol. 6, No. 3, 2006, pp. 331–335.

[35] Odd Arne Westad, *The Global War: Third World Interventions and the Making of Our Times*, New York: Cambridge University Press, 2005, p. 27.

As a result, in Africa, just as across much of the developing world, the two rival superpowers supported coups, helped client governments put down rebellions, and backed opposing claimants to political power in violent struggles.[36] For example, the United States and the Soviet Union backed opposing sides in the Ethiopia-Somalia war, or the so-called Ogden War, in 1977–1978. There, the Soviet Union provided crucial support to Ethiopia in the form of military supplies and Soviet advisers, as well as by supporting soldiers deployed by its ally Cuba. The Soviet intervention was largely motivated by long-term promotion of Marxist ideology, because the new Ethiopian government was modeled on Marxist-Leninist ideology and the Russian Revolution; the Soviet engagement in the Horn of Africa more broadly was viewed by Moscow's decisionmakers as establishing Moscow as a major power in Africa and globally and offering an alternative to the United States and Western influence.[37] Meanwhile, the United States supported the opposing side—Somalia. In particular, Washington opposed the Soviet- and Cuba-supported Ethiopian forces and used the axing of Somalia-Soviet military cooperation as an opportunity to do so.[38] During Angola's civil war in 1975, which was fought mainly along ethnic and political lines, the United States supported the National Front for the Liberation of Angola; the Soviet Union supported the Popular Movement for the Liberation of Angola, which maintained Marxist ideology; and China supported the National Union for the Total Independence of Angola, which had splintered off the National Front for the Liberation of Angola.[39] Furthermore, Soviet leaders viewed Angola as an opportunity to expand Soviet influence in Southern Africa while also blocking China's attempts to gain influence in countries with movements supported by the Soviet Union.[40] The United States, already concerned about the future of the West's access to the Red Sea and Africa's raw materials, saw an opportunity to prevent an increase in the Soviet Union's influence and its supported movements in Angola and to show that the United States could still meaningfully influence events in secondary theaters, after the events in Vietnam.[41] Meanwhile, China likely was motivated by its competition with the Soviet Union for influence in Africa and the perception that the Soviet Union building influence in Africa could also undermine Chinese socialism.[42]

Although the Cold War dynamics largely pitted the United States against its main rival the Soviet Union, China too became involved in conflicts in Africa during that era—notably

---

[36] Kanet, 2006.

[37] Westad, 2005.

[38] Gebru Tareke, "The Ethiopia-Somalia War of 1977 Revisited," *International Journal of African Historical Studies*, Vol. 33, No. 3, 2000.

[39] Office of the Historian, "Milestones: 1969–1976—The Angola Crisis 1974–75," U.S. Department of State, undated-a.

[40] Westad, 2005, p. 215.

[41] Westad, 2005, pp. 212–222.

[42] Westad, 2005, pp. 226–227.

between 1949 and the mid-1970s.[43] China was more focused on East Asian conflicts, but it also rendered support to Maoist and other insurgents in African countries via military training and material support.[44] China supported Maoist groups in Algeria, Ghana, and Tanzania, as well as revolutionary groups in countries under white minority governments (e.g., Rhodesia, Namibia, and South Africa) and Portuguese rule (e.g., Angola, Cape Verde, Guinea-Bissau, Mozambique, and São Tomé).[45] The United States and China were not always on opposite sides of conflicts in Africa; because of a common anti-Soviet sentiment after the split between China and the Soviet Union, China had even shifted its support from one local actor to another to avoid siding with the Soviet Union. In the 1970s, for example, both the United States and China supported the groups in Angola fighting against the Soviet- and Cuba-supported People's Movement for the Liberation of Angola, while in Sudan China praised the fall of the Soviet-supported Sudanese Communist Party in 1971.[46]

Great-power involvement in foreign conflicts during the Cold War era had a central distinguishing feature. As political scientist Karl Deutsch explained,

> international conflict between two foreign powers . . . [was] fought out in the soil of a third country[,] disguised as a conflict over an internal issue of that country; and using some of that country's manpower, resources and territory as a means for achieving preponderantly foreign goals and foreign strategies.[47]

U.S. and Soviet involvement in third countries was largely driven by the imperative to prevail in the all-encompassing geopolitical and ideological struggle, as the two rivals sought to bal-

---

[43] In the 1980s, Deng Xiaoping's reform and opening-up philosophy refocused China to a path of forging economic development and integration with the West (Cohen, Treyger, et al., 2023).

[44] Cohen, Treyger, et al., 2023; Chris Saunders, "SWAPO's 'Eastern' Connections, 1966–1989," in Lena Dallywater, Chris Saunders, and Helder Adegar Fonseca, eds., *Southern African Liberation Movements and the Global Cold War "East": Transnational Activism 1960–1990*, Berlin: De Gruyter, 2019; and David Shinn, "China-Africa Ties in Historical Context," in Arkebe Oqubay and Justin Yifu Lin, eds., *China-Africa and an Economic Transformation*, Oxford, United Kingdom: Oxford University Press, 2019. The intensity of China's presence in Africa was also interrupted by the Cultural Revolution in China, which resulted in China recalling its ambassadors and leaving the chargés d'affaires to lead the embassies; several diplomatic faux pas followed. One such event, when a letter from the Chinese embassy accused a Kenyan minister of sabotaging China-Kenya relations, led to the expulsion of the Chinese embassy's chargé d'affaires (Ian Taylor, "Taylor on Chau, 'Exploiting Africa: The Influence of Maoist China in Algeria, Ghana, and Tanzania,'" *H-Asia*, April 2015).

[45] See, for example, Joshua Eisenman, "Comrades-in-Arms: The Chinese Communist Party's Relations with African Political Organisations in the Mao Era, 1949–76," *Cold War History*, Vol. 18, No. 4, 2018.

[46] Eisenman, 2018; and Sofia Fernandes, "China and Angola: A Strategic Partnership?" in Marcus Power and Ana Cristina Alves, eds., *China & Angola: A Marriage of Convenience?* Oxford, United Kingdom: Pambazuka, 2012.

[47] Karl W. Deutsch, "External Involvement in Internal Wars," in Harry Eckstein, ed., *Internal War: Problems and Approaches*, New York: Free Press of Glencoe, 1964, p. 102.

ance each other's influence across much of the world.[48] Because of the global and zero-sum nature of this struggle—that is, a communist government anywhere was viewed as a loss to the United States, just as a capitalist nation was viewed as a loss to the Soviets—great-power entanglement in conflicts all over the world was rather frequent.[49] As a result, the political fates of countries and regions that should have been secondary to the great powers' core national security concerns acquired greater importance.

In the recent, post–Cold War past, the United States, China, and Russia have supported actors involved in conflicts on the continent in a variety of ways. Since the early 2000s, U.S. engagements in Africa have been focused on counterterrorism.[50] Washington has preferred to carry out its military interventions through smaller task forces by using special operations forces for limited engagements, deploying remotely piloted aircraft, or simply supporting African forces with training or equipment in their fight against violent extremist organizations (VEOs).[51] For example, the United States has employed small numbers of special forces in Somalia since the mid-2000s to fight al-Qaeda and help the Somalian government develop the capacity to fight al-Shabaab.[52] Especially since the establishment of AFRICOM in 2007, increasing numbers of U.S. military personnel were employed to support African states in the context of the global war on terrorism.[53] The United States has similarly used special forces in Uganda, sending about 100 special forces soldiers to support President Yoweri Museveni in his campaign against Joseph Kony and the Lord's Resistance Army.[54]

---

[48] The causes and drivers of the U.S. and Soviet involvement in the multitude of conflicts across the world between the end of World War II and the end of the Cold War remain subject to debate among historians; however, there is little doubt that ideological and geopolitical aspects of the Cold War rivalries and the contest over newly independent countries were paramount. For a seminal historical treatment of the U.S. and Soviet interventions of the late Cold War, see Westad, 2005.

[49] We are indebted to our colleagues for tabulating the incidence of proxy wars over time; see Stephen Watts, Bryan Frederick, Nathan Chandler, Mark Toukan, Christian Curriden, Erik E. Mueller, Edward Geist, Ariane M. Tabatabai, Sara Plana, Brandon Corbin, and Jeffrey Martini, *Proxy Warfare in Strategic Competition: Overarching Findings and Recommendations*, Santa Monica, Calif.: RAND Corporation, RR-A307-1, 2023.

[50] In 2002, the George W. Bush administration launched a counterterrorism program known as the Pan Sahel Initiative, which aimed to help the forces of Chad, Mali, Mauritania, and Niger build their capacities to fight terrorist groups (Office of Counterterrorism, "Pan Sahel Initiative," U.S. Department of State Archives, November 7, 2002; and Annika Lichtenbaum, "U.S. Military Operational Activity in the Sahel," *Lawfare*, January 25, 2019).

[51] Barbara Salazar Torreon and Sofia Plagakis, *Instances of Use of United States Armed Forces Abroad, 1798–2021*, Washington, D.C.: Congressional Research Service, R42738, September 8, 2021; Lichtenbaum, 2019; and Stephen Burgess, "Military Intervention in Africa: French and US Approaches Compared," *Journal of European, Middle Eastern, and African Affairs*, Vol. 1, No. 1, Spring 2019.

[52] Stephen M. Schwartz, "The Way Forward for the United States in Somalia," Foreign Policy Research Institute, January 12, 2021; and Meghann Myers, "US Troops Now 'Commuting to Work' to Help Somalia Fight Al-Shabab," *Military Times*, April 27, 2021.

[53] Lichtenbaum, 2019.

[54] Torreon and Plagakis, 2021, p. 27.

China and Russia also have been involved in African conflicts over the past couple of decades, though certainly less so than the United States has—and generally without resorting to direct, kinetic military action via official military forces. More-recent Chinese involvement in African conflicts and support to local actors in Africa largely has been carried out through participation in UN peacekeeping operations or via political support in elections.[55] For example, in 2006 in Zambia, China vocally opposed the election of Michael Sata (who was critical of China and its policies regarding Taiwan), and during the 2018 presidential elections in Sierra Leone, China allegedly provided material and financial assistance to the country's ruling party, with which China has had long-standing relations.[56]

Russia has been involved in several recent African conflicts in a more aggressive manner than China has. Although the role of the Russian state in some conflicts cannot be fully confirmed, Russian state and state-affiliated actors—notably, private military and security companies (PMSCs)—have supplied military equipment, provided advising and training, and even taken part in kinetic operations.[57] Russia's most infamous PMSC, the Wagner Group, and other Russian actors have supported the regimes of Sudan, the Central African Republic (CAR), the DRC, and Mozambique against popular uprisings and violent rebels alike.[58] More recently, Wagner made an appearance in Mali, likewise supporting the government.[59]

Most of the U.S., Chinese, and Russian engagements described here, however, have not drawn the three competing powers into opposing each other in the same conflict. The African conflict that most distinctly presented such an opportunity, and one that drew Russia, the United States, and other external powers, is the conflict in Libya. Like the Syrian civil war in the neighboring Middle East, the conflict grew out of unrest from the Arab Spring in 2011. In this case, although assistance from the United States and its NATO allies led to the death of longtime Libyan ruler Muammar al-Qaddafi, the end of Qaddafi's rule did not stabilize the country. Libya descended into a bloody civil war; the United States, along with Turkey, backed the Government of National Accord; and Russia, the United Arab Emirates (UAE), Saudi Arabia, and others backed the Libyan National Army under General Khalifa Haftar.[60]

---

[55] Judd Devermont, director, Africa Program, Center for Strategic and International Studies, "China's Strategic Aims in Africa," testimony before the U.S.-China Economic and Security Review Commission, Washington, D.C., May 8, 2020a. See also Cohen, Treyger, et al., 2023, Appendix B.

[56] Will Green, Leyton Nelson, and Brittney Washington, *China's Engagement with Africa: Foundations for an Alternative Governance Regime*, Washington, D.C.: U.S.-China Economic and Security Review Commission, May 1, 2020. Later, after Sata was elected president of Zambia in 2011, he become supportive of China.

[57] For more detail, see Cohen, Treyger, et al., 2023, Appendix C.

[58] Cohen, Treyger, et al., 2023.

[59] Cohen, Treyger, et al., 2023.

[60] Frederic Wehrey, "'Our Hearts Are Dead.' After 9 Years of Civil War, Libyans Are Tired of Being Pawns in a Geopolitical Game of Chess," *Time*, February 12, 2020. To be sure, Russia did not decisively side with Haftar until relatively late in the conflict (see Jalel Harchaoui, "The Pendulum: How Russia Sways Its Way to More Influence in Libya," *War on the Rocks*, January 7, 2021).

A decade later, the conflict had produced a death toll in the thousands and displaced well over a quarter million people.[61]

Although the United States and Russia ultimately are backing opposing parties in Libya, their involvement there is not driven by an overriding zero-sum logic of competition.[62] This is in contrast with the Cold War–era conflicts noted earlier. Although U.S. policy has consistently called for the withdrawal of foreign forces from Libya—seeking to squeeze out Russia's mercenaries, among others—it is motivated largely by regional counterterrorism and stability concerns.[63] Gaining influence in a country strategically located on NATO's southern flank is a motivation for Russia's involvement, but Russia is also motivated by the need to boost its economy, as it seeks to recoup losses caused by the UN-authorized removal of the Qaddafi regime in 2011, as well as an interest in boosting Russia's regional standing and ability to operate in Africa more broadly.[64]

Reflecting the relatively muted role of great-power competition behind their involvement, the United States and Russia have generally been cautious about each other's presence in both Libya and Syria. Neither side has viewed the conflicts primarily as a way to impose costs on a competitor.[65] U.S. involvement in Libya has been minimal overall. And although the United States noted the increased presence of Russia's Wagner mercenaries in Libya and explicitly called for their withdrawal, it has not chosen to increase its own involvement in Libya to bring about that outcome.[66]

The war in Libya, like the war in Syria, demonstrates that conflicts that draw in great-power competitors can erupt outside of the primary theaters of competition, including in Africa. Yet the nature of these powers' involvement in Libya—and the great powers' participation in other conflicts—raises questions about the dynamics of great-power involvement in future conflicts. To be sure, Africa has transformed since the end of the Cold War; many of its countries are richer and more influential and have stronger political leadership.[67] Moreover, African leaders and residents have their own views about managing great-power competition and seizing the strategic opportunities to pursue their own national interests that such com-

---

[61] Center for Preventive Action, "Instability in Libya," Council on Foreign Relations, May 12, 2022.

[62] For a discussion of the powers' involvement in Syria, see Cohen, Treyger, et al., 2023.

[63] Christopher M. Blanchard, "Libya and U.S. Policy," Congressional Research Service, IF11556, last updated September 2, 2021.

[64] Harchaoui, 2021.

[65] This is also the case with the Syrian civil war, where U.S. and Russian interests are more in tension. For discussion, see two of the companion volumes in this series: Cohen, Treyger, et al., 2023; Rhoades et al., 2023.

[66] AFRICOM, "Russia, Wagner Group Continue Military Involvement in Libya," press release, July 24, 2020; and Blanchard, 2021.

[67] Besides that, the creation of the African Continental Free Trade Area might increase the currently rather low intra-Africa trade, thus diversifying trading partners.

petition might offer.[68] Nonetheless, many countries in the region experience multiple sources of instability that could offer opportunities for external powers to intervene in their internal conflicts in some way.

The United States and its competitors have a variety of interests that might provide the motivation to take advantage of those opportunities. The United States, for example, retains its interests in stability and the prevention of violent extremism that have driven many of its interventions since the Cold War.[69] For China, economic interests could push it to take sides in an African conflict; indeed, the need to protect these interests and Chinese citizens overseas have already motivated China to expand its ability to project power farther from its territory.[70] For Russia, too, building influence as a power of consequence, gaining footholds in strategic regions of Africa, and pursuing economic interests likely would provide motivation for further meddling in countries' internal affairs.

More to the core concern of this study, competition among the powers might generate its own logic, motivating great-power support for local actors in internal conflicts. Although the ideological aspect of great-power competition in Africa has diminished, along with the Cold War zero-sum dynamics, the allegiances of the wars of liberation are still reflected, to some extent, in the historic ties and memories that the United States, Russia, and China are able to build on across the continent, as well as in the local security dynamics.[71] As strategic competition intensifies globally, will Africa's conflicts come to resemble the proxy wars and military interventions of the Cold War, where rival powers supported parties on opposite sides of conflicts, driven predominantly by geopolitical and ideological goals rooted in competition? Or will future conflicts more closely resemble the civil war in Libya, where rival great powers may be backing different parties, but it is not primarily for reasons related to competition or intended to impose costs on their competitors?

With this study, we aim primarily to explore these questions, but we should note that the competition between the United States on the one hand and China and Russia on the other does not represent the full extent of international competition that is developing on the continent. There are many other important external players in Africa, including the European Union (EU), France, Turkey, the UAE, Iran, India, and Israel. In fact, some of the more intense conflicts waged by Russian PMSCs put Russia in opposition not to the United States but to France. Notably, Russia has been maneuvering to discredit France—and, indirectly,

---

[68] See, for example, Mjumo Mzyece and Mzukisi Qobo, "US-China Tension Creates Opportunities Africa Must Seize," Africa Report, June 22, 2020.

[69] Cohen, Treyger, et al., 2023.

[70] Kristen Gunness, "The PLA's Expeditionary Force: Current Capabilities and Future Trends," in Joel Wuthnow, Arthur S. Ding, Phillip C. Saunders, Andrew Scobell, and Andrew N. D. Yang, eds., *The PLA Beyond Borders: Chinese Military Operations in Regional and Global Context*, Washington, D.C.: National Defense University Press, 2021; and Jiang Zemin, "Report at the 16th Party Congress," China Internet Information Center, November 17, 2002.

[71] Brown, 2016.

France's Western partners—in Mali. Specifically, the entrance of the Wagner Group into Mali contributed to France losing its role of a key security provider, and France considers "cohabitation with Wagner impossible."[72] France's position on Wagner's presence in Mali also has been shared by the countries that contribute to the European Takuba Task Force, such as Sweden, Germany, and the United Kingdom.[73] Although such actions may not affect the United States directly, they may affect the ability of the United States to achieve and maintain influence in the region. These broader dynamics are outside of the scope of this report, but the experiences of U.S. allies and partners in Africa may offer insights into the military clashes in which the United States may become involved.

Definitions of Key Concepts

We begin by defining the concepts that are key to this research. First, we adopt the definition of *competition* proposed by Michael Mazarr and his co-authors in a 2018 RAND study:

> Competition in the international realm involves the attempt to gain advantage, often relative to others believed to pose a challenge or threat, through the self interested pursuit of contested goods such as power, security, wealth, influence, and status.[74]

Second, we define the set of relevant conflicts. Cold War–era conflicts noted earlier are often described as *proxy wars*. What precisely makes external powers' involvement in a foreign conflict a proxy war is a matter of some debate.[75] For instance, some definitions of proxy wars limit them to cases in which external powers support non-state actors but not states.[76] However, most discussions of proxy wars distinguish this form of involvement from direct military interventions: In proxy warfare, the external power intervenes through only indirect support—such as with arms and other resources—and delegates the fighting to a local actor.[77]

In practice, the line between indirect and direct or military support may not be a firm one, as indirect support to proxies can subtly escalate to military action. Moreover, one power may intervene in a conflict solely through indirect support of a proxy actor, whereas

---

[72] Yves Bourdillon, "La Russie Pousse Ses Pions En Afrique Via Ses Mercenaires" ["Russia Pushes Its Pawns in Africa via Its Mercenaries"], *Les Echos*, December 13, 2021.

[73] Bourdillon, 2021.

[74] Michael J. Mazarr, Jonathan Blake, Abigail Casey, Tim McDonald, Stephanie Pezard, and Michael Spirtas, *Understanding the Emerging Era of International Competition: Theoretical and Historical Perspectives*, Santa Monica, Calif.: RAND Corporation, RR-2726-AF, 2018, p. 5.

[75] See, for example, Andrew Mumford, *Proxy Warfare*, Cambridge, United Kingdom: John Wiley & Sons, 2013, p. 1.

[76] See, for example, Dominic Tierney, "The Future of Sino-US Proxy War," *Texas National Security Review*, Vol. 4, No. 2, Spring 2021; and Mumford, 2013, p. 1.

[77] See, for example, Tierney, 2021; Mumford, 2013, p. 1.

its rival power might intervene more directly. For example, in Afghanistan in the 1980s, the Soviet intervention entailed a substantial deployment of Soviet troops, whereas the U.S. involvement was largely confined to supporting the *mujahedeen* (Islamic guerrilla fighters).[78] Then too, the risks that attend the spillover of competition into foreign conflicts—risks of escalation into direct conflict and mounting costs of involvement—may exist whether rival powers become involved directly or indirectly. Thus, in this series of reports, we investigate the prospects for great-power involvement in conflicts in secondary theaters, whatever form this involvement takes.

More specifically, we consider *whether and under what conditions the United States could expect to become involved in a secondary-theater conflict in which at least one of its two main competitors is also involved.* Great-power involvement in conflicts might take the shape of proxy warfare—that is, support for a state or a non-state actor by means short of direct military intervention. This might include covert or overt action. In particular, it might include purely indirect aid, such as training, equipping, advising, selling arms, and providing financial assistance, but it might also involve combat or military action—so long as that action is carried out by non-state groups, such as PMSCs, affiliated with and operating on behalf of the external power.[79] Great-power involvement in conflicts might also take the shape of direct military interventions—although we deemphasize the prospects of major military interventions.

Importantly, we do not limit our investigation to the potential involvement in third-party conflicts for "foreign goals," as per Deutsch's description of Cold War proxy wars noted earlier. In the future, great powers may become embroiled in conflicts in pursuit of a variety of goals, and we do not want to exclude any possibilities from consideration. Similarly, emphasizing the degree to which the proxy, or local actor, must be an agent that wholly does the external principal's bidding, rather than pursuing its own agenda, would unduly narrow the scope on the basis of factors that are difficult to parse even in historical cases—and much more so in hypothetical future conflicts.[80]

Methodology

To study great-power competition and potential conflict in Africa (and the other two secondary theaters studied in this series), we devised a three-stage methodology. First, we relied on publicly available data to measure the relative potential for great-power competition across

---

[78] See, for example, Mumford, 2013, p. 14.

[79] Some definitions of *proxy warfare* treat PMSCs and similar actors as the proxies that are being supported by the external powers, on par with local actors (see, for example, Mumford, 2013). We think that this lens is not helpful for the present context and consider such actors as Russia's PMSCs to be a potential instrument of support to local actors rather than a party to the conflict in their own right.

[80] For an example of such an emphasis, see Douglas A. Ollivant and Erica Gaston, "The Problem with the Narrative of 'Proxy War' in Iraq," *War on the Rocks*, May 31, 2019.

all the countries in the region; second, we relied on conflict risk assessments to measure the relative risk of internal conflict across all the countries in the region; and third, we combined the two measures to identify *competition flashpoints*—that is, places where more than one of the three powers (the United States, China, or Russia) would most plausibly become involved in conflicts. We address the first stage here and the latter two in the subsequent subsection.

Measuring the Potential for Competition

In the first stage, we sought to measure the relative *potential for competition* among the United States, China, and Russia, across multiple domains, for all the countries in Africa. Because great-power competition takes place across multiple domains, measuring the potential for competition is a data-intensive task. Moreover, measuring competition itself is a difficult proposition; whether one state is in competition with another is as much a function of perceptions of a zero-sum game as it is of concrete, measurable factors. Our approach was therefore to rely on data that enabled us to measure the degree of great-power involvement in each state, relative to other states in the region. That is, we identified states in the region in which the United States, China, and Russia have been most involved, using each of the four main tools of national power— diplomacy, information, military, and economics (often known by the acronym DIME). States that attract the greatest degree of involvement from all three powers are thus the sites of potentially acute great-power competition. Potential, of course, need not mean actual; it is possible that the objectives that underlie each great power's involvement do not clash. However, there is more opportunity for competition where great powers are most extensively involved.

Moreover, measuring involvement captures *influence-seeking* rather than influence itself. Although we measured how much time and resources the United States, China, and Russia have been investing in a location, we did not measure to what extent these investments have paid off in terms of each great power gaining influence on the ground.

In the appendix to this report, we provide more-detailed information about the definitions, sources, and data used to capture influence-seeking. Table 1.1 identifies the variables used to measure involvement or influence-seeking across the four domains of national power, as well as the time frame of the data used.

To measure diplomatic involvement, we relied on some traditional indicators, such as the amount of foreign aid each great power directed toward countries in the region.[81] We also captured whether states had an embassy in each country and reciprocal visa-free travel, on the assumption that the presence of such agreements indicates more people-to-people ties. In addition, we captured the number of high-level diplomatic visits by heads of state, top for-

---

[81] Although we sought data for the most recent year, the most recent data for China's foreign aid assistance were from 2014. Thus, our measures of China's diplomatic influence-seeking may be somewhat distorted, if the relative prioritization of its foreign aid recipients in the region shifted considerably since then.

TABLE 1.1

Measuring Influence-Seeking and Potential for Competition: Variables

Domain	Variable	Time Frame of Data
Diplomacy	Foreign aid and assistance	Most recent year available
	High-level diplomatic visits	Between 2000 and 2020
	Presence of embassy	As of 2020
	Visa-free travel	As of 2020
Information	State-sponsored media	As of 2020
Military	Involvement in post–Cold War conflicts	Since 1991 (binary)
	Arms exports	2014–most recent year available
	Presence of military forces and bases	2014–2020
	Military agreements	As of 2020
	Military exercises	2014–2020
	PMSCs	Recent years
	Military access	As of 2020
Economics	Trade volume	2018
	Investment	Most recent year available
	Critical infrastructure	Russia only, as of 2020

eign policy officials, and (for the United States) top military officials, because one of the most valuable diplomatic commodities is senior leader time.

Of the four main tools of state power, informational activities proved most challenging for us to measure. For Russia, we determined whether a state-sponsored media outlet (RT, Sputnik, or TASS) had a cooperation agreement with local media. For China, we determined whether the China Global Television Network, China Radio International, or Xinhua was present in the country. And for the United States, we identified countries where Voice of America had a bureau, had transmitters, owned FM frequencies, or had contracts with local radio or television affiliates that retranslate. Although this measure of information does not capture many channels of informational influence and narrative dissemination, it does provide a rough approximation of where great powers have chosen to devote their informational resources. Because of the difficulty of collecting reliable information on all three great powers' online-based information activities across African countries, we could not incorporate online-based influence-seeking activities into the information variable.

We collected multiple indicators for the potential for military competition. Given the military focus of this work and the aim of exploring the possibilities for conflict in Africa, we relied on a larger number of metrics than for other domains of national power. Most of the indicators—notably, military agreements, arms exports, military access, military exercises, and the presence of military forces and bases—bear a direct relationship to the state of military-to-military ties. We also included a variable for prior or ongoing great-power involvement in a conflict in each country after the Cold War. Lastly, given the importance of gray-zone tactics, we included the reported presence of U.S., Chinese, and Russian PMSCs.[82]

Finally, on economic measures, we relied on bilateral merchandise trade volume and direct investment. On the latter, although direct investment position data were available for the United States, and partly available for Russia, this was not the case for China; thus, for China, we relied on the most comprehensive independent effort to catalog China's global investments, compiled by the American Enterprise Institute and the Heritage Foundation. Because Russia's direct investment position data are particularly patchy and likely do not adequately represent countries in which Russian entities have an economic stake, we supplemented the investment measure with another variable that captured an important aspect of economic involvement: the presence of Russian companies in critical infrastructure sectors of each country. For the United States and China, these investments generally are included in their respective investment data.

A few caveats about these data and our approach are in order. First, given the extensive geographic scope and differences between what data the United States, China, and Russia make public, not every variable was available for each of the three great powers, and not all the data were of equal quality or completeness.[83] Second, even when the data were available and complete, many of the variables are not directly comparable across the competing powers. Unlike the trade volume metric, for instance, the presence of PMSCs does not represent the same kind of influence-seeking for each great power; whereas the United States and Russia might both have PMSCs in a given country, the former's may be performing embassy security, while the latter's may be training local military factions or participating in combat. Third, not all variables proved of equal utility by region. For example, if the United States has an embassy in every country in Africa, the variable does not help identify where the United States focuses its efforts there.

Despite these limitations, these variables offer a reasonable approximation of where each power is focusing its efforts. To synthesize this broad set of variables, we constructed metrics, or indices, measuring great-power influence-seeking in each of the four domains (diplomacy, information, military, and economics) and overall, and those indices capture where in the region each power focuses its activities. The *influence-seeking indices* (i.e., scores) for each of the three powers across the four domains provide a numeric indication of how involved a given great power is in a particular country relative to other countries in that region. The influence-seeking metrics *for all three* competing powers are then combined to produce *indices for competition potential* in each domain and overall for a given country.

---

[82] As noted earlier, see the appendix for sources and definitions for all the variables discussed in this section.

[83] For example, both the United States and Russia decline to publicly report foreign investments for certain countries because of confidentiality concerns.

In constructing the influence-seeking and competition-potential indices, we accorded each variable equal weight. Military access, for example, counts as much as the presence of PMSCs in the military influence-seeking index and the military competition-potential index, and direct investment counts as much as arms exports in the overall competition-potential index. The appendix describes our approach in greater detail.

To be sure, how much each activity should matter in determining a country's importance to competing powers is an open question. In the absence of a strong theoretical reason to value any one factor as significantly more important than others, we opted for equal weights. The resulting indices are just one way, and certainly not the only way, of capturing influence-seeking and potential competition. Thus, our approach does not pursue a nuanced weighting of different activities. However, it does provide a succinct measure of where the three competitors are focusing their efforts, which accounts for different ways in which states build influence and relations. That is, we can identify the most likely competition flashpoints (i.e., the countries where all three powers have a relatively high level of involvement).

Measuring the Potential for Conflict

A high potential for competition among two or more great powers in a given country does not necessarily make that country a very likely location for a proxy war or military intervention. Great-power support for local actors in power struggles in secondary regions requires both motive *and* opportunity. Opportunity, in this case, would stem from a high risk of conflict. External powers' support for proxies or more-direct interventions are predicated on an underlying internal conflict or civil war, or at least conditions where such a conflict might be plausibly catalyzed by external powers.[84] External powers, then, can exploit these dynamics to their advantage; they might choose to back a party whose victory might confer benefits on the external power or a party that is in a position to inflict costs on a rival great power.[85]

Thus, in the second stage of our methodology, we assessed the *potential for conflict* erupting in each of the countries relative to the rest of the region, particularly where that might invite external intervention or produce proxy wars. To do so for countries in Africa, we relied on the University of Uppsala's Violence Early-Warning System (ViEWS), a well-regarded tool for forecasting the probability of internal conflict on the basis of a large set of variables found to be correlated with conflict.[86] ViEWS assesses the prospective risk of conflict over three years and "provides early warnings for three forms of political violence: armed conflict involving states

---

[84] In theory, an inter-state war can also have elements of a proxy war; here, however, we focus largely on internal conflicts, although we do consider inter-state or cross-border dynamics in some of the scenarios examined.

[85] See, for example, Idean Salehyan, Kristian Skrede Gleditsch, and David E. Cunningham, "Explaining External Support for Insurgent Groups," *International Organization*, Vol. 65, No. 4, Fall 2011.

[86] ViEWS: The Violence Early-Warning System, web tool, Uppsala University Department of Peace and Conflict Research, undated; and Uppsala University Department of Peace and Conflict Research, "About ViEWS," webpage, last modified April 25, 2022.

and rebel groups, armed conflict between non-state actors, and violence against civilians."[87] (The appendix presents the ViEWS predicted conflict probabilities in greater detail).

Choosing and Analyzing Countries and Conflict Scenarios

In the third stage, using the results from our analysis of the potential for competition and the potential for conflict, we selected two cases to present some of the more plausible conflict scenarios, where great powers might become involved. To do so, we first limited the potential set to the one-third of countries with the highest conflict potential. This helped ensure that the conflict scenarios we examined are sufficiently foreseeable and based on existing dynamics, so that we could identify the most likely causes of conflict; in other words, this subset of states is most likely to present actual, rather than merely speculative, opportunities for great powers to become involved in conflicts.

We then ranked this set of most-conflict-prone states in the region by competition potential, from highest to lowest. This enabled us to also identify which states have been the sites of the most extensive great-power influence-seeking and are therefore theoretically more likely to attract great-power attention if conflict breaks out. A high potential for competition does not *ensure* that any of the three powers has sufficient motivation to become involved, but it should make it more likely on average.[88]

Rather than simply picking the states with the greatest competition potential among the most-conflict-prone states, we adopted a somewhat more qualitative approach. We consulted with regional subject-matter experts and our analyses of China's and Russia's approaches to supporting proxy actors (see the summary volume of this series[89]) to select countries (1) where the likelihood of significant conflict, especially with some transborder or broader regional implications, is indeed present and (2) that present at least theoretically plausible contexts for great-power involvement in conflicts. From among countries that met those general criteria, we further sought to select cases that were sufficiently different from each other to stress the Department of the Air Force in different ways.

After selecting the countries for analysis of potential great-power involvement in internal conflicts, we drew on a variety of sources to develop plausible scenarios for what these conflicts might look like. First, we explored local political dynamics and identified which local actors have ties to which great power, if any. We relied on expert analyses of each coun-

---

[87] The project incorporates a "variety of variables to specify the models that are then used to predict the risk of armed conflict. Such variables contain data on a range of aspects that might influence the risk of conflict occurrence in a particular grid-cell or country" (Uppsala University Department of Peace and Conflict Research, "Independent Variables," webpage, undated).

[88] To be sure, in an atmosphere of acute rivalry resembling periods of the Cold War, it is possible that a great power would support local actors purely for competitive reasons in countries where it lacks any other interests. Where this might occur, however, is essentially unpredictable; thus, we focus on identifying the more plausible cases based on factors (i.e., influence-seeking) that we can observe.

[89] Cohen, Treyger, et al., 2023, Appendixes B and C.

try's political dynamics and assessments of conflict risks. Our conflict scenarios are based on causes of conflict identified as salient or most likely in such analyses.[90] Sparks that start armed conflicts are not always predictable; for example, the outbreak of a series of uprisings of the Arab Spring in 2011 was largely unexpected to most analysts, including intelligence analysts.[91] Thus, we do not claim to predict precisely how conflicts will unfold or to cover the full spectrum of possible scenarios that might come to pass. Instead, we focus on the dynamics of discord that are evident at present and identified by regional experts as the most-plausible sources of substantial violent conflict in the foreseeable future.

Second, we assessed each great power's overarching interests in the country, which help inform what objectives, if any, each might have in a hypothetical conflict. We then explored what type of posture and access each great power might have and what types of capabilities it might be able to bring to bear on the given scenario. Next, we explored how such a conflict might unfold and what factors might affect its ultimate outcome. To focus analysis here, we accorded more attention to scenarios that we assessed were more likely to draw in the United States and at least one of its two key competitors. That is, even where multiple, equally plausible conflict scenarios existed, we focused on the scenario where the great powers were more likely to have sufficient motivation for involvement. To empirically ground these assessments, we drew on a variety of sources to better understand how China and Russia—as well as the United States—have approached conflicts in secondary theaters in the past. These analyses included research into how Chinese and Russian experts—as well as Western ones—write about the subject today, which is included in the summary volume in this series.[92] Because of the global coronavirus disease 2019 (COVID-19) pandemic, our research team was not able to travel to Africa to carry out field research there. However, we carried out interviews with U.S.-based experts on the countries selected for study and on Chinese and Russian influence in the region, and those experts represented both academia and former U.S. government and military officials. Finally, we assessed the implications of each conflict scenario for the U.S. government at large, the joint force, and the Department of the Air Force, and particularly what the scenarios might mean for future military posture, capabilities, and capacity.

Lastly, we want to emphasize that this report is prepared from the point of view of great-power competition, so it focuses on the interests and capabilities of the United States, China, and Russia. As a result, we do not engage the perspectives of African countries in depth.

---

[90] In this, we drew on our interviews with regional experts, scholarly and policy research on each country, and the research that produced the assessments of political risk on which we relied to rank countries in each region. The views of the anonymous interviewees are solely their own and do not represent the official policy or position of DoD or the U.S. government.

[91] Jeff Goodwin, "Why We Were Surprised (Again) by the Arab Spring," *Swiss Political Science Review*, Vol. 17, No. 4, 2011.

[92] For these analyses, see Cohen, Treyger, et al., 2023.

Overview of Report Structure

The report is organized as follows. In Chapter Two, we describe the results of our analysis of the United States', China's, and Russia's interests in Africa across the four primary domains of influence-seeking (diplomacy, information, military, and economics), review the potential for conflict across the African continent, and identify two countries for more in-depth study. We find that the great powers' interests converge most significantly in South Africa, Nigeria, Sudan, and Kenya; that is, the potential for competition is the highest in the largest economies, the largest energy or mineral producers, or the countries that are in strategically important locations. Our analysis also reveals that the countries where the potential for competition is greatest are not necessarily those with the highest potential for conflict. To identify countries that are among the more plausible locations for potential future conflicts with great-power involvement, we combined the potential for competition and the potential for conflict and selected two countries, Nigeria and Mozambique, for more in-depth exploration of potential conflict scenarios involving some or all of the three great powers.

In Chapters Three and Four, we explore the most likely conflict scenarios in these two countries and assess the plausible features of great-power involvement in such. These chapters include a discussion of each great power's interests in Nigeria and Mozambique and the most likely path to conflict that might lead to the involvement of more than one great power. In both cases, we find that, if they were to become involved, the great powers (1) are likely to support the same government actors even if their motivations and interests may be different and (2) would be unlikely to commit large resources or find themselves in a direct confrontation. We also find that the United States would likely have to face deconfliction and harassment issues, compete for access to ports or airports, and face potential competition for political access.

Finally, in Chapter Five, we summarize Chapters Two through Four and offer recommendations on how the U.S. government, the joint force, and the Department of the Air Force could better prepare for potential future competition and conflict in Africa.

CHAPTER TWO

Identifying Regional Competition Flashpoints

The increase in the strategic relevance of Africa has been discussed by policymakers and analysts for more than a decade.[1] This is a change from the 1990s, when the United States and Europe were focused on the reconstruction of Eastern Europe following the end of the Cold War and the collapse of the Iron Curtain, as well as security issues in Southeast Europe; Russia had retrenched from its global role and was restructuring after the collapse of the Soviet Union; and China and other countries in Asia were benefiting from foreign investment and increased globalization.[2]

Today, however, there is again increased influence-seeking on the continent by China and Russia, among others. In this chapter, we discuss key aspects and trends in great-power competition and influence-seeking across the diplomatic, informational, military, and economic domains of influence. This analysis helps us identify the relative *potential for competition* among the United States, China, and Russia, across the domains, for all the countries in Africa (as defined in this report; see Chapter One). The countries that we identify as having the most potential for acute great-power competition on the continent are likely to present the greatest motivation for potential great-power involvement in future conflicts in the region.

Next in the chapter, we provide an assessment of which countries present the highest potential for experiencing an internal conflict, thus offering the opportunity for the three great powers to participate in a proxy conflict. Lastly, by overlaying the potential for competition with the potential for conflict, we identify two countries that could be plausible candidates for potential future conflicts with great-power engagement. That exercise then forms the basis for the scenarios analyzed in Chapters Three and Four.

Regional Competition Landscape

To understand how the United States, China, and Russia might compete in Africa, we represent the potential for competition by capturing the three powers' influence-seeking activities

---

[1]   We emphasize that this report is written from the perspective of great-power competition rather than the perspective of African studies.

[2]   Jennifer Giroux, "Africa's Growing Strategic Relevance," *CSS Analyses in Security Policy*, Vol. 3, No. 38, July 2008.

or involvement in countries across the continent. In this section, we present the potential for competition as a snapshot in time within each of the four domains (diplomacy, information, military, and economics) and across all four domains. For each domain, we present a map that depicts the competition-potential index (or score) for each country, identify the main characteristics of the three great powers' influence-seeking activities, and describe key trends.

Diplomacy

Figure 2.1 illustrates the potential for competition in the diplomatic domain for the United States, China, and Russia collectively across Africa; darker shades represent a higher potential for competition.

Across the region, diplomatic involvement by the three powers seems to converge in East and Southern Africa, specifically in Kenya, Ethiopia, South Africa, and Tanzania (countries that are among the largest economies in Africa) and Mozambique, Uganda, Zimbabwe, and Nigeria.[3] Kenya is an unsurprising diplomatic priority for the United States. It is a U.S. strategic ally today and was also allied with the West during the Cold War.[4] Since al-Qaeda detonated a bomb outside the U.S. embassy in Nairobi in 1998, the two countries have cooperated on fighting terrorism and building security in Kenya. Kenya is also among the top countries for U.S.-Africa high-level visits and recipients of U.S. foreign aid.[5] However, Kenya is also a top country for diplomatic activity from China; in particular, it is among the largest recipients of China's foreign aid and is an active partner for high-level visits.

Although great-power interests converge most clearly in those countries, the convergence does not mean that all the countries are equally prioritized by each great power. The United States' diplomatic involvement, for example, is highest in Kenya, Ethiopia, and Tanzania (followed by Nigeria), which are also among the top recipients of U.S. foreign aid.[6] Russia's diplomatic interests seem to be highest in Mozambique, Madagascar, and South Africa, while China's are in Namibia, Sierra Leone, and Kenya, in both cases largely because the amount of foreign aid and assistance and the number of high-level visits are higher there. Of these six countries, only Kenya and South Africa are among the countries with the ten highest scores for U.S. diplomatic influence-seeking. The focus on converging priorities—and those that

---

[3] In regional terms, Nigeria ranks the highest for West Africa, Kenya ranks the highest for East Africa, South Africa ranks the highest for Southern Africa, and Tunisia ranks the highest for North Africa.

[4] Both countries have been close allies since Kenya's independence in 1963; the relationship became even closer after Kenya's democratic transition in 2002, and Kenya and the United States agreed in 2018 to become strategic partners (Bureau of African Affairs, "U.S. Relations with Kenya: Bilateral Relations Fact Sheet," U.S. Department of State, last updated August 21, 2020b).

[5] Throughout this chapter, we describe results from our analyses of the measures that constitute the competition-potential index; for the variables and data sources, see Table A.1 in the appendix to this report. Note that, unless otherwise indicated, data are current as of the time frames outlined in Table 1.1. (For example, whether a great power had military access in a given country was current as of 2020.)

[6] ForeignAssistance.gov, "Data," webpage, last updated April 22, 2022, Country Summary Excel file.

FIGURE 2.1

Diplomatic Competition Potential in Africa

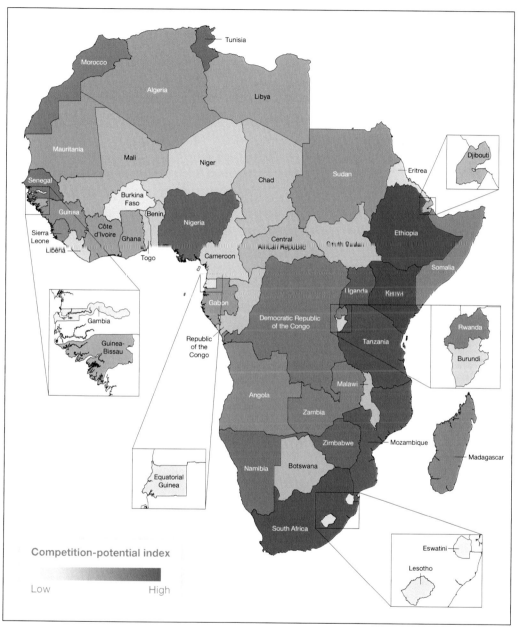

Competition-potential index

Low　　　　　　　High

may be captured by the available data—means that some countries that one might expect to see among those with the highest potential for diplomatic competition do not in fact appear at the top. For example, Libya, though a site of ongoing great-power involvement in its conflict, ranks in the middle in terms of potential for diplomatic competition. This is partly because Libya has not drawn a great deal of diplomatic influence-seeking from China and, compared with many other countries in the region, has not attracted as much foreign aid from China or the United States.[7]

Although Figure 2.1 offers a snapshot of where influence-seeking activities are most intense for the three powers collectively, it does not depict trends. Our data, however, suggest that China has been expanding its influence in Africa. We cannot make precise quantitative comparisons among the three powers in terms of diplomatic engagements, but evidence strongly suggests that Beijing is allocating the most resources to nurture long-term elite-to-elite relations, evidenced by China maintaining a regular high-level meeting schedule with more visits per year to African countries than the United States made.[8] It has invested a lot of resources and time in developing its presence across Africa, specifically in countries where it has economic interests (e.g., large trading partners, countries with extraction industries) and countries with significant regional influence (e.g., South Africa, Nigeria, Kenya, and Algeria). Thus, although the United States has the largest embassy network across the continent, China has been catching up since the early 2000s and has managed to establish embassies in all the reviewed countries except for Eswatini, which continues to maintain diplomatic relations with Taiwan.[9]

Russia's overall diplomatic engagement with African countries falls behind that of China and, in some respects, the United States. This may be explained by the fact that Russia is more focused on security and economic cooperation.[10] Russia's performance across the diplomatic means of influence-seeking is not uniform. On the one hand, since 2010, Russia has surpassed the United States in the number of high-level visits, and the number peaked in 2019,

---

[7] See Table A.2 in the appendix for the list of each African country's influence-seeking indices, by great power, and overall competition potential for the diplomatic domain.

[8] In 2016, for example, China conducted more than four times as many high-level visits as the United States did. China has even been reported to have used its technology companies, specifically Huawei, in helping some African governments spy on their political opponents (former U.S. Department of State official, interview with the authors, July 2021; Joe Parkinson, Nicholas Bariyo, and Josh Chin, "Huawei Technicians Helped African Governments Spy on Political Opponents," *Wall Street Journal*, August 15, 2019; and Judd Devermont, Marielle Harris, and Alison Albelda, "Personal Ties, Measuring Chinese and U.S. Engagement with African Security Chiefs," Center for Strategic and International Studies, August 2021).

[9] J. D. Moyer, D. K. Bohl, and S. Turner, "Diplometrics Diplomatic Representation," data set, Frederick S. Pardee Center for International Futures, 2016; and Thiam Niaga and Tim Cocks, "China Opens Embassy After Burkina Faso Severs Ties with Taiwan," Reuters, July 12, 2018.

[10] Russia tries to build on old Cold War ties with Africa and is developing relationships with several client states for its government-owned or -linked enterprises (particularly in the energy, nuclear energy, extractive industry, space, and machinery sectors) and countries where it has energy-related interests (former U.S. Department of State official, interview with the authors, July 2021).

the year of the first Russia-Africa summit.[11] Moreover, Russia and China maintain relations with a major African power, South Africa, via the BRICS (Brazil, Russia, India, China, and South Africa) group, as well as relations with the African Union.[12] On the other hand, Russia provides less foreign aid than the United States, China, or European countries as a group.[13] Russia has resident embassies in 36 of the 48 countries included in this report. This represents a respectable network of representation in Africa, but it does slightly fall behind the pan-African embassy networks of the United States and China. Moreover, Russian authors assess that, at least compared with China, Russia is not very successful in implementing a unified approach to its economic representation, because only its embassy in South Africa has a trade mission in sub-Saharan Africa.[14] Furthermore, Russian authors note that Russia's expertise on Africa is underdeveloped and that Russia is unable to keep on top of the dynamic changes in Africa, which impede strategic-level thinking about Africa.[15]

Meanwhile, the United States remains a key foreign aid provider to Africa. In fact, the U.S. foreign aid to Africa has increased since early 2000.[16] However, the United States falls behind the other two powers (and particularly China) in terms of the other factors analyzed for the diplomatic parameter, and there is a risk that the U.S. diplomatic position in Africa could weaken.[17] Among the great powers, the United States conducted the lowest number of high-level visits in our data set, and the number of meetings per year has fallen since 2012 and 2013, when the U.S. Secretary of State and President Barack Obama visited the continent. Our interviewees also noted that the United States has not always been able to maintain the kind

---

[11] The U.S. meeting numbers have been lower than China's, peaking in 2012 and since dropping, particularly between 2016 and 2020.

[12] "African Union Prioritizes Russia's Role in Ensuring Stability in Africa," TASS, May 5, 2021.

[13] Russia is selective when it provides foreign aid and tends to prioritize countries with previous Soviet links. In 2019, of the countries reviewed in this report, Madagascar, Mozambique, and South Sudan received the most foreign aid and assistance, followed by the DRC, Guinea, and Sierra Leone (Organisation for Economic Co-operation and Development, "Aid (ODA) Disbursements to Countries and Regions [DAC2a]," webpage, undated).

[14] G. G. Shalamov, "China's Presence in Africa: Lessons for Russia," *Russia and the Contemporary World*, Vol. 4, No. 101, 2018.

[15] That is cited by Russian researchers as at least one reason that Russia essentially missed the Oromo Revolution in Ethiopia in 2014–2018, despite Ethiopia having a special role in Russia-Africa dynamics as the birthplace of the great-grandfather of legendary Russian poet Alexander Pushkin (Ivan Loshkaryov, "Russia's Policy in a Dynamic Africa: Searching for a Strategy," Russian International Affairs Council, October 9, 2019; and Alexandra Fokina and Ekaterina Pervysheva, "Bratya Po Oruzhiyu. Rossiya Pitayetsya Vosstonovit Vliyaniye V Afrike. Pochemu Eyo Presledyyt Neydachi?" ["Brothers in Arms: Russia Is Trying to Restore Influence in Africa. Why Does It Fail?"], Lenta Ru, November 21, 2020).

[16] U.S. Agency for International Development (USAID), "U.S. Overseas Loans and Grants: Obligations and Loan Authorizations, July 1, 1945–September 30, 2019," webpage, February 24, 2021a.

[17] Judd Devermont, "The World Is Coming to Sub-Saharan Africa. Where Is the United States?" Center for Strategic and International Studies, August 24, 2018; and former U.S. Department of State official, interview with the authors, July 2021.

of long-standing diplomatic attention and engagement that is expected by African leaders.[18] Furthermore, U.S. authors note that the United States underuses the ability of senior officials to forge and maintain relationships (rather than just seal deals) and, particularly since the attack on the U.S. facilities in Benghazi, Libya, limits the ability of senior diplomats stationed abroad to spearhead meaningful developments in bilateral relations. One interviewee also noted that, for medium-level meetings, the United States often chooses representatives who may not be at the equivalent level to the representative from the African partner country.[19]

Lastly, when comparing the three great powers, we did not identify a discernable difference in the practices of visa-free travel programs in various African countries.[20] Great-power competitors' visa-free travel programs are one-way, meaning that U.S., Chinese, or Russian citizens may visit certain countries without a visa, but the citizens of these countries may not visit the United States, China, or Russia without a visa.

Information

Figure 2.2 illustrates the potential for competition in the informational domain for the United States, China, and Russia collectively across Africa.

Across the informational means of influence, the greatest potential for competition is concentrated in South Africa.[21] As noted in Chapter One, our methodology for informational influence was limited to government-owned media presence, so we were not able to pick up differences in competition related to other types of informational activities.[22] Therefore, sev-

---

[18] Former U.S. Department of State official, interview with the authors, July 2021.

[19] Judd Devermont, "A New U.S. Policy Framework for the African Century," Center for Strategic and International Studies, August 7, 2020b; and former U.S. Department of State official, interview with the authors, July 2021.

[20] Besides that, expatriate communities may be a significant force of lobbying the foreign policy and economic interests of their countries of origin. Although precise data are difficult to find, the available information suggests that Libya and South America may host the largest U.S.-, Chinese-, and Russian-born communities. Unofficial sources suggest that Russian immigration to Africa may have peaked in the early 1990s and has since fallen, but there has been an increase in the number of Chinese migrant workers, along with China's growing economic and diplomatic presence (in addition to the sources of analysis outlined in Table A.1, see United Nations Department of Economic and Social Affairs, "International Migrant Stock: The 2017 Revision," webpage, undated).

[21] See Table A.3 for the list of each African country's influence-seeking indices, by great power, and overall competition potential for the informational domain.

[22] Our quantitative methodology did not include analysis of the use of internet-based platforms for informational influence, because internet penetration in Africa was only 39.6 percent in 2019 (admittedly with large variation among countries) and because of the limited availability of comparable data across all African countries and the three great powers within the time frame of the project. However, Russian and Chinese government-linked media outlets do make information available online in English, French, and Portuguese, making it potentially available for African internet users. More has been written about Russia-linked online information influence activities on online networking sites; over the past few years, such activities have been detected in several African countries. Facebook has deactivated accounts that were displaying

FIGURE 2.2

Informational Competition Potential in Africa

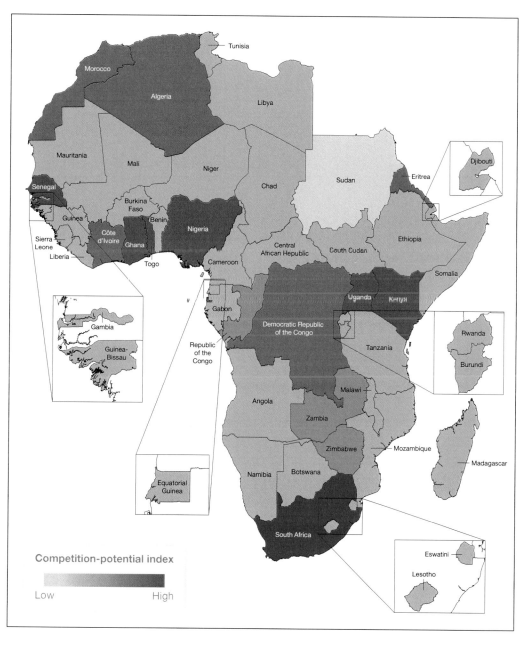

Competition-potential index

Low   High

SOURCE: Authors' analysis of the influence-seeking measures described in this report; for data sources, see the appendix. Base map: Esri, Garmin, and CIA, 2019.

eral countries—Ghana, Kenya, and Nigeria—rank at the same level, just below South Africa. All four countries, as well as Senegal and Uganda, are among the most rapidly growing African entertainment and media markets.[23] Because Voice of America and the Middle East Broadcasting Networks (both funded by the U.S. government) cover nearly every reviewed country, directly or through affiliates, measuring their presence did not meaningfully help us identify which countries received greater attention from the United States in this domain.[24] The organizations offer programs specifically for Africa in English and French, as well as several African languages.[25]

Although neither China's nor Russia's media has a geographical span comparable to that of Voice of America, both countries have been active in seeking influence through government-owned or government-linked media over the past two decades. China's largely government-owned media presence in Africa started in the early 2000s and has particularly intensified over the past decade. As of this research, its media was present directly or through affiliates in nine countries.[26] We detected the presence of China's media in Ghana, Kenya, Nigeria, Senegal, South Africa, Togo, Uganda, Zambia, and Zimbabwe. China's aim is pri-

---

inauthentic behavior and were linked to Russian actors; those accounts specifically targeted Cameroon, CAR, Côte d'Ivoire, the DRC, Libya, Madagascar, Mozambique, and Sudan (Africa Center for Strategic Studies, "Russian Disinformation Campaigns Target Africa: An Interview with Shelby Grossman," February 18, 2020). For an analysis of Kremlin-linked media about UN and EU missions in Mali and CAR, see Tomass Pildegovičs, Kristina VanSant, and Monika Hanley, eds., *Russia's Activities in Africa's Information Environment—Case Studies: Mali and Central African Republic*, Riga, Latvia: NATO Strategic Communications Centre of Excellence, 2021.

[23] In addition, Ghana, South Africa, and Senegal were among the African countries with the highest ranking in the 2021 World Press Freedom Index, while Kenya, Nigeria, and Uganda rated significantly lower (Reporters Without Borders, "World Press Freedom Index," webpage, undated, from 2021; and Andrea Ayemoba, "Ghana's Entertainment and Media Revenue to More Than Double over the Next Five Years—PWC Report," Africa Business Communities, September 21, 2017).

[24] Voice of America has a significant network of affiliates, FM frequencies, and transmitters. It is available in English, French, and numerous African languages (Voice of America, "Programs," webpage, undated; and U.S. Agency for Global Media, *FY 2020 Performance and Accountability Report*, Washington, D.C., November 16, 2020).

[25] Voice of America Afrique, homepage, undated.

[26] For example, China Radio International covers Kenya; China's news agency Xinhua has entered into a partnership with Kenya's most-read newspaper, *Daily Nation*; and China's television station CNC World has been broadcasting to African satellite and cable viewers since 2011. The Beijing-based and technically private StarTimes Group, which has become popular among cable and satellite viewers, also produced content in local languages and included ideological elements (Chrispin Mwakideu, "Experts Warn of China's Growing Media Influence in Africa," Deutsche Welle, January 29, 2021; Eric Olander, "China's StarTimes Is Now One of Africa's Most Important Media Companies," *Medium*, August 26, 2017; Herman Wasserman and Dani Madrid-Morales, "How Influential Are Chinese Media in Africa? An Audience Analysis in Kenya and South Africa," *International Journal of Communication*, Vol. 12, May 14, 2018; and Gerrit Wiesmann, "Joseph Odindo on China's Influence on African Media," Mercator Institute for China Studies, January 29, 2021).

marily to "tell China's stories well,"[27] promote a China-friendly discourse, and tell the story of China as a positive economic cooperation partner and a benign actor. Its media strategy is based on the longer-term goal of gaining support for China's economic and political objectives and includes journalist training and cultural exchanges.[28] Kenya has been the object of the most-intense Chinese media relations; activities include entering into partnerships with local media, establishing local affiliates or new media channels, and creating local content in local languages.[29] Importantly, Kenya hosted the first-ever foreign-based broadcasting hub of China Central Television following the establishment of the Africa-based network in 2012, and the leading English-language state newspaper *China Daily* is also published in Kenya.[30] But China's media presence is broader than just government-owned platforms: The technically private media company StarTimes has a foothold in both Kenya and South Africa.[31]

Russia seeks to ensconce Africa's media within Russia's information space, and we identified Russia's state-linked media presence in Algeria, Côte d'Ivoire, the DRC, Eritrea, Morocco, the Republic of the Congo, and South Africa. Moscow aims to reduce the threat of what it perceives as foreign disinformation against Russia, nurture support for Russia's foreign policy in Africa and elsewhere, and boost its reputation while positioning itself as a symbol of "the opposite of everything bad—colonialism, capitalism and inequality"—a reputation that Russian experts fear is slowly perishing because of the generational change among African elites.[32] Russia is perhaps more active in Africa via online, rather than print, media. For example, Russian government–supported online media and television broadcasts are distributed in English, French, and Portuguese.[33] We identified seven countries in which Russia-

---

[27] The phrase was introduced by President Xi Jinping in a speech to the National Propaganda and Ideology Work Conference on August 19, 2013 (China Media Project, "Telling China's Story Well," April 16, 2021).

[28] Louisa Lim and Julia Bergin, *The China Story: Reshaping the World's Media*, Brussels: International Federation of Journalists, June 2020; and Jorge Marinho, "China in Africa (2019): Facebook and Twitter as Part of Public Diplomacy," *CPD Blog*, University of Southern California Center on Public Diplomacy, August 14, 2020.

[29] Andrew Jacobs, "Pursuing Soft Power, China Puts Stamp on Africa's News," *New York Times*, August 16, 2012.

[30] Michael Leslie, "The Dragon Shapes Its Image: A Study of Chinese Media Influence Strategies in Africa," *African Studies Quarterly*, Vol. 16, No. 3–4, December 2016.

[31] There, China or Chinese companies own or have stakes in television and printed media. In smaller nations, China tends to have re-broadcasting agreements (Wasserman and Madrid-Morales, 2018).

[32] Fokina and Pervysheva, 2020; and Nataliya Bugayova and Darina Regio, *The Kremlin's Campaign in Africa: Assessment Update*, Washington, D.C.: Institute for the Study of War, August 2019.

[33] Russian researchers have lamented that Russia is not paying enough attention to television and radio media; in particular, they have argued that Russia should add Africa to its existing list of focal areas for information distribution (which currently includes Europe and the United States). Indeed, in 2019, Africa had the lowest percentage of individuals using the internet (28.6 percent), compared with 76.7 percent in the United States and 82.5 percent in Europe (International Telecommunication Union, "Statistics," webpage, undated; and Nikita Panin, "Vozmozhen Li Afrikanskii Gambit Vo Vneshnei Politike Rosii?" ["Is the African Gambit Possible in Russian Foreign Policy?"], Russian International Affairs Council, April 23, 2021).

linked media outlets have been present recently, and most of those instances are joint media projects carried out by Sputnik or RT.[34] Compared with China's, Russia's media presence is more limited; its outlets are in fewer countries, the scale and methods of engagement are more limited, and the activities are focused mostly on content-sharing, joint program development, and training for journalists.[35] Yet Russia also has additional cultural tools of influence. The Federal Agency for the Commonwealth of Independent States Affairs, Compatriots Living Abroad, and International Humanitarian Cooperation (Rossotrudnichestvo)—better known as the soft-power arm of Russia's foreign policy and information operations—is present in Ethiopia, Morocco, the Republic of the Congo, South Africa, Tanzania, Tunisia, and Zambia, mostly in the form of Russian centers for science and culture.[36] These centers may help Russia create better political relations with the host countries.[37]

As we noted in Chapter One, influence-seeking should not be conflated with influence. In this regard, despite the gains made by China and Russia in the information sphere, the United States appears to maintain a good deal of influence in Africa, judging by public opinion polls. Public opinion shows, for example, that African populations prefer democracy and accountable governance and are at least slightly more in favor of the U.S. model of development than of China's model in most African countries, particularly among younger Africans.[38]

Military

Figure 2.3 illustrates the potential for competition in the military domain for the United States, China, and Russia collectively across Africa.

Across the region, military involvement by the three powers seems to converge in Sudan, Nigeria, and South Africa.[39] Sudan's high ranking is driven by its high importance for both

---

[34] These seven countries are Algeria, the DRC, Eritrea, Côte d'Ivoire, Morocco, the Republic of the Congo, and South Africa (in addition to the sources identified in Table A.1, see Nataliya Bugayova and George Barros, "The Kremlin's Expanding Media Conglomerate," Institute for the Study of War, January 15, 2020).

[35] Bugayova and Barros, 2020.

[36] Rossotrudnichestvo, "Zarubezhniye Predstavitelstva" ["Overseas Representations"], webpage, undated.

[37] However, despite this presence, some reports suggest that the placement of these offices has not been based on Russia's strategic interests; for example, Rossotrudnichestvo has not announced any plans to create an office in CAR or Sudan (Alexander Petrov, "Tam Horosho, No Nam Tuda Ne Nado" ["It's Good There, but We Don't Need to Go There"], Versia, June 17, 2021).

[38] However, the margin that Africans prefer the U.S. development model over China's is small—32 percent to 23 percent (Josephine Appiah-Nyamekye Sanny and Edem Selormey, "Africans Regard China's Influence as Significant and Positive, but Slipping," Afrobarometer, Dispatch No. 407, November 17, 2020).

[39] See Table A.4 for the list of each African country's influence-seeking indices, by great power, and overall competition potential for the military domain. Note that Djibouti is ranked 17th overall. Competition has been taking place there between the U.S. Combined Joint Task Force – Horn of Africa and the People's Liberation Army (PLA) Advance Base Unit at Doraleh Port, where the sides have made such accusations as using laser pointers to harass aircrews and using other tactics against vessels docked at the Chinese pier. Although there are high levels of military competition in Djibouti currently, the purpose of our methodol-

FIGURE 2.3

Military Competition Potential in Africa

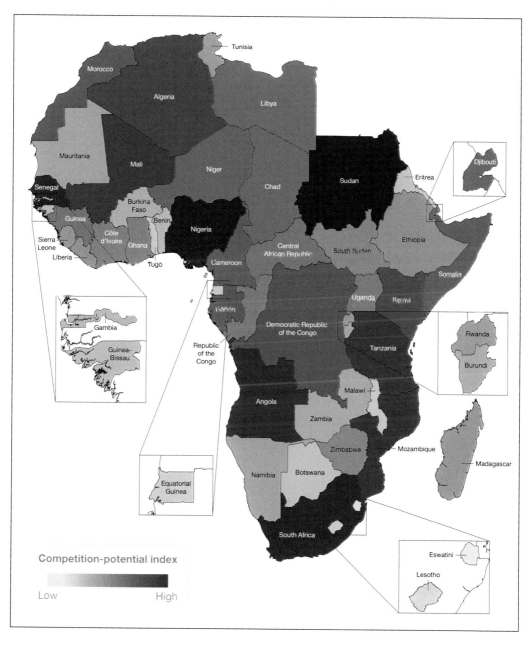

Competition-potential index

Low   High

SOURCE: Authors' analysis of the influence-seeking measures described in this report; for data sources, see the appendix. Base map: Esri, Garmin, and CIA, 2019.

China and Russia. This priority is evidenced in the existence of bilateral military agreements with both powers; the presence of both great powers' PMSCs in Sudan; at least some export of military equipment to Sudan between 2014 and 2020; the presence of China's and, to a much smaller extent, Russia's military forces as part of UN missions; and Russia's involvement in the war in Darfur. China's military footprint in Sudan is largely based on its oil interests. Sudan is also one of the African countries where China participates in a UN mission that allows China to build out-of-area experience, and this presence could allow China to protect its citizens in the country if needed.[40] Russia is primarily interested in Sudan as a geostrategically important location for access to the Red Sea and the Indian Ocean. In 2020, Russia signed an agreement with Sudan to establish a Russian naval outpost there.[41] This outpost could help Russia regain at least some of the military footprint it used to have along the Red Sea during the Cold War.

Meanwhile, U.S. engagement in Sudan has been limited to diplomatic means, although new cooperation opportunities may arise following the removal of Sudan from the U.S. Department of State's list of state sponsors of terrorism in 2020. And although Nigeria and South Africa are important for Russia and China, they rank quite low for the United States. In fact, for the military factor, we observe that there is a higher coincidence of the countries that rank high for both China and Russia than for either China or Russia and the United States. Of the countries with the five highest competition scores for the United States, none is among the countries with the ten highest scores for the other powers, and only one (Sudan) for China and Russia is in the United States' ten highest scores for military influence-seeking.

Sudan, Nigeria, and Tanzania ranked the highest for China, followed closely by South Africa. These are countries where China has at least some military presence (Sudan), has carried out military exercises (Sudan, Nigeria, Tanzania, South Africa), has exported at least some military equipment (Nigeria, Sudan, Tanzania), has a presence of PMSCs (Sudan, Nigeria, Tanzania, South Africa), or has a military or strategic-level agreement that we were able to identify (Sudan, Nigeria, Tanzania). China's post-Maoist military engagement with coun-

---

ogy was to identify potential new areas of competition where a broad set of interests of all three great powers might intersect. Notwithstanding the presence of the U.S. and Chinese troops in Djibouti, China has more troops in five other African countries, and it holds more military exercises in several other countries as well. Djibouti ranked low across the military factors that we analyzed for Russia (former U.S. government official and think-tank expert on Africa, interview with the authors, July 2021; Africa and special operations researcher, email exchange with the authors, December 2021). See also Aaron Mehta, "Two US Airmen Injured by Chinese Lasers in Djibouti, DOD Says," *Defense News*, May 3, 2018.

[40] Richard Gowan, "China's Pragmatic Approach to UN Peacekeeping," Brookings Institution, September 14, 2020.

[41] It is reported that the outpost will be used mainly for logistics, repairs, and resupply; as of this writing, the agreement had not been ratified by Sudan's parliament. More-recent reports suggest that Sudan may refuse hosting a Russian base, following the changes in Sudan's leadership after the coup in 2021 (Amy Mackinnon, "With Base in Sudan, Russia Expands Its Military Reach in Africa," *Foreign Policy*, December 14, 2020; and Amy Mackinnon, Robbie Gramer, and Jack Detsch, "Russia's Dreams of a Red Sea Naval Base Are Scuttled—for Now," *Foreign Policy*, July 15, 2022).

tries in Africa and other countries outside its borders started increasing in the late 1990s as a result of its broader "going out" strategy, which encouraged Chinese firms to invest overseas, and has intensified even more over the past decade.[42] In Africa, it has particularly hinged on participation in multilateral peacekeeping operations under the UN and the African Union, as well as a gradual strengthening of bilateral security relationships. Of the three great powers examined in this report, China is the largest troop contributor to UN peacekeeping operations in Africa. As a result, China has the second-largest military presence of the great powers, after the United States: The number of its uniformed personnel on the continent increased from 1,797 in 2014 to 2,318 in 2020.[43] Chinese PMSCs are also present in Africa, where they tend to be involved in ensuring the safety and security of private companies and their employees. The PMSCs' presence on the continent increased after incidents in Chad (2008), Iraq (2014), Sudan (2008 and 2012), and South Sudan, (2016), when Chinese workers were endangered and needed evacuation.[44] Although China seems to adhere at least rhetorically to a policy of non-interference (thus trying to avoid a potential backlash), and although China wants to tightly control the PMSCs to avoid their blundering into local conflicts, members of Chinese PMSCs and Chinese nationals have been accused of providing illegal military training to a local security firm in Zambia and operating an illegal security firm in Kenya.[45]

Despite China's efforts, the United States and Russia exceed China in military influence-seeking. For example, Chinese PMSCs remain new and weak relative to their U.S. and Russian counterparts, leaving many Chinese firms to rely on local militias, host-country forces, or third-country PMSCs when local law enforcement proves insufficient to defend the firm's employees.[46] Although China also has been aggressively pursuing the African military equipment market since 2010 and considers Africa one of its key arms export markets, today China

---

[42] Devermont, 2020a.

[43] Although China has pulled its military from Liberia and Côte d'Ivoire, its military presence in the DRC, Mali, and Western Sahara has remained constant, while its presence in Djibouti, South Sudan, and Sudan has increased.

[44] Helena Legarda and Meia Nouwens, "Guardians of the Belt and Road: The Internationalization of China's Private Security Companies," Mercator Institute for China Studies, August 16, 2018; Ben Blanchard, "Stranded Chinese Workers in Iraq Being Evacuated," Reuters, June 27, 2014; and Xinhua, "Backgrounder: China's Major Overseas Evacuations in Recent Years," *China Daily*, March 30, 2015.

[45] U.S.-China Economic and Security Review Commission, "China's Strategic Aims in Africa," hearing, Washington, D.C., May 8, 2020a.

[46] For example, DeWe Security Services Group, one of the most well-known Chinese overseas security firms, was founded only in 2011, and the China Overseas Security Group was founded only in 2015. Chinese companies in Africa also tend to hire local guards to assist in securing facilities (Alessandro Arduino, "China's Private Security Companies: The Evolution of a New Security Actor," in Nadège Rolland, ed., *Securing the Belt and Road Initiative: China's Evolving Military Engagement Along the Silk Roads*, Seattle, Wash.: National Bureau of Asian Research, Special Report No. 80, September 2019, p. 98).

is only the fourth-largest arms supplier to Africa after Russia, France, and the United States.[47] However, compared with the United States and even Russia, China seems to be selling weapons to a larger variety of recipients, and its weapons have been found to be used in conflict zones in Côte d'Ivoire, the DRC, Somalia, and Sudan.[48] China also uses arms sales as a means to increase its influence and build economic and political relationships.[49] Another means of engagement is military exercises: Although China's participation in military exercises is ahead of Russia's, China has carried out significantly fewer exercises in Africa than the United States has and has been engaged in the fewest conflicts of the three powers.[50]

As China has been expanding its military presence in Africa, it also has increased the number of countries with which it has military or strategic agreements. More details often are unknown, but China has at least some sort of an agreement in place with 18 countries, and the unifying factor is that these countries have significant quantities of natural resources of interest to China; the exceptions are Senegal, Tanzania, and Djibouti, where it has its only naval base in Africa.[51] China has pursued better access not only through agreements but also through funding; since at least 2015, it has financed military infrastructure projects.[52] Besides that, China reportedly has sought to establish a network of space ground stations and operated satellite tracking stations in Namibia and Kenya.[53]

For Russia's competition-potential indices, Sudan, South Africa, and CAR rank the highest, followed closely by Angola and Nigeria. These countries have high indices because they have at least some military equipment imports from Russia (Angola, Nigeria, Sudan, South

---

[47] The largest African recipients of China's arms in terms of value between 2014 and 2020 were Algeria, Nigeria, Sudan, and Cameroon (Tatiana Kondratenko, "Russian Arms Exports to Africa: Moscow's Long-Term Strategy," *Deutsche Welle*, May 29, 2020; and Andrew Hull and David Markov, "Chinese Arms Sales to Africa," *IDA Research Notes*, Summer 2012).

[48] Colum Lynch, "China's Arms Exports Flooding Sub-Saharan Africa," *Washington Post*, August 25, 2012; and Cohen, Treyger, et al., 2023.

[49] Cohen, Treyger, et al., 2023.

[50] Over the period that we collected data, China participated in one exercise each in Cambodia (Golden Dragon 2019), South Sudan (China-Bangladesh Peacekeeping Training Exercise in 2018), and South Africa (Multinational Maritime Exercise 2019, together with Russia), as well as a maritime drill in the Gulf of Aden in 2020 (see the sources identified in Table A.1, but especially International Institute for Strategic Studies, Military Balance Plus, online database, undated; and Uppsala Conflict Data Program, web tool, Uppsala University Department of Peace and Conflict Research, undated, particularly the Armed Conflict Dataset and the External Support Dataset).

[51] Although Senegal lacks rich natural resources, Beijing is interested in pursuing political and economic interests there (Stefan Gehrold and Lena Tietze, "Far from Altruistic: China's Presence in Senegal," *KAS International Reports*, Vol. 11, November 2011). China also has been interested in Tanzania's port infrastructure (John Hursh, "Tanzania Pushes Back on Chinese Port Project," *Maritime Executive*, December 2, 2019). (In addition, see the sources identified in Table A.1.)

[52] Examples include support to the African Union logistics base in Douala, Cameroon (Devermont, 2020a).

[53] U.S.-China Economic and Security Review Commission, *2019 Report to Congress*, Washington, D.C.: U.S. Government Publishing Office, November 2019.

Sudan), have or have recently had a presence of Russian PMSCs (all five countries), have at least some presence of official Russian military forces (Sudan, CAR), or have participated in an exercise with Russia (Sudan, CAR, South Africa).

The military and security domains are especially significant for Russia's role on the continent, and overall Russia is a significant competitor to the United States in the military domain. Arms sales and transfers and other military assistance (largely in the form of PMSC services) are some of the primary tools of Russia's foreign policy and Kremlin-linked actors in Africa. In fact, Russia's military presence on the continent by far dominates diplomatic activities, informational presence, and even economic influence.[54] Russia's military-technical cooperation is aimed at maintaining and expanding Russia's arms export market, ensuring the presence of Russian military experts and trainers, gaining experience in counterterrorism operations, improving the access of Russian forces to locations that could have strategic and operational meaning, establishing support bases for Russian forces, and improving the system of deployment and basing for the armed forces and thus supporting Russia's image as a great power.[55] In this respect, Russia is building on the Soviet experience of providing military equipment, training, and assistance to revolutionary movements in Africa. Today, however, ideological reasons have given way to economic and geopolitical interests—particularly maintaining good relations with African leaders, maintaining Russia's role as an influential power, and supporting Russia's economic interests.

Russia is the dominant supplier of arms to African countries, not only of the three powers but worldwide. This is a role that Russia has consistently built since the early 2000s.[56] By far the largest recipient of Russian arms is Algeria; other significant buyers include Angola, Nigeria, Sudan, and South Sudan.[57] Although U.S. and international sanctions on Russia theoretically could hamper African states' ability to procure Russian weapons and encourage them to continue cooperation with the United States and other Western countries, Russia's officials

[54] Russian Federation, *Maritime Doctrine of the Russian Federation for the Period up to 2020*, Moscow, July 2015; and Russian Federation, *Military Doctrine of the Russian Federation*, Moscow, December 25, 2014.

[55] Russian Federation, 2014; SNG.Today, "Voyennii Expert Obyasnil, Kak Bazoi V Sudane PF Ochertit Nacionalniye Interesi V Afrike" ["Military Expert Explained How the Base in Sudan Will Help Russia Outline Its National Interests in Africa"], May 14, 2021; and Ksenija Brishpolets, "Strategicheskiye Interesy Rossii V Afrike" ["Russian Strategic Interests in Africa"], *Mezhdunarodnaya Analitika* [*International Analytics*], No. 1-2, 2019.

[56] Pieter D. Wezeman, Alexandra Kuimova, and Siemon T. Wezeman, *Trends in International Arms Transfers, 2020*, Stockholm: Stockholm International Peace Research Institute, March 2021.

[57] Russia's sales between 2014 and 2020 have included submarines, anti-tank missiles, combat helicopters, guided bombs for Uganda's combat aircraft, T-90 main battle tanks to Uganda and Algeria, tank destroyer Khrizantema-S missiles to Libya, and transport helicopters. China's sales over the same period have included air search radars, anti-ship missiles, beyond-visual-range missiles, combat helicopters, fighter aircraft, surface-to-air missile systems, self-propelled guns and mortars, multiple rocket launchers, and short-range air-to-air missiles (per our review of Stockholm International Peace Research Institute [SIPRI], Arms Transfers Database, web tool, undated-a, trend-indicator values of arms exports from Russia, 2014–2020).

have made clear their intentions to counteract these sanctions by offering payment methods and procurement conditions tailored to each buyer.[58]

In terms of the other military factors considered in our analysis, Russia somewhat falls behind the United States. Of the three powers, Russia has the smallest presence of official uniformed personnel on the continent, and those troops are there mainly as part of UN missions. Russia has also participated in the fewest exercises of the three powers; between 2016 and 2020, Russia participated in only one military exercise.[59] Meanwhile, Russian PMSCs are scattered across the region.[60] Using open-source materials, we were able to record their presence in 25 of the reviewed countries, and data suggest that the geographical span of PMSCs has expanded since around 2015. Although the United States has the widest distribution of PMSCs across the continent, Russia's PMSCs may serve as an unofficial arm of the Kremlin's policies and as a means of propping up friendly regimes and leaders. This arrangement helps protect Russia's economic interests and helps Russia limit its financial and political (both domestic and external) costs while maintaining plausible deniability.[61] Russian PMSCs, specifically the Wagner Group, have already been engaged in clashes with U.S. partners in the region. Russian PMSCs in CAR have clashed with French troops and the UN and EU missions in the country. In 2021, for example, the UN Multidimensional Integrated Stabilization Mission in CAR had to force Wagner to return to its base after the PMSC tried to arrest a CAR military official and, as a result, deteriorated the security situation.[62] The EU and UN have expressed concern about the blurring of the line between civil and military operations. Specifically, the UN has been concerned about the interconnection between Russian PMSCs and a Russia-owned CAR-based mineral extraction company, as well as the sometimes blurred lines among private military personnel, CAR's armed forces, and even UN peacekeepers and their violations of human rights and international humanitarian law.[63] Wagner has managed to take over command and supervision of the Central African Armed Forces units (including

---

[58] "Rússia renuncia ao dólar e se flexibiliza na exportação de armas para contrariar sanções" ["Russia Renounces the Dollar and Becomes More Flexible in Arms Exports to Counter Sanctions"], Sputnik, July 21, 2021.

[59] This was the Multinational Maritime Exercise 2019 in South Africa. Its aims were boarding, interoperability, and maritime security (International Institute for Strategic Studies, undated).

[60] Russia maintains the smallest presence of official military forces in Africa of the three powers; the number decreased from 59 in 2013 to 39 in 2020, after a reduction of personnel in the DRC and Côte d'Ivoire. The only locations where Russian force presence increased is CAR (based on data from International Institute for Strategic Studies, undated).

[61] Siegle, 2021.

[62] Rodrigue Forku, "Tensions High Between UN Forces, Russian Mercenaries in C. African Republic," Anadolu Agency, July 12, 2021; and United Nations Office of the High Commissioner for Human Rights, *Public Report on Violation of Human Rights and International Humanitarian Law in the Central African Republic During the Electoral Period, July 2020–June 2021*, Geneva, August 4, 2021.

[63] United Nations Human Rights Council, "CAR: Experts Alarmed by Government's Use of 'Russian Trainers,' Close Contacts with UN Peacekeepers," press release, March 31, 2021.

the National Territorial Battalion 7 that had been trained by the EU) and gain influence over the armed forces' General Staff and government institutions.[64]

To support its aims stated earlier, Russia has signed at least some kind of a military cooperation agreement with at least 33 countries in Africa, and some of these, such as Mozambique and Sudan, allow Russia access to naval or air infrastructure.[65] Thus, Russia loses to the United States in this category only in terms of the coverage of agreements. Overall, Russia seems to prefer a more financially conservative approach to a potential future foothold on the continent—that is, by negotiating access to existing infrastructure rather than constructing its own.[66] Through these agreements, Russia seeks to improve the access of its forces to locations that could have strategic and operational use, establish support bases, and improve the system of deployment and basing of its armed forces.[67] Specifically, it seeks to ensure access for Russian naval and other forces to key remote areas of the world ocean as part of its aim to maintain freedom of navigation and safe navigation, ensure access to vital areas for sea lines of communication, and ensure "on a periodic basis a naval presence of the Russian Federation in the Indian Ocean."[68] In addition, Russia's State Space Corporation, commonly known as Roscosmos, has acknowledged its interest in placing ground stations in Africa to support Russia's Globalnaya Navigazionnaya Sputnikovaya Sistema (or GLONASS) satellite navigation system.[69] South Africa, which is also the location of the U.S. National Geospatial-Intelligence Agency monitoring station, reportedly became the first African country to host a ground station for Russia's system.[70]

This military presence does not necessarily translate to indiscriminate engagement in proxy conflict. More recently, Russia has been selective about involvement in African conflicts and has had fewer engagements than the United States has, though more than China. Russia

---

[64] European External Action Service, "Political and Strategic Environment of CSDP Missions in the Central African Republic (CAR)," November 22, 2021.

[65] Open-source materials suggest that Russia has access to port or airport infrastructure in six countries: Guinea, Madagascar, Mozambique, Sierra Leone, South Africa, and Sudan (in addition to the sources in Table A.1, see "Moskva Zakluchila Soglasheniye Flota V Sudane" ["Moscow Signed an Agreement on the Base of the Russian Fleet in Sudan"], RBK, December 8, 2020).

[66] Africa and special operations researcher, interview with the authors, July 2021.

[67] Russian Federation, 2014; SNG.Today, 2021.

[68] Russian Federation, 2015.

[69] "Russia May Create Glonass Ground Stations in Africa and Asia-Pacific Region," TASS, June 18, 2019.

[70] It has also been reported that Russia is considering establishing another ground station in Africa—in Angola ("Russia to Deploy Space Monitoring Stations in South Africa, Mexico and Chile," Space in Africa, March 7, 2019; Jan Van Sickle and John A. Dutton, "The Control Segment," Penn State College of Earth and Mineral Sciences, 2020; and "Roscosmos to Deploy GLONASS Monitoring Stations in Five Countries," TASS, September 16, 2021).

has been engaged in conflicts in CAR, Côte d'Ivoire, Libya, and Sudan—where its involvement has been through PMSCs, some uniformed personnel, and provision of arms sales.[71]

For the United States, Niger, Senegal, and Kenya rank the highest. These are countries with which the United States has conducted exercises or training (Senegal, Kenya), with significant U.S. military presence (Niger), with at least some U.S. military imports (all three countries), or where we were able to identify current or recent presence of U.S. PMSCs (all three countries).

Overall, the United States continues to lead in terms of its military presence in Africa. In fact, open-source data and expert interviews suggest that the United States is more present on the continent today than it was during the Cold War.[72] U.S. military interests in Africa seem to have increased since 2002, when the United States extended the global war on terrorism to the Sahel region. This interest has generally been in countering VEOs and has involved small-footprint operations: special operations forces, security assistance, and intelligence and logistical support to partner countries.[73]

The United States leads the great powers across almost all of the military variables. It has the largest uniformed presence, it has the largest network of military agreements, and it carried out the most exercises with African countries over our period of data collection. The United States' uniformed presence in Africa has increased, from 3,227 personnel in 2014 to 5,828 in 2020.[74] U.S. PMSCs seem to be present across the continent; however, in contrast with Russian PMSCs, they tend to be involved in ensuring the safety and security of private companies and their employees or carrying out U.S. government contracts aimed at training or supporting local partners.[75] These companies often have multiple divisions that can carry out a broad variety of security tasks,[76] military training and advising efforts, so-called

---

[71] This list does not include purely PMSC contracts and activities. For example, in CAR, Russia has provided assistance in the form of arms supplies and training, via both uniformed personnel and PMSCs, but PMSCs have also been involved in conflicts in the DRC and Mozambique. See Cohen, Treyger, et al., 2023, Appendix C.

[72] International Institute for Strategic Studies, undated (2021 data); Africa and special operations researcher, interview with the authors, July 2021.

[73] However, the U.S. military engagement reflects the same issues that mire overall U.S. foreign policy toward the continent: The involvement tends to lack a comprehensive and strategic view of Africa and is largely piecemeal (Africa and special operations researcher, interview with the authors, July 2021; Office of Counterterrorism, 2002; and Michael Shurkin and Aneliese Bernard, "Ten Things the United States Should Do to Combat Terrorism in the Sahel," *War on the Rocks*, August 30, 2021).

[74] This is mainly because of an increase of personnel in Djibouti and Niger and is likely related to the U.S. military infrastructure in these locations. Elsewhere, however, U.S. military presence has remained constant (e.g., in Cameroon) or has been reduced (e.g., in Liberia).

[75] We identified that the major U.S. PMSCs have operations in 36 African countries.

[76] For example, Shell employs armored personnel to ensure the safety of its operation in the Niger Delta (Africa and special operations researcher, interview with the authors, July 2021).

democracy-promotion activities, safe transportation operations, and maintenance and support for U.S. forces and missions.[77]

Besides having the largest network of military cooperation agreements in place, the United States has the largest network of military bases and outposts, including Camp Lemonnier in Djibouti and Niger Air Base 201 near Agadez, Niger, as well as bases, outposts, or access to infrastructure in Burkina Faso, Ghana, Kenya, and Uganda.[78] At the same time, U.S. access, basing, and presence in Africa are more limited than in other areas of responsibility, and instead of having larger permanent military bases, the U.S. military in Africa tends to have lighter-footprint presence and expansible facilities and access points.[79] More important for operations in Africa are the U.S. bases in Europe, particularly in terms of the location of longer-range U.S. Air Force assets.[80] Of the three great powers, the United States participated in the most military exercises in Africa during our period of data collection. The number of exercises grew from four in 2014 to 20 in 2020.[81] The U.S. exercises are aimed at training counterterrorism and counterinsurgency operations, maritime and navigation, special operations forces, air transport, air combat, or humanitarian assistance and disaster response.[82]

Compared with its great-power competitors, the United States has been more engaged in conflicts in Africa, most recently as part of its focus on the global war on terrorism.[83]

---

[77] For example, some U.S. PMSCs implement U.S. government programs aimed at training and democracy-promotion or provision of operations and maintenance support for U.S. facilities (Kwesi Aning, Thomas Jaye, and Samuel Atuobi, "The Role of Private Military Companies in US-Africa Policy," *Review of African Political Economy*, Vol. 35, No. 118, 2008; and DynCorp International, "DynCorp International Wins $20 Million AFRICAP Task Order in Liberia," press release, January 2010).

[78] See, for example, Stephen J. Townsend, general, U.S. Army, "A Secure and Stable Africa Is an Enduring American Interest," statement before the U.S. Senate Armed Services Committee, Washington, D.C., January 30, 2020; U.S. Africa Command Public Affairs, "AFRICOM Commander Conducts Visit to Manda Bay," U.S. Africa Command, January 17, 2021; Craig Whitlock, "U.S. Expands Secret Intelligence Operations in Africa," *Washington Post*, June 13, 2012; and Peter E. Teil, "United States Africa Command Posture and Requirements and IPL Overview," U.S. Africa Command, 2018.

[79] Michael J. Lostumbo, Michael J. McNerney, Eric Peltz, Derek Eaton, David R. Frelinger, Victoria A. Greenfield, John Halliday, Patrick Mills, Bruce R. Nardulli, Stacie L. Pettyjohn, Jerry M. Sollinger, and Stephen M. Worman, *Overseas Basing of U.S. Military Forces: An Assessment of Relative Costs and Strategic Benefits*, Santa Monica, Calif.: RAND Corporation, RR-201-OSD, 2013.

[80] Lostumbo et al., 2013.

[81] The number for 2020 was for planned exercises, most of which did not happen because of the COVID-19 pandemic (International Institute for Strategic Studies, undated).

[82] Most of the exercises with U.S. participation also have involved European allies (United Kingdom, Spain, France, Belgium) and partners (Georgia) or non-European allies and partners (e.g., Canada, Australia) (International Institute for Strategic Studies, undated).

[83] Uppsala Conflict Data Program, undated, particularly the Armed Conflict Dataset and the External Support Dataset; and data on non-state armed groups, from Dangerous Companions Project, homepage, undated. For more information, see Stina Högbladh, Thérése Pettersson, and Lotta Themnér, "External Support in Armed Conflict 1975–2009, Presenting New Data," paper presented at the 52nd Annual International Studies Association Convention, Montreal, Canada, March 16–19, 2011; and Nina von Uexkull

Over our period of data collection, the U.S. military was engaged in seven countries, where it mostly supported recognized government actors, except for Libya in 2011. U.S. support has mostly taken the form of training, material and logistics support, funding or economic support, and in some cases intelligence and weapon support.[84]

Although the United States is the single largest arms exporter globally, and its arms exports to Africa slightly increased from 2016 to 2020, its sales to Africa remain smaller than those of Russia. The United States exports a lot of armored personnel carriers and all-purpose vehicles, but it tends to limit its sales of kinetic military equipment to Cameroon, Kenya, Morocco, Tunisia, and South Africa—countries that enjoy closer overall security cooperation with the United States.[85] Yet none of the countries is significant for the U.S. export market. The United States also makes selected excess military equipment available to African countries through the Excess Defense Articles program.[86]

Economics

Figure 2.4 illustrates the potential for competition in the economic domain for the United States, China, and Russia collectively across Africa.

In the economic domain, the potential for competition among the three powers is the greatest in Algeria, South Africa, and Nigeria. This reflects the great powers' economic interest in the three largest African economies in terms of gross domestic product (GDP),[87] leading oil producers (Nigeria and Algeria),[88] and significant mineral producers or locations of mineral deposits (e.g., South Africa is a leading platinum and gold producer, and Nigeria has significant yet underdeveloped mineral resources).[89] These are the countries that emerge at the top of economic involvement across all three powers in Africa.

Angola, Nigeria, and South Africa rank the highest for economic influence-seeking for China and reflect the top three countries for China's trade volume in 2018. We also detected Chinese companies present in key infrastructure sectors in these countries. Of the three

---

and Thérése Pettersson, "Issues and Actors in African Nonstate Conflicts: A New Data Set," *International Interactions*, Vol. 44, No. 5, 2018.

[84] Uppsala Conflict Data Program, undated, particularly the Armed Conflict Dataset and the External Support Dataset; Dangerous Companions Project, undated.

[85] These countries have received such products as anti-tank missiles, air-to-air missiles, combat helicopters, fighter aircraft, M1A1 Abrams tanks, and unmanned aerial vehicles. Between 2014 and 2020, Nigeria, Kenya, and Algeria were the largest recipients of U.S. weapons in terms of volume (analysis of data from SIPRI, undated-a).

[86] U.S. Government Accountability Office, *Military Equipment: Observations on the Transfer of Excess Humvees to Foreign Governments*, Washington, D.C., GAO-20-189, February 2020.

[87] World Bank, "GDP (Current US$)," webpage, undated-a.

[88] Grace Goodrich, "Top 10: Africa's Leading Oil Producers in 2021," Energy Capital & Power, June 16, 2021.

[89] Mining Africa, "These Are the Top Mining Countries of Africa," webpage, undated.

FIGURE 2.4

Economic Competition Potential in Africa

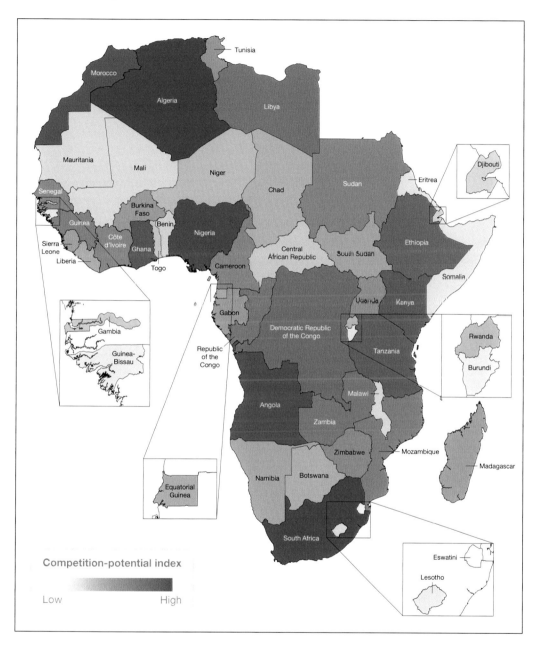

SOURCE: Authors' analysis of the influence-seeking measures described in this report; for data sources, see the appendix. Base map: Esri, Garmin, and CIA, 2019.

powers, China is the largest economic partner for the continent, with increasing trade volumes and large investments, and is behind the United States only in foreign direct investment. China is Africa's largest single-state trading partner, and China-Africa trade more than doubled between 2007 and 2019.[90] In 2019, 16 percent of African exports to countries outside Africa went to China, and 19 percent of African imports from countries outside Africa were from China.[91] China's trade volume with South Africa by far exceeds China's trade with other countries in Africa. Other top trading partners include Angola, Nigeria, Algeria, the DRC, and Ghana, although China maintains substantial trade relations with other African countries.

Our analysis suggests that Chinese companies are present in key infrastructure and resource sectors in at least 33 of the reviewed countries in Africa. China's presence is particularly active in port and airport infrastructure, rail infrastructure, energy, extractive industries and mining, and manufacturing (e.g., cement plants). China is also present in Africa's fishing sector and has encouraged predatory fishing practices in such areas as the Gulf of Guinea.[92] China's fishing practices in South America have already caused diplomatic tensions between the United States and China. Considering that the United States has been assisting African countries in securing their fishing rights, U.S.-China tensions on this matter could continue in Africa.[93] However, Chinese and U.S. companies have collaborated on infrastructure projects. Although China generally prefers financing its own companies, it may resort to using the technical advantages of U.S. companies at least sometimes, particularly for cooperation among large multinational companies in the energy sector.[94] But the line between Chinese companies and the state is blurred, and state-linked companies are often used by the Chinese state and its intelligence services to seek influence and as a means of building China's economic power. Reports suggest a recent increase in the presence of Chinese intelligence personnel in Africa, under the leadership of military and economic intelligence organizations.[95]

Although China has become the largest single-state economic partner for the continent, its economic activities are increasingly scrutinized in Africa, and China has been criticized

---

[90] At the same time, China is only the second-largest import and export partner for Africa, after the EU (Johns Hopkins China-Africa Research Initiative, "Data: China-Africa Trade," webpage, undated).

[91] The U.S. foreign direct investment in Africa reached a peak in 2014 after more than a decade of growth; since then, it has slightly fallen (African Union, *African Trade Statistics: 2020 Yearbook*, Addis Ababa, August 2020; and Statista, "Direct Investment Position of the United States in Africa from 2000 to 2020," August 4, 2021).

[92] Morgan Pincombe, *Casting a Neocolonial Net: China's Exploitative Fishing in the Gulf of Guinea*, Williamsburg, Va.: Project on International Peace and Security, Brief No. 13.5, May 2021.

[93] For example, Chinese fishing boats could clash with African maritime forces trained by U.S. forces.

[94] Yun Sun, "American Companies and Chinese Belt and Road in Africa," Brookings Institution, July 11, 2018.

[95] Executive Research Associates, *China in Africa: A Strategic Overview*, Craighall, South Africa, October 2009; and U.S.-China Economic and Security Review Commission, 2020a.

as using *debt trap–style investments* (long-term loans rather than grants) to create strategic dependency relationships.[96] There is also a perception of a decline of China's influence on national economies over the past few years, and the largest falls have been in Sierra Leone, Botswana, Malawi, and Mali.[97] Moreover, since 2016, China's competitor India is the largest trading partner for sub-Saharan Africa and the second-largest destination for African goods after China (notwithstanding the joint EU market), so China might be more motivated to compete with India than with the United States in Africa.[98]

Algeria, Morocco, and South Africa rank the highest for Russia's economic influence-seeking activities, and these are the top three countries for Russia-Africa trade volume in 2018. We also detected Russian companies present in key infrastructure and economic sectors, as well as at least some foreign direct investment in 2018 and 2019 in these countries. Russia is interested in diversifying its trade and economic relations in order to counteract the impact of sanctions and the fall of oil prices on Russia and to strengthen the client base of its largely state-owned enterprises.[99] Russia-Algeria trade volume by far exceeds Russia's trade with any other country in Africa, followed by Morocco, South Africa, and Tunisia, illustrating Russia's traditionally more-developed trade relations with North Africa.[100] Notwithstanding its role as an arms exporter, Russia has very few products that interest African countries, and, compared with the trade balance of China, the United States, and the EU, Russia's trade balance is modest.[101] The competitiveness of Russa's products and its economic presence in Africa are inferior to those of China, Western countries, and other BRICS (Brazil, Russia, India, China, and South Africa) member states, but Russian officials and researchers still consider Africa to be a potentially promising market for Russian trade and an important supplier of products of extractive services.[102]

---

[96] Views on China's use of debt-trap diplomacy as a policy tool differ among researchers and analysts; some view it as a deliberate lending policy, and some view it as an uncoordinated policy that puts the blame on the receiving governments (Michael Shurkin, Alexander Noyes, and Mary Kate Adgie, *The COVID-19 Pandemic in Sub-Saharan Africa: An Opportunity to Rethink Strategic Competition on the Continent*, Santa Monica, Calif.: RAND Corporation, PE-A1055-1, July 2021; and Sanny and Selormey, 2020).

[97] Sanny and Selormey, 2020.

[98] Devermont, 2018; African Union, 2020.

[99] Fokina and Pervysheva, 2020.

[100] For this project, Egypt is considered part of the Middle East (see the companion report Rhoades et al., 2023; and Kester Kenn Klomegah, "Russia's Strategy to Enter the African Market," *Modern Diplomacy*, May 21, 2021).

[101] Main export industries include agriculture, mechanical engineering, chemical, timber, and metallurgical industry products.

[102] Lora Chkoniya, Gabriel Kotchofa, and Dmitry Ezhov, "Kompetencii Afriki. Chto Afrika Mozhet Predlozhit Rosii I Miru?" ["Africa's Competence. What Can Africa Offer Russia and the World?"], in Andrey Kortunov, Nataliya Zaiser, Elena Kharitonova, Lora Chkoniya, Gabriel Kotchofa, and Dmitry Ezhov, *Afrika-Rosiiya+: Dostizheniya, Problemi, Perspektivi* [*Africa-Russia+: Achievements, Problems, Prospects*], Moscow: Russian International Affairs Council, Report No. 53, 2020.

Russia's state-owned or -linked companies are active in geological exploration, nuclear energy, oil and gas, hydroelectric power, extractive industries and mining (including diamond-, gold-, and uranium-mining), and some budding car manufacturing and assembly. At times, Russian companies cooperate with Western companies on the exploration of energy and mining sites, potentially to squeeze into the rather contested upstream mining landscape, and could eventually use the opportunities to increase their presence in the African oil and gas extractive industries opened by U.S. and other Western companies that may seek to divest.[103] Moscow's energy diplomacy also includes promoting Russia's nuclear power capabilities, particularly by courting Algeria, the DRC, Ethiopia, Ghana, Kenya, Nigeria, Rwanda, South Africa, Sudan, Uganda, and Zambia to build nuclear power plants.

Both China and Russia emphasize the role of the state in developing bilateral business relations.[104] To improve trade, China and Russia have sought to improve trade and business relations both bilaterally (e.g., by developing bilateral elite-to-elite relations and establishing the Russian Export Center) and multilaterally (e.g., via the Forum on China-Africa Cooperation and the Eurasian Economic Commission).[105] Lastly, both China and Russia have sought to offer their space capabilities and knowledge to the budding African space sector and to develop good relations with the African countries that hold space-relevant positions at the UN.[106] Overall, however, China, the United States, and European countries have been more successful in developing good working relations in this realm than Russia has.

South Africa, Nigeria, and Algeria rank the highest for the United States' influence-seeking activities, and they also reflect the top three countries in terms of U.S.-Africa trade

---

[103] For example, in Botswana, a subsidiary of Alrosa (Russian) and Botswana Diamonds Plc (British) was created in 2013 to explore promising deposits; in Ghana, Lukoil entered an offshore exploration project operated by a Norwegian company; and in Nigeria, Lukoil co-funded a deepwater oil project with U.S.-based Chevron ("Krupneishiye Rosiiskiye Proyekti V Afrike" ["The Largest Russian Projects in Africa"], October 23, 2019; Lukoil, "Ghana," webpage, undated-a; Lukoil, "Nigeria," webpage, undated-b; and Etienne Kolly and Justin Michael Cochrane, "To Deal or Not to Deal, That Is the Question . . . ," IHS Markit, July 9, 2002).

[104] For example, China emphasizes state-owned enterprises or companies connected to them, and Russia emphasizes intergovernmental commissions.

[105] For example, in 2019, the Eurasian Economic Commission and the African Union signed a memorandum of understanding on economic cooperation to bolster cooperation on infrastructure, agriculture, trade, and other areas (Eurasian Economic Commission, "EEC and African Union Commission Signed Memorandum of Understanding," press release, October 24, 2019; "Kompetencii Rossii Dlya Afriki" ["Russian Competences for Africa"], Roscongress, October 23, 2019; and U.S.-China Economic and Security Review Commission, *2020 Report to Congress*, Washington, D.C.: U.S. Government Printing Office, December 2020b).

[106] A representative from Burkina Faso is the Deputy Chairman of the 1st Committee, which, among other things, covers disarmament in space; a representative of Cameroon is the vice president of the 4th Committee, which works on international cooperation in space; and South Africa chairs the Scientific and Technical Subcommittee of the UN ad hoc Committee on the Peaceful Uses of Outer Space. One Russian source suggests that "diplomatic blunders in Africa could greatly affect the prospects of mining on the moon," particularly from the international agreement and cooperation perspective ("Rossiya, SSHA Ili Kotai—Kto Pobedit V Afrikanskoi Kosmicheskoi Gonke," FAN, June 27, 2020).

volume in 2018. However, the United States has a smaller presence than China. In 2019, the United States ranked third after China and India in terms of imports to Africa (Russia ranked 14th). In terms of exports, China ranked first as the single largest national exporter; the United States ranked sixth, and Russia ranked 31st.[107]

U.S.-Africa trade should also be put into perspective. As noted earlier, U.S. economic interests in Africa are low compared with such interests in other regions in the world. Between 2008 and 2018, U.S. trade volume with Africa declined in absolute terms,[108] and it has been hovering between 1.5 and 2 percent of the U.S. global trade since 2007.[109] The U.S. energy and mineral imports from Africa are also very small; for example, U.S. imports of crude oil and crude oil products dropped by one-third between 2006 and 2021. South Africa was the only single African country among the top ten exporters of minerals to the United States in 2019, while Africa was the source of only 11 percent of the U.S. mineral imports.[110] In fact, Africa is not the leading trading partner for any of the three great powers; their trade with each other (e.g., the United States and China,[111] Russia and China[112]) or with other regions (e.g., Asia or Europe) exceeds their trade with Africa.[113] To change this, during the U.S.-Africa Business Summit in 2019, the Trump administration launched its Prosper Africa initiative, which was intended to double trade with Africa by aiding U.S. businesses there; the effort was later revived by President Joe Biden.[114] It remains to be seen what results the initiative will achieve, but observers suggest that its $50 million support pledge cannot compete with China's investments, which amount to billions.[115]

Overall Competition Potential in Africa

In this section, we present the overall potential for competition—that is, across the four domains (diplomacy, information, military, and economics). First, we examine the potential for competition for the three great powers collectively. Then, we break down the potential for competition separately for (1) the United States and China and (2) the United States and Russia. Figure 2.5 illustrates the overall competition-potential indices across Africa.

---

[107] African Union, 2020.

[108] U.S. Census Bureau, "Trade in Goods with Africa," webpage, last updated 2021a.

[109] U.S. Census Bureau, undated, full data set for all countries from 2021.

[110] U.S. Energy Information Administration, 2021; World Integrated Trade Solution, undated-c.

[111] Office of the United States Trade Representative, "The People's Republic of China," webpage, undated-b.

[112] World Integrated Trade Solution, "Russia Trade," webpage, undated-b.

[113] "Russia in Africa: What's Behind Moscow's Push into the Continent?" BBC News, May 7, 2020.

[114] Tom Sheehy, "U.S.'s 'Prosper Africa' Initiative Launches in Mozambique, Fighting Uphill Battle Against Corruption," Foreign Policy News, June 17, 2019; and Doyinsola Oladipo and Andrea Shalal, "Biden Revives Trump's Africa Business Initiative; Focus on Energy, Health," Reuters, July 27, 2021.

[115] Lauren Baker, "Bridging Perceptions: China in Mozambique," Marco Polo, August 27, 2019.

FIGURE 2.5

Overall Competition Potential in Africa

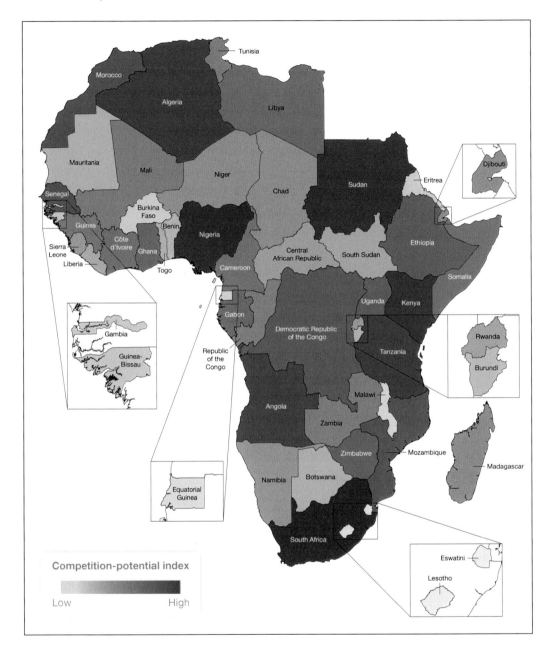

SOURCE: Authors' analysis of the influence-seeking measures described in this report; for data sources, see the appendix. Base map: Esri, Garmin, and CIA, 2019.

The country with the greatest potential for competition across all four domains of influence-seeking and across all three great powers is South Africa, closely followed by Nigeria, Sudan, and Kenya. Table 2.1 presents the 15 countries with the highest competition-potential indices overall and shows how each country ranked for the U.S.-China competition and the U.S.-Russia competition.

Our analysis shows that Kenya, Nigeria, Senegal, and South Africa rank the highest overall for the United States. For China, the highest-ranking countries are Nigeria, South Africa, and Tanzania. Russia is most involved in South Africa, Sudan, and Algeria. Although this list should be viewed in the context of the methodology that we used, it does show that the attention of all three powers converges on Africa's largest economies: Nigeria, South Africa,

TABLE 2.1

The 15 Countries with the Highest Competition Potential Overall and Their Rankings for Bilateral Competition Potential

Country	Competition-Potential Ranking		
	Overall	U.S.-China	U.S.-Russia
South Africa	1	2	1
Nigeria	2	1	2
Sudan	3	9	4
Kenya	4	3	6
Algeria	5	6	5
Tanzania	6	4	15
Angola	7	7	10
Morocco	8	8	3
Senegal	9	5	8
Mozambique	10	12	9
DRC	11	15	7
Uganda	12	10	12
Ethiopia	13	13	16
Ghana	14	11	18
Zimbabwe	15	20	28

NOTE: The rankings were calculated by adding the standardized indices capturing the involvement in each African country across all four domains (diplomacy, information, military, economics) for the relevant combination of great powers specified in each column and ranking them from highest total (top ranking) to lowest.

and, to a lesser extent, Morocco.[116] In addition, high-ranking countries are among the largest energy or mineral producers or possess other significant natural resources (e.g., Algeria, Nigeria, South Africa),[117] or they are countries with strategically important locations (e.g., Sudan's access to the Red Sea and the Gulf of Aden, North African countries' access to the Mediterranean Sea, and Tanzania and Kenya's significance for the Indian Ocean). As we noted earlier, because of the focus on convergent priorities—specifically ones that may be captured by available data—some countries that might be expected to show a high rate of diplomatic or military influence-seeking activity, such as Libya and Djibouti, do not have high overall competition-potential indices.[118]

As illustrated in Figure 2.6 (and Table 2.1), the potential for U.S.-China competition is highest in Nigeria, South Africa, and Kenya. The potential for competition between these two powers is also relatively high in many other countries, including Tanzania and Senegal.[119] This reflects the United States' and China's interests in the largest sub-Saharan African economies and in countries that have significant media and other sectors that may help their influence activities spill over to smaller neighboring countries. The fact that sub-Saharan African countries top the list of locations for potential U.S.-China competition reflects the importance of the region for China: Nigeria is an important energy and infrastructure partner, South Africa is an important trading partner, and Kenya is not only a trade and infrastructure partner but also a media partner. Furthermore, China has established close political and trade relations with Senegal in West Africa. There, it supports the so-called Plan for an Emerging Senegal with China—which targets opening highways, a theater, a museum, and a children's hospital—while Senegal co-chairs the Forum on China-Africa Cooperation.[120] Tanzania has historical and military ties with China and is a strategic location for the Belt and Road Initiative, even if Tanzania-China relations have been bumpy recently.[121] Nigeria, South Africa, Kenya, and Senegal also rank the highest for the United States. Kenya is the

---

[116] Of these three countries, Morocco ranks rather high for the United States and Russia but much lower for China.

[117] U.S. Energy Information Administration, "Total Energy Production 2019," webpage, 2019.

[118] Thus, for example, although Libya is the location of great-power involvement in conflict, it draws less influence-seeking activity from China and does not rank highly across all the considered factors for the United States and China. And although Djibouti has been the location of military competition between the United States and China, influence-seeking activities across other factors are lower than they are for other African countries.

[119] The lowest potential for competition with China was recorded in Eswatini—likely related to the fact that Eswatini has diplomatic relations with Taiwan, although it also has among the lowest competition-potential indices for the United States.

[120] Xing Jianqiao, "China, Senegal Continue to Deepen Comprehensive Strategic Cooperative Partnership in 2019," Xinhua, December 27, 2019; and Eric Olander, "Tanzania's Relationship Status with China: It's Complicated," *China in Africa Podcast*, January 29, 2021.

[121] David Shinn, "China in Africa," testimony before the U.S.-China Economic and Security Review Commission, Washington, D.C., May 8, 2020.

FIGURE 2.6

U.S.-China Competition Potential in Africa

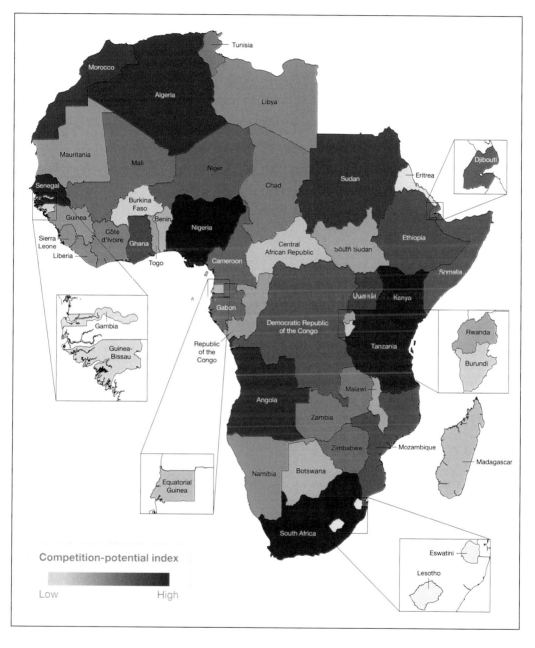

SOURCE: Authors' analysis of the influence-seeking measures described in this report; for data sources, see the appendix. Base map: Esri, Garmin, and CIA, 2019.

United States' ally against Islamic terrorism and used to be viewed as a strategic location against communism during the Cold War.[122] Meanwhile, South Africa is the United States' largest trading partner in Africa, and the United States is the largest foreign investor in Nigeria (in terms of foreign direct investment).[123]

Potential for U.S.-Russia competition is the highest in South Africa, Nigeria, and Morocco (see Figure 2.7 and Table 2.1). This reflects the high rankings of South Africa and Nigeria for both powers (higher for the United States, slightly lower for Russia) across the four influence-seeking domains. Morocco is in the top three because both powers' economic and military interests converge there, and Russia has a strong informational presence in the country.

Regional Potential for Internal Conflict

The relative intensity of influence-seeking across the region indicates the relative motivation for conflict. As we noted earlier, great-power involvement in conflicts, whether through proxy support or limited military interventions, requires *opportunity*. To assess the potential for conflict across Africa, we relied on Uppsala University's ViEWS assessments, as described in Chapter One.[124] We used ViEWS assessments of the probability of internal conflict for the forthcoming 36 months (starting in April 2021) that encompassed three main forms of political violence (armed conflict involving states and rebel groups, armed conflict between non-state actors, and violence against civilians).[125] Figure 2.8 depicts the relative probabilities of internal conflict across the continent; darker shades represent a higher probability of conflict.[126] Table A.6 in the appendix presents the underlying data for each country.

According to the ViEWS assessments, the highest potential for fatal political violence over the forecasted years is in Nigeria, the DRC, and Somalia, where the probability of conflict breaking out or continuing is 90 percent or more. The probability of conflict is also assessed to be very high—60 percent or more—in Mali, Cameroon, Burkina Faso, South Sudan, and

---

[122] Linnet Hamasi, "Kenya-US Relations Under Joe Biden's Presidency: Prospects and Challenges," *Kujenga Amani*, February 10, 2021; and Bureau of African Affairs, 2020b.

[123] Bureau of African Affairs, "U.S. Relations with South Africa: Bilateral Relations Fact Sheet," U.S. Department of State, last updated January 14, 2020a; and Bureau of African Affairs, "U.S. Relations with Nigeria: Bilateral Relations Fact Sheet," U.S. Department of State, last updated April 29, 2021a.

[124] ViEWS: The Violence Early-Warning System, undated.

[125] Specifically, the ViEWS project "generates monthly probabilistic assessments of the likelihood that fatal political violence will occur in each country and 55x55 km location throughout Africa—during each of the next 36 months" (ViEWS: The Violence Early-Warning System, undated).

[126] We relied on the average monthly predicted probabilities to generate overall country-level conflict potential.

FIGURE 2.7

U.S.-Russia Competition Potential in Africa

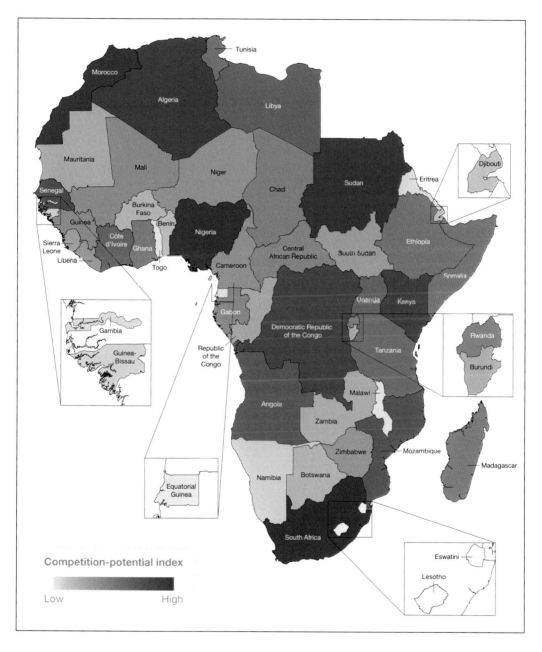

Competition-potential index

Low   High

SOURCE: Authors' analysis of the influence-seeking measures described in this report; for data sources, see the appendix. Base map: Esri, Garmin, and CIA, 2019.

FIGURE 2.8

Conflict Potential in Africa

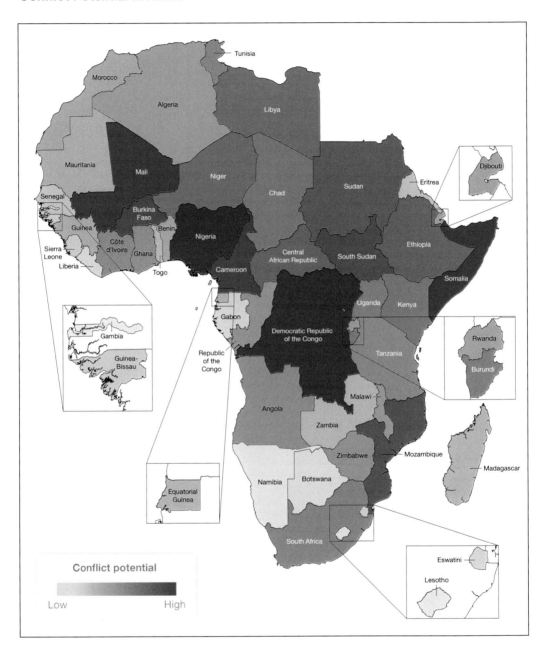

SOURCE: ViEWS: The Violence Early-Warning System, undated (data from 2021). Base map: Esri, Garmin, and CIA, 2019.

Mozambique. Countries with the highest conflict potential are highlighted in Table 2.2.[127] As the probabilities of conflict show, instability continues to hinder many countries in Africa; for 11 countries, the probability of violent conflict is above 50 percent (CAR is the 11th country).

The recent conflict landscape in Africa is characterized by a very low incidence of inter-state conflicts and a much higher rate of intra-state conflicts. The analysis of researchers from Peace Research Institute Oslo suggests that the number of state-based internal conflicts (a conflict where at least one party is a state) has increased, from 21 state-based conflicts recorded in 2018 to 25 in 2019.[128] By contrast, there has been a very low incidence of inter-state wars; since the 1990s, Africa has witnessed only seven inter-state wars, and the most recent as of this writing was in 2016, between Ethiopia and Eritrea. Intra-state conflicts, however, continue to ravage the continent. Since 2004, African conflicts also have become

TABLE 2.2
The Ten African Countries with the Highest Conflict Potential

Country	Overall Conflict-Potential Ranking	Probability of Conflict
Nigeria	1	0.96
DRC	2	0.95
Somalia	3	0.90
Mali	4	0.76
Cameroon	5	0.71
Burkina Faso	6	0.67
South Sudan	7	0.67
Mozambique	8	0.61
Sudan	9	0.59
Ethiopia	10	0.57

SOURCE: ViEWS: The Violence Early-Warning System, undated.

[127] ViEWS has been refined over time and demonstrated to perform well relative to alternatives (such as the individual models that constitute the ViEWS approach). For details, see Håvard Hegre, Curtis Bell, Michael Colaresi, Mihai Croicu, Frederick Hoyles, Remco Jansen, Maxine Ria Leis, Angelica Lindqvist-McGowan, David Randahl, Espen Geelmuyden Rød, and Paola Vesco, "ViEWS2020: Revising and Evaluating the ViEWS Political Violence Early-Warning System," *Journal of Peace Research*, Vol. 58, No. 3, 2021. While there is no clear way to translate probabilities into predictions of events, we will note that many of the countries with high estimated probabilities of conflict have indeed experienced outbreaks or continuation of conflict, such as escalating violence in the Sahel region (see Nosmot Gbadamosi, "Violence Spreads in the Sahel," *Foreign Policy*, December 15, 2021).

[128] This discussion is based on Júlia Palik, Siri Aas Rustad, and Fredrik Methi, *Conflict Trends in Africa, 1989–2019*, Oslo: Peace Research Institute Oslo, 2020.

more internationalized; in 2019, 14 conflicts brought external involvement from neighboring countries. These internationalized conflicts generally tend to drag on for longer periods and could lead to greater damage. And a substantial number of state-based conflicts are due to the expansion of VEOs, such as the Islamic State; for example, in 2019, nine countries (Burkina Faso, Cameroon, Chad, Libya, Mali, Mozambique, Niger, Nigeria, and Somalia) were involved in conflicts with the Islamic State in their territories. Moreover, experts suggest that the COVID-19 pandemic may have contributed to increased state violence against civilians, as a result of governments either trying to enforce pandemic-related restrictions or using them to achieve other aims.[129]

Identifying Competition Flashpoints

As described in Chapter One, by looking at the overlap of potential motivation and opportunity, we identified two African countries in which competing great powers might become involved in conflict, whether through indirect support to proxies or through limited military interventions. To do this, we first limited the potential set of countries to the one-third of countries with the highest conflict potential and then ranked these more-conflict-prone states by competition potential, from highest to lowest, as depicted in Table 2.3.

As illustrated in the table, among the one-third of African countries with the highest conflict potential, Nigeria, Sudan, Kenya, and Mozambique are the ones that present the greatest potential for great-power competition.[130] Of these four, we first chose Nigeria—a country that very clearly topped both the conflict- and the competition-potential rankings. We did not select higher-ranking Kenya, because its conflict potential was anomalously low for a state at the top of combined rankings; because Kenya was toward the bottom of the 16 countries that we ranked for conflict potential, identifying plausible conflict scenarios in Kenya would have been a more speculative enterprise compared with doing so for the other three countries. Both Sudan and Mozambique were qualitatively good candidates for closer study. We opted for Mozambique because of the conflict potential, the character of great-power involvement, and the potential it offers for insights into the military-related challenges associated with operating in that part of the continent; in particular, the operational considerations, including the requirements for U.S. Air Force resources, appeared more dissimilar to those for Nigeria.[131]

---

[129] For a more detailed discussion of how the pandemic has affected Africa, see Shurkin, Noyes, and Adgie, 2021.

[130] We did not select Libya for our scenario analysis for a few reasons. For instance, it is already host to an ongoing proxy conflict, and there is less to be gained from examining scenarios of its future course than from considering scenarios that have probably attracted less attention from U.S. decisionmakers and policy elites. Moreover, Libya's proximity to the Mediterranean Sea and to Europe means that it poses fewer operational challenges than some of the other countries higher on the list of candidate countries.

[131] In selecting countries for closer study, we consulted with the sponsor of this project.

TABLE 2.3

Africa Case Selection

Country	Overall Conflict-Potential Ranking	Overall Competition-Potential Ranking
Nigeria[a]	1	2
Sudan	9	3
Kenya	15	4
Mozambique[a]	8	20
DRC	2	11
Ethiopia	10	13
Libya	12	17
Somalia	3	18
Cameroon	5	21
Mali	4	22
Chad	14	28
Niger	13	29
CAR	11	33
South Sudan	7	34
Burundi	16	40
Burkina Faso	6	44

SOURCE: Conflict-potential ranking is based on ViEWS: The Violence Early-Warning System, undated (data from 2021). Competition-potential ranking is based on authors' analysis of the influence-seeking measures described in this report; for data sources, see the appendix.

NOTE: We ranked 48 countries in Africa by conflict potential (1 = highest risk) and competition potential (1 = highest).

[a] We selected this country for scenario analysis.

CHAPTER THREE

Conflict Scenarios with Great-Power Involvement: Nigeria

In 2021, Nigeria was the most populous country in Africa and the sixth most populous country in the world. It is projected to become the third most populous country in the world by 2050, with more than 400 million people, replacing the position currently held by the United States.[1] Although Nigeria has the largest economy in Africa, heavy dependence on petroleum production has constrained economic growth and development.[2] This overreliance on oil, coupled with political instability, has threatened the nation's future.[3] More than 20 years after the end of brutal military rule, Nigeria continues to suffer from widespread systemic corruption, political instability, lack of accountability, governance issues, and criminal activity that hinder its national development and long-term stability.[4]

Nigeria also faces other challenges to its national security and prosperity: Rising ethno-religious tensions, violent extremism, and insurgency have plunged the country into insecurity. Nigerian security forces have been engaged in a protracted fight with terrorist organization Boko Haram and its factions in the northeast since 2009, resulting in an estimated 27,000 people killed by 2020.[5] The Islamic State's Africa franchise, the Islamic State – West Africa Province (ISWAP), has further plagued the northeast, contributing to the violence, insurgency, and chaos in the region. The Nigerian military's inability to quash this insurgency has highlighted the government's incompetence and the military's shortcomings. In addition to failing to defeat Boko Haram and ISWAP, the security forces have been accused

---

[1]   World Population Review, "Nigeria Population 2021 (Live)," webpage, last updated 2021.

[2]   Tomás F. Husted and Lauren Ploch Blanchard, *Nigeria: Current Issues and U.S. Policy*, Washington, D.C.: Congressional Research Service, RL33964, September 18, 2020.

[3]   Petroleum exports account for about 95 percent of Nigeria's total exports, and the collapse in the global price of oil and the impact of the COVID-19 pandemic have significantly damaged Nigeria's economy; its GDP was projected to decline by 5.4 percent in 2020 (see Husted and Blanchard, 2020, p. 2).

[4]   Ejiroghene Augustine Oghuvbu and Blessing Oluwatobi Oghuvbu, "Corruption and the Lingering of Insecurity Challenges in Nigeria," *Journal of Public Administration, Finance and Law*, No. 18, 2020; and Omololu Fagbadebo, "Corruption, Governance and Political Instability in Nigeria: A Dysfunctional Conundrum," *Current Research in Education and Social Studies*, Vol. 1, November 2019.

[5]   Human Rights Watch, "Nigeria," in *World Report 2020: Events of 2019*, New York, 2020.

of human rights abuses and crackdowns that have created a dangerous environment for the local population, who are unable to rely on the Nigerian government to ensure their safety.[6]

On top of the growing violence and despite the potential that Nigeria has to become an economic powerhouse, Nigeria's development and security are further challenged by the ongoing climate crisis and the ensuing water shortages and pollution in the Niger Delta, the country's most important oil-producing region.[7] In this chapter, we examine what a conflict with great-power involvement centered in Nigeria might look like. First, we present an overview of local political dynamics to identify the more likely among several plausible causes of internal conflict. We then examine the interests and objectives of the three great powers in the country, their relative abilities to project power, and the capabilities they might bring to bear in such a conflict. Next, we assess how each power might choose to become involved in the conflict, if at all, and consider the factors that might affect the United States' ability to achieve its aims. To empirically ground these assessments, we drew on a variety of sources to better understand how the United States, China, and Russia have approached proxy wars and limited conflicts in the past. This research included interviews with experts and an exploration of how Chinese and Russian experts—as well as Western ones—write about the subject today; those discussions are included in the summary volume of this series.[8]

We find that, although Nigeria continues to have numerous internal security issues and the great powers have interests in the country, great-power involvement in Nigeria's conflicts—particularly in ones where the United States faces China, Russia, or both—is likely to be limited. Both China and Russia have economic and geopolitical interests in the country and are primarily interested in maintaining a level of stability that allows them to pursue these interests. Moreover, in the most likely scenario of engagement, the great powers are unlikely to engage in a proxy war that leads them to support opposite sides. Instead, they could find themselves in situations that require deconfliction for infrastructure or potential operational entanglement.

Overview of Local Political Dynamics

Since Nigeria achieved its independence from the United Kingdom in 1960, its power dynamics have been driven and defined by its various ethnic factions. The ethnic groups have in place a power-sharing agreement with the Nigerian government to make sure that each of

---

[6] Human Rights Watch, 2020.

[7] The river delta has been a major flashpoint between the local populations, criminal gangs, international corporations, and the Nigerian government (Amnesty International, "Niger Delta Negligence," webpage, March 2018).

[8] Cohen, Treyger, et al., 2023, Appendixes A, B, and C.

the major groups is represented.[9] However, the power-sharing agreement has not prevented political conflict; President Buhari first won office in 2015, but his re-election in 2019 was marked by the spread of disinformation and widespread violence, causing some to view his re-election as a step backward for Nigerian democracy.[10]

Although Nigeria's political system is based on the principle of federalism, the country remains highly centralized. As we discuss later, this has led to dissatisfaction among different ethnic and regional groups, calls for greater federalization of the country, and even some talks of potential secession.[11] At the same time, Nigeria's ethnic, regional, and religious scene is complex, and Nigeria has approximately 250 ethnic groups; the Hausa, Fulani, Igbo, and Yoruba are the major ones.[12] These groups dominate the country's political scene. In regional terms, Nigeria could be viewed as being made up of the mostly Muslim northern states, mostly Christian southeastern states, religiously mixed central and southwestern states, and mostly Christian Niger Delta region.[13] All major ethnic groups have formed militias to protect their interests because the Nigerian government is unable to adequately handle security issues.[14]

Sharia law has been adopted in 12 of the country's 36 states, mostly in the north.[15] The application of Sharia law to governmental jurisdictions resulted in the Trump administration placing Nigeria on a special watch list because of violations of religious freedoms.[16] Meanwhile in the southeast, where the main ethnic group is the Igbo—who are Christian, are staunch opponents of Sharia law, and were the primary backers of the secessionist movement in Biafra—Biafran activism has emerged.[17] Instead of seeking "a seat at the table," Biafran activists seem to aim to "overturn the table altogether," according to one historian of Africa,

---

[9] For example, President Muhammadu Buhari is an ethnic Fulani Muslim, and Vice President Yemi Osinbajo is ethnically Yoruba.

[10] Husted and Blanchard, 2020.

[11] John Campbell and Nolan Quinn, "What's Behind Growing Separatism in Nigeria?" Council on Foreign Relations, August 3, 2021.

[12] Erima Comfort Ugbem, Ayokunle Olumuyiwa Omobowale, and Akinpelu Olanrewaju Olutayo, "Racial Politics and Hausa-Fulani Dominant Identity in Colonial and Post-Colonial Northern Nigeria," *Nigerian Journal of Sociology and Anthropology*, Vol. 17, No. 10, June 2019.

[13] Commonwealth Initiative for Freedom of Religion or Belief, "CIFORB Country Profile: Nigeria," University of Birmingham, undated.

[14] "Ethnicity in Nigeria," PBS NewsHour, April 5, 2007.

[15] Katrin Gänsler, "Nigeria Looks Back on 20 Years of Sharia Law in the North," Deutsche Welle, October 27, 2019.

[16] Husted and Blanchard, 2020.

[17] Biafra is a state in West Africa that declared independence and prompted a 30-month war with the Nigerian government from 1967 to 1970. The Nigerian government eventually won the conflict, but it took a heavy toll on the area; hundreds of thousands of Igbo died from starvation during the war. Nigeria does not officially commemorate the conflict, and it continues to be a powerful cause among the Igbo population.

and do not have one single aim, while most activism takes place online.[18] President Buhari has continuously rejected calls for a referendum on and demands for Biafra separatism.[19] In 2017, an Abuja high court declared the Indigenous People of Biafra to be a terrorist organization. Experts, however, suggest that whether the pro-Biafra movement will expand may depend on the reaction of the Nigerian government; increased attention to encouraging a stronger sense of national belonging may prevent future escalations.[20] The United States does not consider the Indigenous People of Biafra to be a terrorist organization, but Washington is committed to supporting a united Nigeria.[21]

There also have been calls for giving Nigeria's regions more autonomy in Yorubaland. However, there are few indications that these calls would instantly turn into violent separatist movements.[22] Yoruba are generally located in the urban centers and dominate the area surrounding Lagos, the most developed region of the country. In recent times, ethnic tensions have been mitigated by the pluralism and mixture of Islam and Christianity in Yoruba culture.[23]

Home to most of Nigeria's oil, the Niger Delta has become a source of conflict as oil spills have disrupted the communities of Ijaw who live off the river. In addition, criminal gangs have exploited the situation to illegally harvest oil in the Niger Delta, thereby adding to the pollution of the river and violence in the region. More recently, the Ijaw have expressed dissatisfaction with the opportunities for political representation and the development of infrastructure, as well as resentment about the inability to ensure that the wealth from oil production stays in the region. Some Ijaw statesmen have spoken about the need for greater federalization of Nigeria and, if that is unsuccessful, potential secession from Nigeria.[24]

Despite these circumstances and the fact that Nigeria ranks low in global political stability indices, experts conclude that support for secession is not widespread, and few Igbo and

---

[18] Samuel Fury Childs Daly, "Unfinished Business: Biafran Activism in Nigeria Today," *Georgetown Journal of International Affairs*, April 7, 2021. Pro-Biafran protests have been met with harassment and violence; in 2016, Nigeria's security forces were accused of "extrajudicial executions and violence resulting in the deaths of at least 150 peaceful pro-Biafra protesters" (Amnesty International, "Nigeria: At Least 150 Peaceful Pro-Biafra Activists Killed in Chilling Crackdown," November 24, 2016; see also Patrick Egwu, "50 Years On, Biafra's Pain Is Still Fresh," *Foreign Policy*, June 11, 2020).

[19] Egwu, 2020.

[20] Nnamdi Obasi, "Nigeria: How to Solve a Problem Like Biafra," International Crisis Group, May 29, 2017.

[21] Egwu, 2020.

[22] John Campbell, "Yoruba Debate 'Restructuring' of Nigeria or 'Autonomy,'" Council on Foreign Relations, April 16, 2021.

[23] "Ethnicity in Nigeria," 2007.

[24] Michael Egbejule and Adeyemi Adepetun, "IYC Laments Alleged Marginalisation of Ijaw in Political Appointments," *The Guardian*, October 11, 2021; and "Ijaw Leaders Plan Secession from Nigeria, Meet British Government with Demands," Sahara Reporters, July 6, 2021.

Yoruba are in favor of separatism.[25] Political risk analysis also does not seem to place Nigeria among the African countries with the highest risk of a coup.[26] Although, in the future, the situation might change as a result of such factors as changes in the federal structure of the country, internal and external dynamics of the separatist movements, and the ability of expatriate communities in Europe and the United States to gather support for these movements, experts do not view secession as an immediate security threat to Nigeria.[27]

Beyond the ethnic groups, other major stakeholders with political influence in Nigeria are the multinational oil companies operating in the country. Because Nigeria's budget is dependent on oil revenue, oil companies hold a large share of power there.[28] The two largest companies operating in the Niger Delta are British-Dutch multinational oil and gas company Royal Dutch Shell and Italian multinational company Eni.[29] Both have been accused of causing oil spills in the river delta and being slow to clean them up.[30] The Niger Delta is increasingly a source of conflict as the government is forced to deal with the growing pollution problem and the need for oil revenue from the oil companies.

Boko Haram, a Salafist Sunni Muslim terrorist organization, rose to prominence in 2009 when it launched an insurgency in northeast Nigeria.[31] Following the rise of the Islamic State core in Iraq and Syria, Boko Haram's then-leader Abubakar Shekau pledged allegiance to the Islamic State in 2015 and rebranded Boko Haram as ISWAP.[32] However, infighting among the group soon resulted in ISWAP splitting back into Boko Haram and ISWAP; Islamic State core leadership appointed a different leader for ISWAP, and Shekau reassumed leadership of

---

[25] Campbell and Quinn, 2021. For global political stability indices, see, for example, World Bank, "Worldwide Governance Indicators," webpage, undated-c; and Clayton Besaw, Matthew Frank, Eric Keels, Jay Benson, John Filitz, and Jonathan Powell, *Annual Risk of Coup Report*, Broomfield, Colo.: One Earth Future, April 2019.

[26] See, for example, Sam Haynes, "The Countries to Watch for a Coup: Political Risk Outlook 2019," Verisk Maplecroft, February 5, 2019.

[27] Campbell and Quinn, 2021.

[28] Crude oil production is dominated by large Western transnational oil companies that have joint venture partnerships with the Nigerian government. The downstream sector is mostly dominated by the federal government (Anjli Raval and Neil Munshi, "Nigeria Set to Sell Down Stake in Oil Ventures to Boost Finances," *Financial Times*, March 20, 2019).

[29] In 2021, Shell announced its plans to divest its operated joint venture licenses as it seeks to implements its net-zero emissions policy (Gail Anderson, "Shell to Divest Its Entire Nigeria Joint Venture Portfolio," Wood Mackenzie, August 16, 2021).

[30] Amnesty International, 2018.

[31] Claire Klobucista, "Nigeria's Battle with Boko Haram," Council on Foreign Relations, Backgrounder, August 8, 2018; and Tomás F. Husted, "Boko Haram and the Islamic State's West Africa Province," Congressional Research Service, IF10173, last updated March 26, 2021, p. 1.

[32] Husted, 2021, p. 1.

Boko Haram.[33] ISWAP has since cultivated a larger membership (estimated between 3,500 and 5,000 fighters as of 2020) and presence than Boko Haram has and is reportedly one of the Islamic State's most active affiliates globally.[34] Although smaller in personnel size (estimated between 1,500 and 2,000 fighters) and facing organizational issues following the loss of its leader Shekau, Boko Haram remains a significant threat in Nigeria and the broader region.[35] Boko Haram and ISWAP are based in northeastern Nigeria in the Lake Chad basin, an area that borders Cameroon, Chad, and Niger. Collectively, by mid-2021, the violent insurgency waged against the Nigerian government and the numerous terrorist attacks conducted by the two groups since their rise had resulted in more than 350,000 deaths, 3 million internally displaced people, and a burgeoning humanitarian crisis.[36] The Nigerian military has faced considerable struggles in its fight against Boko Haram and ISWAP. ISWAP has launched several attacks against both military and civilian targets and even managed to seize Nigerian military bases and equipment, which has stressed the Nigerian military's readiness and damaged some of its capabilities.[37] Currently, both Boko Haram and ISWAP are relatively local in their reach and ambitions. ISWAP, however, maintains ties to other Islamic State affiliates in Africa, including the Islamic State – Greater Sahara and, of course, the Islamic State core in the Middle East, which provides some degree of financial and technical support to all its affiliates.[38]

Lastly, several militias have surfaced in recent years to fight Boko Haram and ISWAP, essentially to plug the gaps in the Nigerian military's capabilities and inefficient response to the VEOs.[39] Indeed, in many areas, these militias are the main security providers. Government and international actors often engage with them for intelligence-gathering, defensive operations, offensive operations, and assistance in delivering aid.[40] The main militia groups are the Civilian Joint Task Force; the Vigilante Group of Nigeria; and three smaller local militias called the hunters (*kungiyar maharba*), the vigilante (*yan banga*), and the Shuwa vigilante

---

[33] Shekau purportedly died in a battle between Boko Haram and the Islamic State in March 2021. News of his death has been met with some skepticism, however, as the Nigerian government has declared his death on at least five occasions in the past (Paul Carsten, "ISWAP Militant Group Says Nigeria's Boko Haram Leader Is Dead," Reuters, June 7, 2021).

[34] Husted, 2021, p. 1.

[35] Husted, 2021, p. 1; and Fergus Kelly, "AFRICOM Shifts Strategy from Degrading to Containing West Africa Insurgents, OIG Report Says," *Defense Post*, February 12, 2020.

[36] "350,000 Killed, 3M Displaced in Nigeria, Boko Haram Conflict," *The Star Democrat*, July 4, 2021.

[37] Thomas D. Waldhauser, general, U.S. Marine Corps, "A Secure, Stable, and Prosperous Africa Is an Enduring American Interest," statement before the U.S. Senate Committee on Armed Services, Washington, D.C., February 7, 2019, p. 30.

[38] Vincent Foucher, "The Islamic State Franchises in Africa: Lessons from Lake Chad," International Crisis Group, October 29, 2020.

[39] Vanda Felbab-Brown, "Militias (and Militancy) in Nigeria's North-East: Not Going Away," Brookings Institution, April 14, 2020.

[40] Felbab-Brown, 2020.

(*kesh kesh*). The Civilian Joint Task Force has garnered international support, even meeting with the UN to discuss humanitarian efforts.[41] However, this and other militias have also been purveyors of human rights abuses, and although they are helping the Nigerian military in its counterterrorism efforts, they also contribute to instability in the region.

Overall, although there are multiple sources of violence and instability in Nigeria, the violence perpetrated by extremist organizations, specifically Boko Haram, has attracted the most international attention and is the greatest concern for the international community because of Boko Haram's allegiance to the Islamic State, the cross-border character of the threat in the region, and the potential that violence will spill over to other countries and regions.[42]

Comparative Analysis of Great-Power Interests and Objectives, Posture and Access, and Capabilities

In this section, we provide an overview of the interests and objectives, posture and access, and capabilities of the United States, China, and Russia in Nigeria.

Interests and Objectives

U.S., Chinese, and Russian interests and objectives in Nigeria fall under three main interrelated categories: strategic and geopolitical, security, and economic interests. The geopolitical and security objectives of all three powers in Nigeria largely mirror their interests across sub-Saharan Africa, although Nigeria is of particular interest given its status as the largest economy and the most populous country in Africa. Common themes include countering VEOs, supporting development efforts, and seeking economic gain through investment in the energy sector and other natural resources.

United States' Interests and Objectives

The United States' primary objectives in Nigeria are focused on stability in the country through providing foreign aid and assistance and countering VEOs. Washington also maintains economic interests in the country, particularly in trade relations and the oil industry.[43] U.S. geopolitical and strategic interests in Nigeria are driven by the country's large size (both geographically and in terms of population), its economic potential, and the high level of influ-

---

[41] United Nations Children's Fund, "Civilian Joint Task Force in Northeast Nigeria Signs Action Plan to End Recruitment of Children," press release, September 15, 2017.

[42] Expert on Africa and non-state actors, interview with the authors, July 2021; former U.S. government official and think-tank expert on Africa, interview with the authors, July 2021.

[43] Bureau of Political-Military Affairs, "U.S. Security Cooperation with Nigeria: Fact Sheet," U.S. Department of State, last updated March 19, 2021; and former U.S. Department of State official, interview with the authors, July 2021.

ence that Nigeria wields throughout Africa.[44] Additionally, the largest African-born population in the United States is from Nigeria, boosting U.S. political interest in the country.[45]

The overarching U.S. objectives in Nigeria are to promote stability and to ensure access, though not exclusive, to Nigeria's natural resources.[46] In pursuit of its higher-level objectives, the United States also seeks to improve governance in Nigeria, chiefly through combating political corruption and supporting free and fair elections, helping prevent human rights abuses (especially by Nigerian security forces against the people), improving humanitarian conditions, and supporting development efforts. As in the rest of Africa, the U.S. Department of State and USAID lead U.S. efforts to help Nigeria achieve its development goals. In 2020, USAID and the State Department allocated more than $450 million in foreign assistance to Nigeria in order to support "programs focused on health, good governance, agricultural development, law enforcement and justice sector cooperation."[47] Moreover, Nigeria consistently ranks among the top annual recipients of U.S. foreign aid globally: Since the early 2000s, U.S. foreign aid to the country has increased dramatically and, between 2007 and 2021, almost doubled.[48] In addition to the usual pots of foreign assistance, the United States provided Nigeria with $42 million in U.S. health and humanitarian aid in fiscal year 2020 in response to the COVID-19 pandemic.[49]

The key U.S. security objective in Nigeria is to counter VEOs—specifically, Boko Haram and ISWAP—and the threat they pose to U.S., partner, and allied interests.[50] To accomplish this objective, AFRICOM pursues a "Diplomacy, Development, and Defense approach" aimed to employ all levers of the U.S. government to counter and mitigate drivers of conflict and extremism, including "helping to counter incentives offered by" VEOs.[51] Other U.S. security objectives include enhancing maritime and border security, combating transnational crime

---

[44] Chris Olaoluwa Ogunmodede, "Biden's 'Low Bar' for Improving Ties with Nigeria," *World Politics Review*, January 26, 2021.

[45] Carlos Echeverria-Estrada and Jeanne Batalova, "Sub-Saharan African Immigrants in the United States," Migration Policy Institute, November 6, 2019.

[46] Bureau of Political-Military Affairs, 2021; and former U.S. Department of State official, interview with the authors, July 2021.

[47] Ogunmodede, 2021.

[48] Husted and Blanchard, 2020; USAID, 2021a.

[49] Other U.S. providers of financial assistance to Nigeria include DoD, the Department of Justice, the Department of Health and Human Services, and the Department of Homeland Security; together, these agencies provided more than $50 million of technical and financial support in fiscal year 2020. U.S.-supported health programs and aid have focused on providing treatment and preventing the spread of HIV and AIDS in Nigeria, which has the second-largest caseload in the world (Husted and Blanchard, 2020; Ogunmodede, 2021).

[50] Waldhauser, 2019, p. 7.

[51] As part of that approach, AFRICOM engages in programs to improve job opportunities, clean water, and education, for example (Waldhauser, 2019, p. 7).

(including human-trafficking, drug-trafficking, and child soldier recruitment), and countering rampant cybercrime.[52]

More broadly, the United States seeks to build partner capacity in Nigeria, particularly in the areas of peacekeeping, counterterrorism capabilities, and civilian law enforcement. Nigeria receives security aid through the U.S. Department of State, including through International Military Education and Training funding for the Nigerian military.[53] In addition, the United States has donated military equipment to Nigeria as part of the assistance to help fight Boko Haram and offered technical assistance and intelligence-sharing as a reaction to Boko Haram's kidnapping of 276 schoolgirls from Chibok, Nigeria, in 2014.[54] Although the United States engages in a substantial amount of security cooperation with Nigeria in support of these goals, deeper cooperation has been constrained by U.S. concerns over the high level of government corruption in Nigeria and reports of human rights abuses by the country's security forces.[55] Concerns over human rights abuses by the Nigerian military have also negatively affected arms sales. For instance, the transfers of U.S.-manufactured military helicopters were blocked or suspended on multiple occasions because of human rights issues, such as the Nigerian military striking an internally displaced persons camp in 2017.[56] Capacity and corruption issues have created a policy dilemma for the United States: Washington wishes to help the Nigerian military fight Boko Haram and ISWAP, but equipment provided to the military may also inadvertently help perpetuate human rights abuses.

---

[52] U.S. Embassy and Consulate in Nigeria, "U.S. Government Supports Nigeria in Fight Against Cybercrime and Financial Fraud," May 24, 2017.

[53] For example, in 2019, 129 Nigerians attended various U.S. foreign military training programs (Bureau of Political-Military Affairs, 2021; and DoD and U.S. Department of State, *Foreign Military Training Report, Fiscal Years 2018 and 2019, Joint Report to Congress, Volume I,* Washington, D.C., March 13, 2019).

[54] For example, the United States donated what are now NNS *Thunder* in 2012 and NNS *Okpabana* in 2014 to the Nigerian Navy, and in 2016, the United States donated mine-resistant and armor-protected vehicles to Nigeria via the Excess Defense Articles Program (Temitayo Famutimi, "U.S. Donates 24 Armored Personnel Carriers to Nigeria," U.S. Africa Command, January 11, 2016).

[55] For example, the so-called Leahy Law includes two statutory provisions prohibiting the U.S. government from using funds for assistance to units of foreign security forces where there is credible information implicating the unit in the commission of gross violations of human rights. The Trump administration also placed visa restrictions on individuals who allegedly meddled in or otherwise compromised Nigeria's 2019 elections (Ogunmodede, 2021; Bureau of Democracy, Human Rights, and Labor, "About the Leahy Law: Fact Sheet," U.S. Department of State, January 20, 2021a).

[56] Furthermore, in 2021, U.S. lawmakers blocked another proposed U.S. sale of 12 AH-1 Cobra attack helicopters and related equipment, as well as precision-guided munitions, over human rights concerns. At the same time, Nigeria received A-29 Super Tucanos after President Trump unfroze a sale that had been paused by President Obama (Husted and Blanchard, 2020; and Doyinsola Oladipo and Mike Stone, "Proposed U.S. Arms Sale to Nigeria on 'Hold' over Human Rights Concerns—Sources," Reuters, July 30, 2021).

As noted earlier, the United States also has economic interests in Nigeria,[57] which has become the United States' second-largest trading partner in Africa and the third-largest destination for U.S. foreign direct investment in the region.[58] Nigeria also has become a tech hub within Africa, and Uber, Google, Facebook, and other U.S. companies have selected Nigeria to host their African headquarters. However, the instability and government corruption in Nigeria have discouraged some U.S. business ventures; Twitter, for example, selected Ghana over Nigeria to host its headquarters.[59] Even if expansion into other business sectors remains constrained by these concerns, the United States has a clear interest in maintaining robust trade ties and access to Nigeria's natural resources, given Nigeria's status as Africa's leading oil producer. However, our interviewees noted that the United States does not seek to achieve exclusive access to Nigeria's energy resources and is in fact drawing down its presence in the sector.[60]

Moreover, these U.S. economic interests should be put into broader perspective. Although Nigeria is a key trading partner for the United States in the region, it was the United States' 52nd goods export market globally in 2019.[61] U.S. energy imports from Africa are very low compared with U.S. imports from other regions, and U.S. crude oil and petroleum product imports from Nigeria have fallen dramatically since 2010, as the United States has been seeking to reduce its energy imports and was successful in economically producing shale oil.[62] Nigeria ranks only 12th in terms of the already rather low U.S. mineral imports from Africa, which are by far dominated by South Africa.[63] Meanwhile, U.S.-Africa trade volume seems to have followed the broader U.S.-Africa trade trends: an increase in trade volume between 1999 and 2008 and a large decline since then.[64]

---

[57] The two countries have been party to a bilateral Trade and Investment Framework Agreement since 2000 (Office of the United States Trade Representative, "Nigeria," webpage, undated-a).

[58] Most trade is in the energy and agricultural sectors (Office of the United States Trade Representative, undated-a; Husted and Blanchard, 2020).

[59] "Twitter's Decision to Base in Ghana Raises Questions About Nigeria's Role as West Africa's Tech Hub," 14 North, April 26, 2021.

[60] Former U.S. Department of State official, interview with the authors, July 2021; expert on Africa and non-state actors, interview with the authors, July 2021.

[61] Office of the United States Trade Representative, undated-a.

[62] For example, U.S. crude oil and oil product imports in July 2010 were 36,409 barrels (and hovered around the 30,000 mark in 2010) and had reduced to 6,091 barrels in June 2021, after a persistent downward trend (U.S. Energy Information Administration, 2021; and Oil and Gas 360, "US Slashes Nigerian Oil Imports by 11.67m Barrels," August 23, 2020).

[63] World Integrated Trade Solution, undated-c.

[64] U.S. trade volume with Nigeria fell from $42.170 billion in 2008 to $4.287 billion in 2020. U.S. exports to Nigeria increased between 1999 and 2013, after which exports declined by almost half (U.S. Census Bureau, 2021a; and U.S. Census Bureau, "Trade in Goods with Nigeria," webpage, last updated 2021b).

China's Interests and Objectives

In a similar vein to the U.S. objectives, China's primary geostrategic objective in Nigeria is to maintain stability to ensure the security and profitability of China's economic activity in the country and maintain Nigeria as a partner in regional and international forums, such as the UN.[65]

Economic interests have been described as the foundation of Chinese objectives in Nigeria and are clearly the driving force behind China's engagement in Nigeria.[66] Some of these interests are quite obvious. Nigeria is a major exporter of oil, and China is the world's largest importer.[67] Although China does not import a particularly large portion of its oil from Nigeria, it is trying to diversify its suppliers away from the Persian Gulf, so petroleum supplies in Nigeria have a strategic significance greater than mere import volumes would indicate.[68] And Nigeria is a key source of other natural resources, including about one-third of China's imports of niobium, tantalum, and vanadium ores, which are extremely rare metals essential for defense applications.[69]

More broadly, Beijing expects Africa generally and Nigeria in particular to become one of the most economically dynamic places on earth over the next 20 years and plans to both facilitate and take advantage of this rise.[70] It plans to do so by increasing trade, ensuring that Chinese companies are able to operate effectively in Nigeria, financing and building infrastructure to connect Nigeria to the rest of Africa and the world, and providing expert advice as needed.[71] In fact, experts note trade as key to China's economic interest in Nigeria.[72] China hopes to midwife an African economic miracle, be well paid for its trouble, and then enjoy the strategic benefits of friendship with a grateful and powerful continent.

As the largest economy in Africa, Nigeria is an attractive market for Chinese exporters.[73] Although China-Nigeria trade makes up a pittance compared with China's trade with such countries as Japan, Germany, and the United States, it makes Nigeria the second most

---

[65] Page, 2018.

[66] Page, 2018, p. 1.

[67] Observatory of Economic Complexity, "Nigeria," webpage, undated-c.

[68] Page, 2018, pp. 5–6.

[69] Observatory of Economic Complexity, undated-a; and Office of the Secretary of the Interior, "Final List of Critical Minerals 2018," *Federal Register*, Vol. 83, No. 97, May 18, 2018.

[70] Ma, 2020b.

[71] Su Xiaohui [苏晓晖] and Zhu Zhongbo [朱中博], "Summary of the 2015 International Situation and Chinese Diplomacy Forum" ["2015年国际形势与中国外交研讨会纪要"], China Institute of International Studies [中国国际问题研究院], January 15, 2016; and Zhang, 2018.

[72] Page, 2018.

[73] In 2019, Chinese exports to Nigeria reached $15.5 billion, up from $13.6 billion in 2018 and $12.2 billion in 2017 (Deloitte, *So, Nigeria Is the Largest Economy in Africa. Now What?* Johannesburg, South Africa, 2014).

common destination for Chinese exports in Africa, only slightly behind South Africa.[74] As noted earlier, trade with Africa is considered a strategic, though low-volume, investment because of expected future growth, and this is especially true of trade with Nigeria.[75] Beijing is working to support free trade agreements among African nations in order to reduce trade barriers and spur economic growth on the continent.[76]

Beijing also hopes to capitalize on Nigeria's rise by positioning itself as one of the country's chief financiers. From 2015 to 2020, China invested $22.5 billion in Nigeria, making it Beijing's top destination for investment in sub-Saharan Africa and among the largest recipients of Chinese financing in the world.[77] Beijing also hopes to capitalize on Nigeria's rapidly growing digital economy and demand for information technology infrastructure. Nigeria is already one of the top countries in Africa in terms of internet users, and about half of its population still does not have reliable internet access.[78] China hopes to provide the phones, data centers, cell towers, and other infrastructure that these users will need to get online through its Digital Silk Road initiative.[79] Beijing has already established a presence in the Nigerian space sector by launching Nigeria's communications satellites in 2007 and a replacement in 2011, as well as by training Nigerian scientists, thus essentially pushing Russia out of the Nigerian space sector.[80]

China hopes that these efforts will help better link the Nigerian and Chinese economies and improve economic integration across Africa, improving the business climate there for Chinese and other businesses.[81] Beijing, Abuja, and a host of Chinese firms and local gov-

---

[74] Observatory of Economic Complexity, undated-a.

[75] Not only is Nigeria Africa's most populous nation, but its population is also still rapidly growing. Furthermore, Nigeria is a key player in regional and continental markets (Zhao, 2019; Su and Zhu, 2016; Page, 2018, p. 4; Ma, 2020b).

[76] Ma, 2020b.

[77] Much of this investment was in transportation and power-generating infrastructure. Chinese companies have either built or financed (or both) the $2.8 billion Ajaokuta-Kaduna-Kano gas pipeline, the $200 million Nnamdi Azikiwe International Airport, the Lekki Port's new deepwater harbor, and the Mambilla Dam. By 2018, China had financed as much as $20 billion in rail projects around the country. To put this in perspective, China invested $7.93 billion in Japan, $25.61 billion in Pakistan, $30.61 billion in Brazil, and $64.97 in the United Kingdom between 2015 and 2020. See American Enterprise Institute and Heritage Foundation, "China Global Investment Tracker," webpage, undated; and Page, 2018, p. 7.

[78] Huang, 2019.

[79] Huang, 2019.

[80] Russia launched the first satellite in Nigeria in 2003; since then, however, China has been more successful in Nigeria. Chinese manufacturer China Great Wall Industry Corporation is reported to own an equity stake in Nigerian Communications Satellite, or NigComSat (Julie Michelle Klinger, "China, Africa, and the Rest: Recent Trends in Space Science, Technology, and Satellite Development," Washington, D.C.: SAIS China-Africa Research Initiative, Policy Brief No. 45, May 2020; and "Nigeria's Nigcomsat to Receive $550 Million Investment from China Great Wall Industry Corporation," Spacewatch Africa, April 2018).

[81] Huang, 2019.

ernments have sought to build a welcoming regulatory environment for Chinese businesses operating in Nigeria by constructing a variety of special trade zones around the country.[82] As China works to build a friendly regulatory environment for its own firms, it views some U.S. plans, such as the Power Africa initiative, with trepidation, fearing that they will be used by Washington to interfere in economic cooperation between China and African states.[83]

Nigeria's precarious security situation already poses a threat to China-Nigeria cooperation, both scaring off potential investors and interfering with Nigerian petroleum exports.[84] Chinese businesses in Nigeria face armed attacks on at least an annual basis.[85] China also seeks stability in Nigeria because it hopes to gain politically from its relationship with Nigeria and other African states. One of Beijing's key political objectives is to maintain close relations with African states to facilitate greater economic interaction and to parry any attempts by Western nations to interfere in that economic cooperation.[86] More broadly, the sheer number of African states (and their attendant voting power in the UN) makes the continent an important arena of international political competition for Beijing. China hopes to work with Africa's many developing states to push for reforms in the UN and other international institutions to make them more responsive to the needs of China.[87] China also hopes that African nations will help deflect criticism and negative narratives about its human rights abuses or other problems. Nigeria's voting pattern at the UN often has been aligned with that of China, and this is not particularly different from most other African countries that tend to vote more with China than with Russia or the United States. In 2019, Nigeria was among many African states that defended China's behavior in Xinjiang, but it did not sign onto a similar statement in 2020.[88]

China's main security objectives in Nigeria center on countering VEOs. Protecting the 20,000–50,000 Chinese nationals in Nigeria and their "legitimate interests" from attacks by VEOs is likely the top military or security concern of Chinese policymakers, and some Chinese scholars affiliated with the Ministry of Foreign Affairs have argued that any threats to these people or interests could justify China violating its long-standing policy of non-

---

[82] Page, 2018, p. 6; Huang, 2018.

[83] Wang, 2018.

[84] Wang, 2018; Page, 2018, pp. 2–3.

[85] Wang, 2018.

[86] Wang, 2018.

[87] Chen Xulong [陈须隆], "Proposals for U.N. Reform" ["联合国改革的出路"], China Institute of International Relations [中国国际问题研究院], October 28, 2015; Zhang, 2018.

[88] Zachary Basu, "More Countries Join Condemnation of China over Xinjiang Abuses," Axios, October 8, 2020; and Yiqin Fu, "UNView: United Nations General Assembly Voting Patterns (1946–2019)," webpage, undated.

interference.[89] To achieve its security objectives, China has declared rhetorically that it seeks to stabilize Nigeria and strengthen the Nigerian authorities so that they can more effectively fight transnational terror groups operating in Nigeria, but specific examples of such assistance are lacking, save for the potential impact of Chinese investment on economic development.[90] Chinese analysts have noted with alarm that there has been a sharp uptick in terrorist activity in Nigeria, especially following Boko Haram's swearing of loyalty to the Islamic State in 2014.[91] Chinese authorities fear not only that the Islamic State or other groups like it could destabilize other African states in the region but also that their extremist ideology or actions could spread to regions closer to China's borders, or even to Muslim minorities living within China.[92]

Russia's Interests and Objectives

Russia's primary objectives in Nigeria are based on Moscow's economic interests in securing natural resources and in seeking clients for Russia's government-owned businesses, as well as geopolitical interests in positioning Russia as an alternative global leader to the United States and in mitigating the country's increasing international isolation. The modern rebirth of the Nigeria-Russia relationship may be traced back to 2001, when President of Nigeria Olusegun Obasanjo visited Russia and signed the Declaration on Principles of Friendly Relations and Partnership and several other agreements that established the legal basis for bilateral relations.[93] In line with Russia's overall policy toward Africa, Russia seeks to promote itself as a dependable security partner that supports global stability and is willing to cooperate with any regime against a common threat.[94] Russia's officials emphasize that Russia's relationship with Nigeria is based on friendship, mutual respect, and "reciprocally beneficial cooperation where interests coincided," while Moscow explores the opportunities of developing this relationship left by the West's reluctance to sell arms to Nigeria (because of human rights abuses).[95]

---

[89] Zeng Aiping [曾爱平], "China and Africa Explore Exchanges on Governance Experience" ["中国非洲治国理政经验交流初探"], China Institute of International Studies [中国国际问题研究院], October 31, 2016; He Dan [何丹], "China Shows Greater Care in Protecting Overseas Interests" ["中国海外利益保护更加温暖人心"], China Institute of International Studies, May 19, 2021; and Page, 2018, p. 6.

[90] Economist Intelligence Unit, "China Offers Help Against Boko Haram," May 9, 2014.

[91] Manyuan, 2014.

[92] Manyuan, 2014.

[93] Edgar Agubamah, "Nigeria-Russia Relations: After and Now," *European Scientific Journal*, Vol. 10, No. 14, May 2014; and President of Russia, "Top-Level Russian-Nigerian Talks Were Held in the Kremlin," March 6, 2001.

[94] Simon Allison, "Russia in Africa: Soft Power Comes with Hard Edges," *Mail & Guardian*, October 24, 2019.

[95] Aidoghie Paulinus, "Atomic Partnership with Russia'll Propel Nigeria's Economy—Sherbashin Russian Envoy," *The Sun*, March 14, 2021; and Sunday Omotuyi, "Russo/Nigerian Relations in the Context of Counterinsurgency in Nigeria," *Jadavpur Journal of International Relations*, Vol. 23, No. 1, 2019.

By gaining Nigeria as a political partner, Russia seeks to mitigate the West's economic sanctions and the increasing international isolation. It courts Nigeria largely because of Nigeria's economic importance on the continent.[96] Nigeria is Russia's fourth-largest trading partner in Africa and its largest trading partner in Western Africa.[97] Russia's trade with Nigeria has increased over the past 20 years, yet the African country ranked just 82nd in terms of Russia's global trade volume in 2019.[98] Russia's companies have been increasingly interested in Nigeria since 2007, and Russia seeks to use its mostly state-owned enterprises to diversify its trade; acquire alternative sources of energy supply and revenue, thus compensating for the high energy extraction costs in Russia; and diversify and expand the business of its energy companies. Russia's companies are present in the Nigerian energy extraction sector and are pursuing the opportunity to develop Nigeria's nuclear energy sector.[99]

Furthermore, Russia has capitalized on the history of arms supply to Nigeria at moments when the United States and other Western countries declined Nigeria's requests for weapons and builds on anti-Western sentiments in order to mitigate Russia's increasing international isolation. For example, Moscow emphasizes that, within the UN, Russia and Nigeria are both interested in humanitarian, ecological, and political issues and the eradication of terrorism and that they enjoy practical project-based cooperation. Mathew Page of Chatham House notes that "Russia and the African countries are natural business partners because the Russians sell more economically priced military equipment," with no or little demand for political accountability, changes in the rule of law, or requirements for democratic values.[100]

Posture and Access

At present, U.S., Chinese, and Russian posture and access in Nigeria are limited. However, China and Russia have been making strides to deepen their access and increase their military presence throughout Africa, while the United States has been scaling back generally across the theater.

---

[96] Omotuyi, 2019.

[97] World Integrated Trade Solution, web tool, undated-a.

[98] Nigeria's exports to Russia are dominated by plant products, while Russia's exports to Nigeria are dominated by wheat, refined petroleum, fish, and iron products (Observatory of Economic Complexity, "Russia/Nigeria Trade," webpage, undated-d).

[99] Lukoil has identified Nigeria as one of the most desirable prospective sites for the expansion of Lukoil business, but because competition with other actors is considerable, Russia may not be well positioned to compete in the Nigerian extractive sector (Oil Capital, "Западная Африка—наиболее перспективный район для инвестиций ЛУКОЙЛа" ["West Africa—The Most Promising Region for LUKOIL Investments"], October 18, 2019; and Sergey Sukhankin, "Russian Inroads into Central Africa (Part Two)," Eurasia Daily Monitor, Vol. 17, No. 59, April 29, 2020b).

[100] Will McBain, "Skepticism Follows Russia-Nigeria Deal Announcements," African Business, December 9, 2019.

United States' Posture and Access

Although the United States does not have any bases in Nigeria or any combat troops permanently stationed there, the U.S. military has engaged in high levels of security cooperation with Nigerian forces for more than 50 years.[101] Washington has provided some assistance to Nigeria to fight Boko Haram but has been cautious about providing direct counterterrorism support to Nigeria (again, because of the poor human rights record of Nigeria's military forces).

Currently, the California National Guard conducts many of these security cooperation efforts, as it is Nigeria's state partner under the Guard's State Partnership Program. These efforts are focused on training and advising, specifically to improve Nigeria's medical and emergency capabilities and management, UN peacekeeping operations, and counternarcotics capabilities, as well as to improve "Nigerian security procedures, rule of law, aviation maintenance, human rights, and service member welfare."[102] The United States also carries out security cooperation efforts under the auspices of AFRICOM. These include high-level meetings,[103] military exercises, and the provision of intelligence support to the Nigerian Air Force.[104] AFRICOM also supports the Multinational Joint Task Force—a force comprising Nigeria, Benin, Cameroon, Chad, and Niger that has been a key actor in the fight against Boko Haram and ISWAP and that helps coordinate operations and facilitate intelligence-sharing through exercises, limited operations, and security assistance to counter-VEO efforts.[105] In conjunction with USAID, AFRICOM has worked with the members of the Multinational Joint Task Force to deliver humanitarian support and international relief efforts to the areas most affected by VEO activity.[106] Efforts to deliver aid, however, have been routinely disrupted by ongoing violence, instability, and growing levels of internal displacement. To further support counterterrorism efforts, AFRICOM provides intelligence support, via funding from Title 10 and Title 22 of the U.S. Code, to the Nigerian Air Force (as mentioned earlier) with the aim of bolstering its intelligence, surveillance, and reconnaissance (ISR); intelligence collection; counter–improvised explosive device; and air-ground integration capabilities.[107] In the past, the United States has also sent troops to Nigeria to

---

[101] U.S. military personnel are able to operate in Nigeria based on the status of forces agreement signed in 2000 (Bureau of Political-Military Affairs, 2021).

[102] AFRICOM, "State Partnership Program," webpage, undated.

[103] For example, U.S. Army Africa co-hosts an annual African Land Forces Summit with the Nigerian Army to "provide a forum to develop cooperative solutions for improved trans-regional security and stability" (Waldhauser, 2019, p. 30).

[104] Waldhauser, 2019, p. 30.

[105] Waldhauser, 2019, p. 7; and Samantha Reho, "Senior African Military Intelligence Directors Discuss Lake Chad Region Threat Environment," U.S. Africa Command, August 14, 2019.

[106] Waldhauser, 2019, p. 29.

[107] Waldhauser, 2019, p. 31.

aid in counterterrorism efforts. Under the Obama administration, for example, the United States deployed an interagency team, 80 U.S. troops, and an unmanned aerial vehicle to support search efforts in the aftermath of Boko Haram's kidnapping of the 276 schoolgirls from Chibok, Nigeria, in 2014.[108] It is plausible that similar small-scale deployments could occur if the fight against Boko Haram and ISWAP escalates.

Additionally, the Nigerian military participates in three AFRICOM-led U.S. military exercises: African Lion, Flintlock, and Obangame Express. However, as with other security assistance to the Nigerian armed forces, U.S.-Nigeria military training relations have not always been smooth. For example, in 2014, Nigeria abruptly canceled ongoing training by U.S. soldiers for countering Boko Haram, claiming the reason to be "purely strategic action," although the decision might have been a reaction to the U.S. decision not to sell lethal weapons to Nigeria because of the Leahy Law.[109]

One important development to U.S. posture and access in Nigeria occurred in March 2021, when the U.S. Army Corps of Engineers established a permanent presence in Abuja, Nigeria, to manage AFRICOM projects, including the "construction of new facilities for the A-29 Super Tucano wing at Kainji Airbase."[110] This permanent presence and the building of new facilities could lay the groundwork for increased U.S. engagement in Nigeria, particularly by the U.S. Air Force, if security and political conditions allow for it. The construction of an air base in the Agadez region of neighboring Niger in 2019 may also facilitate the potential use of drone operations.[111] Nigeria had initially opposed locating AFRICOM's base in Africa in 2007, considering such presence to be a potential interference with national sovereignty and fearing that it could make Africa a target; however, President Buhari has since suggested that AFRICOM should relocate to "closer to the theatre of operations," which could be a result of the increased security threats from the Islamic insurgency.[112]

Provided there is the need and the motivation, the United States could project power into Nigeria from other locations. In this respect, the United States has significantly more experience than Russia or China does, gained through decades of expeditionary operations of different scales. The United States maintains the most capable navy in the world, which supports

---

[108] Husted and Blanchard, 2020.

[109] "Nigeria Ends US Mission to Counter Boko Haram," *Defense News*, December 1, 2014.

[110] Alfredo Barraza, "USACE Establishes Permanent Presence in Africa to Support Key Missions," U.S. Army, March 2, 2021.

[111] DoD Inspector General, *Evaluation of Niger Air Base 201 Military Construction*, Washington, D.C.: U.S. Department of Defense, DODIG-2020-077, March 31, 2020; and Oriana Pawlyk, "US Begins Drone Operations out of New Niger Air Base," Military.com, November 1, 2019.

[112] Patrick Smith, "US/China/France: Africa's Security Woes Complicated by Foreign Boots," Africa Report, May 10, 2021.

the "mobile nature of [U.S.] maritime power," even if deploying to Nigeria or other African locations would still require encountering the tyranny of distance.[113]

Nevertheless, overflight rights could complicate the United States' ability to project power into Nigeria. Ideally, the United States would be able to leverage its bases in Europe to fly aircraft and military forces into Nigeria. As described in Chapter Two, Egypt, Algeria, and Libya (or at least the area controlled by Khalifa Haftar's Libyan National Army) all have ties to Russia.[114] If Russia can convince these countries to deny the U.S. Air Force the ability to overfly their countries, the United States would be forced to fly around Africa, adding thousands of miles (and multiple hours) to the trip and minimizing one of the key posture advantages that the United States has in responding to contingencies in this part of the continent.

China's Posture and Access

Nigeria tends to guard its own sovereignty zealously and thus far has not granted the PLA access to its territory for anything other than occasional training exercises or port visits.[115] That being said, Nigeria does frequently support multilateral interventions in other West African countries, so it might be open to providing temporary access to its territory for logistical support of foreign forces participating in such an operation.[116] Extensive Chinese investment in Nigeria's Lekki Port has led some to suggest that this could perhaps be used to service PLA ships in the future, possibly in a commercial capacity, but this is difficult to verify.[117] China is also heavily engaged in other port, airport, and rail infrastructure projects in Nigeria, which are primarily commercial in nature but could give Beijing leverage in a potential future competition with the United States and other countries for access to transport infrastructure for economic access, humanitarian assistance, or contingency response.

At present, the PLA does not enjoy any significant access agreements in West Africa, and although its ships visit West Africa with growing frequency, they do not operate there with the same regularity with which they patrol Africa's eastern coast.[118] China's nearest base is its logistics facility in Djibouti, which would be within air transport range of some airfields in

---

[113] Paul Van Hooft, "Don't Knock Yourself Out: How America Can Turn the Tables on China by Giving Up the Fight for Command of the Seas," *War on the Rocks*, February 23, 2021.

[114] Jared Malsin, "Russia Reinforces Foothold in Libya as Militia Leader Retreats," *Wall Street Journal*, June 29, 2020.

[115] Page, 2018, p. 7.

[116] Adesoji Adeniyi, "Peacekeeping Contributor Profile: Nigeria," Providing for Peacekeeping, April 24, 2015.

[117] Chad Peltier, Tate Nurkin, and Sean O'Connor, *China's Logistics Capabilities for Expeditionary Operations*, Coulsdon, United Kingdom: Janes, 2020, pp. 70–71; Office of the Secretary of Defense, *Military and Security Developments Involving the People's Republic of China 2020: Annual Report to Congress*, Washington, D.C., 2020.

[118] Andrew S. Erickson and Austin M. Strange, "China's Blue Soft Power," *Naval War College Review*, Vol. 68, No. 1, Winter 2015, p. 11.

Nigeria but only if the Chinese were able to significantly expand the airstrip at that facility.[119] It is also possible that the PLA will build a base on Africa's Atlantic coast, possibly in Angola or Namibia.[120] China periodically deploys forces, including groups of up to several hundred soldiers, to West Africa as part of UN peacekeeping forces.[121] Moreover, U.S government reports conclude that, although the PLA is working on the development of power projection capabilities, it is likely to become capable of engaging in only limited wars overseas in the medium term (2030–2035).[122] Moreover, the PLA is not engaged in a peacekeeping mission in Nigeria, but it has significant peacekeeper presence distributed across several UN locations—bases that China could seek to use to pursue not only its economic but also its security interests.[123]

Russia's Posture and Access

Although Russia does not have substantial official military presence in Nigeria or its neighboring countries, it maintains significant presence in Nigeria's security and defense sector through elite-to-elite relations, PMSC presence, training, and arms sales. Russia's current military cooperation with Nigeria is based on the 2017 bilateral Agreement on Military Cooperation, which provides a legal framework for cooperation in such areas as exchange of information, training, activities to combat terrorism and piracy, search and rescue at sea, and cooperation on peacekeeping, thus building on the history of mostly economic and educational cooperation with Nigeria during the Cold War.[124] The Russia-Nigeria military-technical cooperation is further reinforced by the 2021 Agreement on Military-Technical Cooperation, which provides the framework for Russia to supply Nigeria with more military equipment and training.[125]

Russia seeks to ensure elite-to-elite relations through educational, cultural, and economic means of cooperation. For example, Russia regularly hosts the Miss Africa Russia beauty pageant and provides undergraduate and graduate spots for African students in Russian uni-

---

[119] Janes, "XAC Y-20 Kunpeng," *All the World's Aircraft: Development and Production*, December 16, 2021d.

[120] Peltier, Nurkin, and O'Connor, 2020, pp. 66–67, 80.

[121] International Peace Institute, Peacekeeping Database, online database, undated.

[122] U.S.-China Economic and Security Review Commission, 2020b.

[123] Thomas Dyrenforth, "Beijing's Blue Helmets: What to Make of China's Role in UN Peacekeeping in Africa," Modern War Institute at West Point, August 18, 2021; and Africa and special operations researcher, email exchange with the authors, December 2021.

[124] Ministry of Foreign Affairs of the Russian Federation, "Agreement Between the Government of the Russian Federation and the Government of the Federal Republic of Nigeria on Military Cooperation," August 22, 2017.

[125] Odita Sunday, "Nigeria Signs Military-Technical Cooperation Treaty with Russia," *The Guardian*, August 26, 2021.

versities.[126] According to official state sources, Russia provides 100 state scholarships per year for higher education in Russia to Nigerian citizens, and, throughout the years, an estimated 100,000 Nigerians have received higher education in Russia, 12,000 of whom have been sponsored by the Russian government.[127]

Although they are not officially linked to the Russian government, Russian PMSCs in Nigeria fulfill Russian foreign policy objectives—specifically, protecting Russia's oil and gas interests and energy contracts. The presence of Russian PMSCs in the country may be traced back to at least 2010, when the now-obsolete RusCorp reported an office in Nigeria.[128] Russian sources indicate that Moran Security Group was engaged in training Nigerian military personnel, although details are sparse.[129] Open-source reports show a sharp increase in the presence of Russian PMSCs in Nigeria since 2015.[130] Judging from these reports, Russian PMSCs, such as RusCorp, Moran, and RSB Group, have been engaged in anti-piracy activities on behalf of Russian state-owned oil companies, as well as in counterinsurgency operations in support of the Nigerian government.[131] Nigeria also has expressed significant interest in using Russian mercenaries to train its armed forces to fight terrorist groups and insurgents.[132] At the same time, the contingent of Russian PMSCs in Nigeria has been described as "an incoherent mix of people, helicopters and random kit from all sorts of different sources," challenging Nigeria's ability to control the actions of the PMSCs.[133]

Russia also has sought to fill training gaps left by the discontinuation of U.S.-provided training. For example, in 2014, Russia reportedly began training Nigerian special forces

---

[126] RUDN University, "Studencheskii Konkurs 'Miss Afrika'" ["Student Competition 'Miss Africa'"], webpage, undated.

[127] Embassy of the Russian Federation in Nigeria, "Rossiya-Nigeriya" ["Russia-Nigeria"], undated; and Agubamah, 2014.

[128] Tor Bukkvoll and Åse G. Østensen, "The Emergence of Russian Private Military Companies: A New Tool of Clandestine Warfare," *Special Operations Journal*, Vol. 6, No. 1, 2020.

[129] Vladimir Neelov, *Chastniya Voyenniye Kompanyi Rossii: Opit I Perspektivi Ispolzovaniya* [*Private Military Companies in Russia: Experience and Prospects for Use*], St. Petersburg, Center for Strategic Assessments and Forecasts, 2013.

[130] Alessandro Arduino, *The Footprint of Chinese Private Security Companies in Africa*, Washington, D.C.: Johns Hopkins University, Working Paper No. 35, 2020.

[131] Asymmetric Warfare Group and U.S. Army Training and Doctrine Command, *Russian Private Military Companies: Their Use and How to Consider Them in Operations, Competition, and Conflict*, Baltimore, Md.: Johns Hopkins Applied Physics Laboratory, April 2020.

[132] Sergey Sukhankin, "Russian Private Military Contractors in Sub-Saharan Africa," *Russie.Nei.Visions*, No. 120, September 2020d; and Thomas D. Arnold, "The Geoeconomic Dimensions of Russian Private Military and Security Companies," *Military Review*, November–December 2019.

[133] Ulrich Petersohn, "Everything in (Dis)Order? Private Military and Security Contractors and International Order," *Journal of Future Conflict*, 2020; and Asymmetric Warfare Group and U.S. Army Training and Doctrine Command, 2020, p. 16.

in Russia, after the United States stopped providing such training.[134] And Nigeria's media reported that Russia has trained Nigerian police and Department of State Services officials.[135] The fact that the training reportedly takes place in Russia may indicate Russia's reluctance to put official boots on the ground in Nigeria. Although Russia carries out a limited number of military exercises in Africa, both Russia and Nigeria, along with Sudan, Tanzania, and Morocco, participated in Exercise Aman 2017 in the Arabian Sea and Pakistan.[136]

In addition, Russia has sought to fill the gap in arms supply left after the United States and other Western countries refused to sell arms to Nigeria. For example, after the United States refused to sell Cobra attack helicopters in 2014, Russia was quick to sell Nigeria Mi-35 and Mi-17 helicopters.[137] This resulted in Nigeria becoming increasingly reliant on Russian military equipment and was followed by the purchase of another 12 Mi-35 fighter jets in October 2019.[138]

Compared with Chinese companies' ownership stakes in Nigerian transport infrastructure, Russian companies' stakes are small. A more recent development in changing this imbalance is the 2019 Russian and Nigerian memorandum of understanding on railway modernization that involves two Russian companies: Russian joint stock company Russian Railways and Transmashholding.[139] Some experts are skeptical about the project ever reaching maturity, but this cooperation and Russia constructing 1,400 km of rail track from Lagos to Calabar might offer Russian stakeholders better access to key transport nodes.[140]

Lastly, although Russia does not have official military presence in Nigeria, its plans to develop a military base in CAR and its military presence in that country may be instrumental in supporting Russia's official or unofficial military and security force presence in Nigeria.[141] Moreover, Russia's military is optimized for contingencies in or near its territory, so it has devoted less investment to developing the ability to project large-scale military forces to a faraway region. Russia has sought to expand its military presence to areas farther away from its

---

[134] János Besenyő, "The Africa Policy of Russia," *Terrorism and Political Violence*, Vol. 31, No. 1, 2019.

[135] John Campbell, "Nigeria Turns to Russia, Czech Republic, and Belarus for Military Training and Materiel," Council on Foreign Relations, October 29, 2014.

[136] International Institute for Strategic Studies, undated.

[137] Besenyő, 2019.

[138] Samuel Ramani, "Russia Takes Its Syrian Model of Counterinsurgency to Africa," Royal United Services Institute, September 9, 2020.

[139] Railway Pro, "TMH Signed Agreements to Develop Nigerian Railway Industry," October 24, 2019.

[140] "Nigeria, Russia in Rail, Steel, Defence Deals," Agence de Presse Africaine, October 24, 2019; and McBain, 2019.

[141] Aleksandr Gostev, "'Dikiye Gysi' Ili 'Psi Voiny'? Rossiskiye Nayomniki V AFrike: Kto, Gde Pochem" ["'Wild Geese' or 'Dogs of War'? Russian Mercenaries in Africa: Who, Where, How Much"], Radio Liberty Russia, January 11, 2019; and Evgeniy Pudovkin, "CAR Pered Viborami Okazalas Na Grani Politicheskovo Kollapsa" ["Before the Elections CAR Found Itself on the Verge of Political Collapse"], RBK, December 23, 2020.

neighborhood (e.g., by participating in the conflict in Syria and in naval exercises near South Africa), but it lacks the aircraft carriers, aerial-refueling capability, and even overseas basing that benefit the United States.[142] However, Russia has long-range transport aircraft that could be used to support smaller deployments.[143]

Capabilities

As with posture and access, U.S., Chinese, and Russian capabilities in Nigeria are currently minimal in terms of in-country assets. All three powers' ability to engage in direct military action there is limited to varying degrees, but all three powers have a variety of capabilities to support proxies indirectly. China has been cultivating the ability to deploy PLA forces to West Africa, which could lead to increased deployments in the future. Russia, meanwhile, retains levers of political influence in Nigeria.

United States' Capabilities

As noted earlier, the U.S. military does not have any substantial military forces in Nigeria. The presence of a representative of the U.S. Army Corps of Engineers in Nigeria in support of the integration of A-29 Super Tucano aircraft could help further develop U.S.-Nigeria air force relations. However, any U.S. military presence in the country would have to face significant time and distance challenges, even with the reported U.S. military outposts in neighboring countries, such as Cameroon and Niger, while the only permanent U.S. base in the region is located in Djibouti at Camp Lemonnier, more than 3,000 miles away from Nigeria, and is dependent on the use of the civilian runway at the Djibouti international airport.[144] Some of the 4,000 U.S., partner, and allied personnel stationed at Camp Lemonnier could be deployed in support of future operations in Nigeria, but the logistical challenges would be significant.[145] The distance between Camp Lemonnier and Nigeria far exceeds the flight range of most air assets in the theater (without needing to refuel), and one U.S. Air Force expert noted that it would be more likely for such assets to be deployed from U.S. facilities in Europe that have the necessary infrastructure for the takeoff and landing of fixed-wing aircraft.[146] Although the United States could use naval assets (such as aircraft carriers) to project power into Nigeria, the deployment of such capabilities likely would depend on the kinds of missions that the United States would be willing to carry out there and its commitment to expend significant resources.

---

[142] William Heerdt, "Russian Hard Power Projection: A Brief Synopsis," Center for Strategic and International Studies, March 25, 2020.

[143] Expert on the Russian military, interview with the authors, October 2021.

[144] Commander, Navy Installations Command, "Welcome to Camp Lemonnier, Djibouti," webpage, undated.

[145] Commander, Navy Installations Command, undated.

[146] Retired U.S. military officer previously stationed in Africa, interview with the authors, July 2021.

A potential option for operational support may be the California National Guard and any of its accompanying assets, considering its established relations with Nigeria. Although most of the Guard members deployed as part of the State Partnership Program are usually sent to assist with training Nigerian troops, there have been instances in which the Guard has participated in kinetic operations in Africa. For instance, the Connecticut National Guard sent more than 600 troops to Eastern Africa in March 2021 to support counterterrorism operations.[147] Such a deployment is conceivable for Nigeria—provided that the appropriate legal agreements and authorities were in place—if the Boko Haram and ISWAP insurgency escalates.

China's Capabilities

Although China currently does not have a military presence in Nigeria, if Beijing chooses to support the Nigerian government in a future conflict, China would face fewer or at least different legal restrictions than the United States would and could have the means to provide military equipment. At present, China sells large quantities of weapons to the Nigerian government (though not so large as the quantities sent to some other nations), including ships, aircraft, and armored vehicles.[148] In 2020, Nigeria received Wing Loong II armed reconnaissance drones.[149] There is no reason to believe that China would not be able to increase these shipments considerably, especially if Nigeria were willing to pay for the arms. And the nature of the Nigerian military could make Chinese equipment provision especially effective. The Nigerian military has about 100,000 men under arms, but despite its size, its effectiveness is hampered by outdated equipment, a lack of logistical vehicles, and inadequate training.[150] China could also provide smaller training under the umbrella of counterterrorism operations but would not be likely to support the training needs for large-scale combat formations similar to U.S. training in Iraq and Afghanistan.

The PLA's ability to deploy its own forces to West Africa is likely to grow considerably by about 2030. At present, China lacks experience deploying or supporting more than several hundred soldiers in the region as part of various UN peacekeeping missions.[151] (Even so,

---

[147] Christopher Keating, "Nearly 600 Connecticut National Guard Troops Headed to Africa in Global War on Terrorism; Largest Deployment Since 2009," *Hartford Courant*, March 10, 2021.

[148] Page, 2018, p. 10; Janes, "Nigeria: Army," *World Armies*, last updated February 28, 2021a; and Janes, "Nigeria: Air Force," *Sentinel Security Assessment: West Africa*, March 9, 2021b.

[149] Liu Xuanzun, "Nigeria Received China-Made Armed Reconnaissance Drones: Reports," *Global Times*, November 11, 2020.

[150] Corruption is endemic in Nigeria's weapon procurement and distribution systems, and this would likely lead to the diversion of some of Beijing's military aid. But if enough is provided, much of it would likely trickle down, however inefficiently, to frontline units. Some Nigerian troops have complained that local insurgents are better armed than they are, suggesting that even moderate improvements to the weapons available could lead to significant increases in effectiveness and morale (Janes, 2021a).

[151] International Peace Institute, undated.

in the past, forces not much larger have proven decisive in West African conflicts.[152]) The PLA's expeditionary capacity outside of the Indo-Pacific region is still in its infancy, but it likely will include carrier strike groups, sizable amphibious forces that can be stationed and deployed overseas, and a network of air bases, some of which may be within striking range of Nigeria.[153] Nevertheless, China is unlikely to develop a fully global reach and instead is likely to opt for developing a network of access points and bases.[154]

In the meantime, China's ability to support a proxy that does not control civilian ports or other logistical infrastructure will be much more limited. The lack of air bases within striking or transport range of Nigerian territory likely would be a significant challenge, unless a new base is secured or China upgrades its base in Djibouti to service fixed-wing aircraft.[155] With its vast state-owned civilian conglomerates and growing role of special forces, Beijing potentially has considerable resources with which to provide clandestine support but lacks experience or institutions to provide such support far from its own borders. Historically, building such a capability to the point that it is strategically effective can take time.[156] China also could provide considerable financial, diplomatic, and cyber or intelligence support to any proxy it chose, whether government or insurgent.

Russia's Capabilities

Russia's support for Nigeria's security so far has largely been in the form of arms sales and the presence of PMSCs, and Moscow has started to demonstrate some of its means of political and information-related capabilities.

In its relations with Nigeria, Russia builds the information aspect on its history of supplying arms to the country—from the Soviet Union's support supplying military equipment to Nigerian forces during the Nigerian civil war (1967–1970) to the 2014 sale of Mi-35 combat helicopters after the United States and the United Kingdom refused to sell arms to Nigeria

---

[152] David Thomson, "The Slow Decline of French Influence in Africa," France 24, February 15, 2010.

[153] Janes, "China: Navy," *Sentinel Security Assessment: China and Northeast Asia*, May 24, 2021c.

[154] RAND expert on China and Africa, discussion with the authors, August 2021.

[155] Peter A. Dutton, Isaac B. Kardon, and Conor M. Kennedy, *Djibouti: China's First Overseas Strategic Strongpoint*, Newport, R.I.: U.S. Naval War College, China Maritime Report No. 6, 2020, p. 31.

[156] For example, although the United States and the Soviet Union were able to build rudimentary capabilities to support armed non-state actors in far-off countries, it took some time for them to do so to any particular effect. This is especially true of the United States, which, like modern China in Africa, did not have many existing relationships with armed groups to build on. For a treatment of Washington's earlier and less-effective efforts to build its ability to support armed proxies, see, for example, Michael Warner, "Central Intelligence: Origin and Evolution—Historical Perspective," in Central Intelligence Agency, *The Creation of the Intelligence Community: Founding Documents*, Washington, D.C.: U.S. Government Printing Office, 2009, pp. 6–7; and Tim Weiner, *Legacy of Ashes: The History of the CIA*, New York: Anchor Books, 2007, pp. 8–9, 12, 277. Special thanks to the work of our RAND colleagues on the subject, available in Watts et al., 2023.

because of human rights abuses.[157] Analysis suggests that Russia is interested in selling arms to Nigeria mainly because of Moscow's geopolitical interests in reasserting Russia's role as a counterweight to U.S. and Western power and influence, a convergence of Russian and Nigerian interests in fighting terrorism, and a desire to maintain Russia's role as the largest arms supplier to Africa and ensure a market for Russian arms manufacturers. Defense analyst Ben Moores summarized the reasons for Nigeria's interest in Russian arms supplies as follows:

> Russia is known to sell equipment at a relatively low cost; it is known to sell to pretty much anyone without any questions asked. It does not ask for any guarantees in terms of where the equipment will go—how the equipment is used. There is no oversight. They do not have to sign up for agreements. Not only that, but Russia is also able to supply equipment relatively quickly—and to supply equipment that is fairly easy for less technically capable militaries to get that equipment into the frontline at a relatively fast pace.[158]

Russia also has demonstrated to Nigerian leaders its political influence tools, such as election interference and social media networks. For example, Russia-linked operatives funded Ghanaian and Nigerian individuals to pose as Americans on social media prior to the 2020 U.S. presidential election.[159]

How Might a Conflict Unfold?

With persistent ethnic tensions, high levels of government and security-sector corruption, and increasing competition over resources, it is easy to see how low-level conflicts may escalate into a broader or higher-intensity conflict in Nigeria. What is less clear is how severe the conflict would have to be to galvanize any substantial involvement from the United States, China, or Russia. As previously discussed, the United States does not have any core geopolitical, security, or economic interests that would be affected by the outbreak of a conflict in Nigeria. And although China and Russia have demonstrated deeper interests than the

---

[157] Kondratenko, 2020.

[158] Joe DeCapua, "Analysts Weigh Nigeria-Russia Arms Deal," Voice of America, December 10, 2014. According to another analyst, "the military has recorded some successes owing to the arms and weapons systems procurement, like the recovery of more than 22 local government areas under Boko Haram terrorists and ensured that Shekau did not disrupt the 2015 election as he had threatened" (Otu Offiong Duke, "The Role of Military Logistics Supports in Safeguarding National Security in Nigeria," *International Journal of Trend in Scientific Research and Development*, Vol. 3, No. 5, August 2019, p. 838). The recovery of these towns and villages, especially in Borno, Yobe, and Adamawa states, has enabled access and revealed the humanitarian needs of civilians living in territories previously under Boko Haram control and in newly accessible areas that are under military control.

[159] Josh Rudolph and Thomas Morley, *Covert Foreign Money: Financial Loopholes Exploited by Authoritarians to Fund Political Interference in Democracies*, Washington, D.C.: Alliance for Securing Democracy, August 2020.

United States has in Nigeria and in Africa more broadly, neither great power seems to have sufficiently important national interests that would compel it to participate through direct military action in a conflict in Nigeria. That being said, the United States has cause to be concerned about the uptick in Chinese and Russian influence throughout the continent in the context of broader great-power competition. And because Nigeria is one of the largest states in Africa, the U.S. desire to mitigate Chinese and Russian influence is particularly acute there.

Considering these dynamics between the great powers and local actors on the ground in Nigeria, we have identified the most likely paths to larger-scale conflict in Nigeria, as well as the prospects for U.S., Chinese, and Russian engagement in these scenarios. The most likely flashpoint for future larger-scale conflict based on current circumstances in Nigeria is the conflict between VEOs and the Nigerian military in the northeastern Borno State. That is, of the most likely causes of internal conflict in Nigeria, this path has the greatest potential of drawing in U.S., Chinese, and Russian involvement. This escalation of violence could affect the stability of China's economic interests in Nigeria and access to China's natural resource investments. For Russia, such a conflict may allow Moscow to continue to build its relations with the Nigerian government by applying its concessions-for-protection policy. The United States, for its part, could feel motivated to become involved because of its commitment to countering VEOs and preventing Boko Haram and ISWAP from becoming a direct threat to the United States.

We also identified other potential conflicts in Nigeria: the dissatisfaction of several ethnic groups with the centralized governance; the ongoing conflict over land in the Middle Belt region between settled farmers and nomadic herdsmen; the persistent ethno-sectarian conflict between the Muslim Hausa and Fulani peoples in the north and the Christian Igbo in the southeast; and the budding conflict over water or other natural resources, especially in the Niger Delta, as Nigeria's projected boom in population between now and 2050 will place further strain on and generate intensified competition over natural resources and likely will result in an increased percentage of the population living in poverty. However, although some of these other conflicts might prompt deeper engagement by the United States, China, or Russia in terms of diplomatic or economic aid, the counterterrorism fight is the only contingency that may spur all three countries to engage militarily. In the next section, we provide an overview of the current conflict and evaluate the prospects of U.S., Chinese, and Russian engagement in a scenario where the fight intensifies.

Why Would the United States, China, and Russia Get Involved, and Whom Would Each Support?

Boko Haram and ISWAP currently have local reach and ambitions, and ISWAP maintains links to other Islamic State affiliates.[160] Should ISWAP manage to leverage its connections across Africa and beyond to grow into a more global threat with the capability to target the United States or its closest allies, the United States may be motivated to take a more assertive role in the counterterrorism fight in Nigeria. Similarly, should ISWAP or Boko Haram target U.S. facilities in Nigeria, the United States would have an obligation to intervene to defend its citizens. Boko Haram and ISWAP both have attempted to attack or have declared that they would attack the U.S. and U.K. embassies in Abuja before, for instance.[161] Should these groups succeed in launching an attack or if the attempts become frequent or severe enough, the United States likely would have to send military assistance to protect its citizens, particularly given the sensitivities surrounding such an event following the attack on the U.S. facilities in Benghazi. In fact, in 2021, U.S. Secretary of State Antony Blinken called for the U.S.-led global coalition to defeat the Islamic State to "expand on coalition plans for effective[ly] dealing with the threat in Africa," suggesting at least some U.S. government appetite for deeper engagement in counterterrorism operations in Africa, even if not unilaterally.[162]

In the scenario in which Boko Haram and ISWAP activity escalates, U.S. military engagement could take the form of a small troop deployment, likely consisting of special operations forces, aircraft to conduct ISR missions, or air strikes on key Boko Haram or ISWAP targets, while PMSCs could provide increased security at U.S. facilities or the facilities of U.S. companies in Nigeria. For example, the U.S. Army's 3rd Special Forces Group, which has been reported to focus on Africa, could be deployed to train host-nation forces.[163] In addition to these measures, or as a response to a less severe threat, the U.S. military could send advisers and trainers to help the Nigerian military in the counter-VEO fight and provide more training to these troops. Per the earlier discussion of U.S. objectives in Nigeria, most U.S. aid—both military and humanitarian in nature—to the country has revolved around the fight against Boko Haram and ISWAP. Both groups are on the U.S. State Department's list of foreign terrorist organizations, and the United States has conducted limited military engagements in the past in the form of small troop deployments, advisers, and ISR assets to support the Nigerian government in the fight against these terrorist groups. In the event of an escalated threat to U.S. interests posed by Boko Haram or ISWAP, the United States likely would

[160] Foucher, 2020.

[161] "Boko Haram 'Plot to Attack UK and US Embassies Foiled,'" BBC News, April 12, 2017.

[162] Antony J. Blinken, "Secretary Antony J. Blinken Opening Remarks at D-ISIS Meeting Opening Session," remarks in Rome, U.S. Department of State, June 28, 2021.

[163] U.S. Army Special Operations Command Historian, "3rd Special Forces Group History," December 7, 2018.

resume such measures, potentially on a larger scale if the magnitude of the threat warranted increased involvement.

Because the United States does not have deep ties to any particular actor in Nigeria beyond the government, it likely would channel all of its support to the Nigerian security forces. Local militias are, at present, not an ideal proxy force for the United States to support, because they have been reported to engage in human rights abuses and contribute to instability in the region, and there is little information available to suggest that the United States has directly supported any of these groups. Thus, despite the previously discussed U.S. concerns over human rights abuses by the Nigerian military, Washington does not have another viable proxy to support in this fight.

China and Russia are also unlikely to support any proxy other than the Nigerian government. This is primarily because of China's and Russia's reluctance to foment instability in Nigeria, as instability would jeopardize their economic—and potentially security, should Boko Haram and ISWAP become global threats—interests in the country were it to descend into widespread chaos or civil war. China seems particularly averse to potential chaos. Chinese analysts, for instance, see the collapse of the Qaddafi regime in Libya and the ensuing chaos as a disaster that has led to a further spread of extremist groups throughout the region.[164] Moreover, Chinese analysts observe that the involvement of extra-regional states in proxy warfare in Libya has made a resolution of that conflict nearly impossible, as each sponsor sustains the strength of its side to enable continued fighting and eschew negotiations, but no one group has been strong enough to end the conflict.[165]

Consistent with its position elsewhere in the world, Russia is likely to continue its support for the Nigerian forces via PMSCs, which generally tend to have agreements with the official state government, and could even consider providing some special forces. However, in recent years, the performance of Russian PMSCs in Africa has not been uniformly smooth and successful. The groups suffered losses and withdrew from Mozambique and, in Libya, failed to help Haftar seize Tripoli and reportedly used Syrian fighters, to the displeasure of Haftar. If Russian PMSCs, and particularly Wagner, continue to have unsuccessful operations elsewhere in Africa, especially when countering Islamic insurgencies or when protecting local leaders, Nigerian leaders may become less interested in looking at Russian PMSCs as security providers and might entertain alternative offers from regional or other PMSCs.

Considering the character of the counter-VEO scenario, we conclude that both China and Russia would support the Nigerian government, because this is the most likely way to ensure stability in the country and build relationships with influential local actors.[166] However, this could change if the militias take on a larger role and become power brokers in Nige-

---

[164] Manyuan, 2020.

[165] Manyuan, 2020.

[166] In the event of an uprising similar to the Arab Spring, China may also provide military support to help the government crush any popular opposition movement, because the Chinese saw the Arab Spring as a disaster for the region and closely associated with Islamic extremism. Were this to transpire, it is possible

ria or if the specific future conflict situation involves a powerful state (local government) actor.[167] That being said, it is possible that some Chinese business interests could provide low-level support to local militia or perhaps even criminal elements in order to protect their personnel or facilities.[168] There could be some possibility that Russia's PMSCs could establish covert back-channels with non-state militia groups to advance their operational aims (such as reducing the threat to a location that they are protecting) or to help position Russia as a mediator.[169] However, there is no available information to suggest that either China or Russia has already funneled support to the militia groups, so it is difficult to gauge the extent to which this might be happening today or in the future. Indeed, China and Russia have continued to build relationships with both Hausa and Fulani figures who represent the primary political groups in the Nigerian government. Thus, in practice, all three great powers are supporting the Nigerian government and military because those are the primary actors with the capacity and intent to fight Boko Haram and ISWAP. At present, this means that the United States, China, and Russia are aligned on the same side of the counterterrorism fight, even if they are all vying to deepen their influence with the Nigerian government and the more-local groups that each supports.

In terms of material support, China and Russia are far less constrained than the United States in what they are willing to provide to the Nigerian government. In addition to offering training and advisers of their own, they may provide weapons and other military equipment to the Nigerian government to defeat any major new offensive by Islamist insurgents and to constrain instability in the country. This places the United States at a disadvantage because Leahy restrictions prevent the United States from providing certain kinds of weapons to Nigeria as long as human rights abuses persist.[170]

More broadly, if China and Russia are both providing significant support, the United States may be more inclined to increase its military engagement in this counterterrorism scenario so as not to cede leverage to either competitor. However, there is currently very little appetite for any sort of military engagement in Africa, and scant U.S. resources are devoted to the continent. Thus, to justify a substantial intervention in Nigeria (beyond the indirect support currently offered through security cooperation initiatives), the U.S. government would have to be presented with a contingency in which U.S. personnel, facilities, or other core national security interests are threatened. In other words, even though Nigeria ranks very

---

that the United States would find itself supporting the protestors, while China could end up supporting the regime (see Wang, 2018).

[167] Cohen, Treyger, et al., 2023.

[168] Chinese companies tend to rely on local militias or PMSCs for security if law enforcement forces are insufficient, possibly providing a modest stream of income for whichever groups provide such services (Arduino, 2019, p. 98).

[169] Cohen, Treyger, et al., 2023.

[170] Robbie Gramer, "U.S. Lawmakers Hold Up Major Proposed Arms Sale to Nigeria," *Foreign Policy*, July 27, 2021.

high as a country where both great-power influence-seeking and the potential for internal conflict converge relative to the other countries in the region (i.e., for competition potential and conflict potential), the chances that the United States would become involved in a conflict on a side opposing China or Russia are not very high.

Table 3.1 provides a summary of the interests and objectives, posture and access, and capabilities of the three great powers in Nigeria. In this table, by *external* reasons, we mean objectives that pertain to broader geopolitical or other concerns beyond the borders of Nigeria; by *internal* reasons, we mean objectives that pertain to concerns that are largely focused within Nigeria.

TABLE 3.1

Key Characteristics of Possible Conflict Scenarios with Great-Power Involvement in Nigeria

	United States	China	Russia
Why would each power become involved?			
External reasons	Strategic and geopolitical: • Prevent competitors from becoming security partners of choice	Strategic and geopolitical (limited): • Seek political support for China's policies	Strategic and geopolitical: • Seek political support for Russia's policies • Undermine U.S. influence • Build status in the region
Internal reasons	Security: • Combat violent extremism • Ensure regional stability	Economic and security: • Protect or secure access to extractive industries, critical infrastructure investments, and trade • Protect Chinese nationals • Counter international terrorism	Economic and security: • Diversify trade and pursue markets • Counter international terrorism
Whom might each power support?	• Government	• Government	• Government
What form would support likely take?	• Indirect overt support • Limited military support	• Indirect support	• Indirect support (covert and overt)
What capabilities would each power bring?	• Training and advising • Military equipment (limited) • ISR • Special operations forces • Airlift • Air strikes	• Training • Military equipment • ISR • Special operations forces • Financial support	• PMSCs • Training and advising • Military equipment • Special operations forces

What Factors Might Influence the Outcome of the Conflict?

Assuming that the security situation deteriorated enough to motivate the United States and China, Russia, or both to engage in the conflict, the United States would face several strategic, operational, and tactical issues that would place it at a disadvantage vis-à-vis its competitors. Although, as previously discussed, all three powers would likely intervene on the same side of the conflict and support the Nigerian government against Boko Haram and ISWAP, they would probably continue to vie for influence in Nigeria rather than work together. Indeed, the United States likely would intervene as part of the global coalition to defeat the Islamic State or would support a multinational operation, and neither Russia nor China is a member of this coalition. Thus, even in a scenario in which all three powers are notionally on the same side, each would still be engaged in great-power competition and looking for opportunities to exploit the situation to its respective advantage.

The issues facing the United States on a strategic level primarily pertain to the United States lacking core interests across Africa and a comprehensive policy for Africa.[171] As previously discussed, the United States has long overlooked Africa and focused on other regions that it has deemed to be more important for its strategic interests.[172] AFRICOM has been relegated to an economy-of-force command, meaning that it has been tasked with operating under very limited resources in order to free up resources to devote to more-critical missions.[173] Although the U.S. government has recognized the importance of Africa and identified it as a region that will become increasingly strategically relevant in the ongoing strategic competition with China and Russia, Africa is not high on the U.S. military's priority list, and the military continues to scale down its presence there.[174] This is partly because U.S. leaders do not believe that the country has significant core interests at play in Nigeria or Africa more broadly, so they would need a compelling reason to justify more-significant interventions or force presence to a domestic audience that has grown war-weary, especially in relation to seemingly irrelevant wars.

Additionally, although the United States has remained substantially engaged with Nigeria in terms of economic assistance, it has been constrained in the type and level of support that it can provide through arms sales and other military aid. As discussed earlier, legal restrictions prohibit the United States from selling Nigeria lethal weapon systems as long as the

---

[171] Former U.S. government official and think-tank expert on Africa, interview with the authors, July 2021.

[172] Currently, most U.S. strategic focus and most U.S. resources are devoted to the Indo-Pacific and European theaters with the aim of deterring and effectively competing against China and Russia.

[173] Townsend, 2020; see also Tara Copp, "Understaffed AFRCIOM Cutting Hundreds More Troops," *Military Times*, February 20, 2019.

[174] Note that, since the completion of research for this report, President Biden authorized a deployment of U.S. special operations forces to Somalia to support the counter-VEO efforts there. This is at least a partial reversal of President Trump's decision to withdraw U.S. forces from the country in 2020 (C. Todd Lopez, "U.S. to Resume Small, Persistent Presence in Somalia," U.S. Department of Defense, May 16, 2022).

Nigerian government engages in human rights abuses; as a result, there are pending sales that have been put on hold. Given these dynamics, China and Russia both have significantly more avenues of security-focused leverage devoted to the African continent and Nigeria in particular. Because the United States often places many conditions on the aid that it provides, it can be a less attractive partner than China and Russia; in particular, African countries are generally willing to work with any of the three powers and, rather than operating off ideological alignment, typically will work with any partner that can provide them with what they want at the greatest speed and with the fewest restrictions.[175] At the same time, Nigeria's financial and energy dealings with Russia may expose the country to the U.S. 2017 Countering America's Adversaries Through Sanctions Act, preventing U.S. support.[176]

Beyond these strategic issues, there are a host of operational and tactical issues that would pose obstacles to a successful U.S. military intervention, even with a smaller troop deployment. First and foremost, the United States suffers from a lack of bases and presence in West Africa. There are some U.S. troops in neighboring Niger; the United States has been able to use the air base in Agadez, Niger, for ISR operations and other air operations; and the United States has a scattering of smaller-scale cooperative locations, but these are largely small-scale locations with few pre-stationed capabilities. U.S. forces would need to face the tyranny of the vast distances of Africa, as well as low airport density and a lack of infrastructure, particularly in remote areas.[177] Considering that the reported range for the MQ-9 remotely piloted aircraft system is 1,150 miles, U.S. forces would need to ensure that they are based in a location that would allow that range to cover the area for their operations in Nigeria.[178] Moreover, many African countries have expressed sensitivity over the use of drones.[179] That being said, the rescue mission of a U.S. citizen in northern Nigeria carried out by U.S. special operators in 2020 proves the capabilities of the U.S. military in Africa to carry out small-scale precision operations on short notice.[180]

One potential development that could affect the U.S. posture in Africa more broadly is that Nigeria's president has asked the United States to move AFRICOM headquarters from Germany to Africa, marking a big change from Nigeria's previous position against AFRICOM

---

[175] Former U.S. government official and think-tank expert on Africa, interview with the authors, July 2021.

[176] U.S. Department of the Treasury, "Countering America's Adversaries Through Sanctions Act–Related Sanctions," August 2, 2017. According to one interviewee, however, sanctions may not necessarily prevent Western or international organizations' cooperation with African countries that cooperate with other countries that are under Western sanctions (former U.S. government official and think-tank expert on Africa, interview with the authors, July 2021).

[177] Julian Hattem, "Why Is African Air Travel So Terrible?" Bloomberg, November 21, 2017.

[178] U.S. Air Force, "MQ-9 Reaper," webpage, March 2021.

[179] Robert Windrem and Jim Miklaszewski, "Why U.S. Drones Aren't Flying over Nigeria (And What They Could Do If They Were)," NBC News, May 9, 2014.

[180] Idrees Ali, "U.S. Special Forces Rescue American Held in Nigeria: Officials," Reuters, October 31, 2020.

headquarters on the continent.[181] Even if the headquarters were not established in Nigeria, moving the headquarters to Africa would have numerous implications for U.S. posture, access, and capabilities on the continent. And although this move could significantly boost U.S. capabilities and readiness for operations in Nigeria, it also would present Boko Haram, ISWAP, and other nefarious actors with new targets. In the event that these terrorist organizations tried to attack U.S. facilities and threatened U.S. personnel, the United States would be likely to engage in more-significant kinetic action to protect its base and personnel.

Short of this development transpiring, however, the United States would have to deploy troops or air assets from Niger, Djibouti, or Europe, all of which would pose logistical issues, such as cross-border flights from Niger and Europe and deconfliction of access to the civilian airstrip in Djibouti. For example, because the airfield in Djibouti is used by both U.S. and Chinese forces, the two countries could find themselves experiencing airspace deconfliction issues if operations were to ramp up, especially given the already high level of congestion in the civilian airspace above Djibouti.[182] The future of African airport infrastructure development remains problematic and could influence U.S. access to adequate infrastructure and airspace deconfliction.[183]

To support a sudden increase in special operators, the United States likely would need to ensure the necessary capacity in locations that would act as regional hubs, such as the West African Logistics Network site at the Kotoka Airport in Ghana—a location that serves as a regional logistics hub for the African continent.[184] In addition, shortcomings in U.S. posture and access might be addressed by leveraging allied resources in the region, particularly those of France. However, France does not have facilities in Nigeria and has stated that it relies on the U.S. presence in Niger for ISR and logistical support.[185] Nonetheless, France has more influence and a larger footprint across Africa and may be able to reallocate forces from neighboring countries, should the counterterrorism fight escalate. Moreover, France maintains a significant role in West African airport infrastructure with the Agency for Aerial Navigation Safety in Africa and Madagascar (L'Agence pour la sécurité de la navigation aérienne en Afrique et à Madagascar), which manages many airports in the region and is headquartered in Paris.

Even as the United States reduces its presence in Africa, China has been improving its overseas military deployment capabilities (see the earlier discussion). Although China's ability to conduct large military operations in West Africa is unlikely to match the U.S. military's

---

[181] Felix Onuah and Alexis Akwagyiram, "Nigeria Urges U.S. to Move Africa Command Headquarters to Continent," Reuters, April 27, 2021.

[182] Retired U.S. military officer previously stationed in Africa, interview with the authors, July 2021.

[183] Retired U.S. military officer previously stationed in Africa, interview with the authors, July 2021.

[184] 405th Army Field Support Brigade, "405th Army Field Support Brigade LOGCAP Mission on the African Continent Reaches Another Milestone," press release, December 13, 2018.

[185] John Campbell, "Cutting U.S. Military Support for France in West Africa Would Be a Mistake," Council on Foreign Relations, January 28, 2020.

in the next several decades, the PLA might be able to deploy enough troops, ships, and air assets to interfere with U.S. deployments and carry out intentional or unintentional harassment of U.S. forces, and both nations could compete for scant transportation infrastructure, even if nominally being in Nigeria for the same cause of fighting VEOs. Likewise, U.S. forces could find themselves in an operational entanglement with Russian PMSCs that are already present in Nigeria.

CHAPTER FOUR

Conflict Scenarios with Great-Power Involvement: Mozambique

As described in Chapter Two, Mozambique is the second country that we selected for case analysis in Africa, given its overall high ranking for both competition and conflict potential. The country may become an area for great-power competition for several reasons. Because of the rise of VEOs in the country, poor governance, poverty, and the effects of adverse climate changes, the security situation in northern Mozambique has decreased over the past several years. Moreover, the large, untapped potential of minerals and hydrocarbons may attract increasing competition to the country.[1] After the 2010 discovery of substantial natural gas deposits in Mozambique's Rovuma basin, near the northern coast of Cabo Delgado province, international interest increased.[2] Besides that, Mozambique's 2,700-km-long coastline on the Indian Ocean means that it could be a strategically important location for navigation and access to the Indian Ocean, as well as a transit area for access to its neighboring inland countries Malawi and Zimbabwe. Although the role of the Mozambique Channel for commercial shipping declined long ago, its importance has begun to increase again since the discovery of offshore natural gas deposits, and it remains located close to sea transit routes in the southwest part of the Indian Ocean.[3] Despite the large natural gas and estimated untapped coal reserves in Tete province, and the country's comparatively large GDP growth since 2010, Mozambique remains one of the poorest countries in Africa; it had the third-lowest GDP per capita in the world in 2020.[4] The country's growth has stalled because of security issues,

---

[1] Jane Korinek and Isabelle Ramdoo, "Local Content Policies in Mineral-Exporting Countries: The Case of Mozambique," Organisation for Economic Co-operation and Development, Trade Policy Paper No. 209, December 2017.

[2] Mozambique reportedly holds 100 trillion cubic feet of proved natural gas reserves, making it the third-largest owner of natural gas reserves in Africa after Nigeria and Algeria (U.S. Energy Information Administration, "Mozambique," webpage, July 2020).

[3] Additionally, the Mozambique Channel held strategic importance during World War II because of Madagascar's role in Allied shipping routes to India, Australia, and Southeastern Asia. The logjam in the Suez Canal in 2021 served as a reminder of the importance of the shipping route via the Cape of Good Hope (Peter S. Goodman and Stanley Reed, "With Suez Canal Blocked, Shippers Begin End Run Around a Trade Artery," *New York Times*, March 29, 2021).

[4] World Bank, "GDP Per Capita (Current US$)—Mozambique," webpage, undated-b.

severe natural disasters, and macroeconomic factors, as well as persistent governance and corruption issues.[5]

A major security concern is the violent attacks on local inhabitants, foreign workers, and energy-processing installations in Cabo Delgado by the Islamic militia group Ansar al-Sunna Wa Jamma (ASWJ)—also known as Ansar al-Sunna, Mozambican al-Shabaab, and the Islamic State – Mozambique—which began in October 2017 and have killed or displaced thousands of people.[6] Furthermore, there has not been full reconciliation between the Frente de Libertação de Moçambique (FRELIMO, or the Mozambique Liberation Front) and the Resistência Nacional Moçambicana (RENAMO, or the Mozambican National Resistance); the two groups were formerly engaged in the 1976–1992 civil war and are now political parties, and tensions reemerged in 2012.[7] And the consequences of climate change and tropical cyclones on Mozambique's development and security are expected to exacerbate the existing issues.[8]

In this chapter, we provide a concise overview of local political dynamics and actors and then discuss each of the great powers' objectives, posture and access, and capabilities in Mozambique. We then assess the potential avenues for a conflict; whether that conflict might include the United States, China, and Russia; and the factors that might influence the outcome of the conflict—especially the factors that could affect the United States' ability to achieve its aims. As in the previous chapter, our assessments are based on a variety of sources,

---

[5] Javier Eduardo Baez Ramirez, German Daniel Caruso, Chiyu Niu, and Cara Ann Myers, *Mozambique Poverty Assessment: Strong but Not Broadly Shared Growth*, Washington, D.C.: World Bank, October 2018.

[6] ASWJ is a branch of the Islamic State – Central African Province (Tim Lister, "The March 2021 Palma Attack and the Evolving Jihadi Terror Threat to Mozambique," *CTC Sentinel*, Vol. 14, No. 4, April/May 2021; and Nicolas Cook, "Insurgency in Northern Mozambique: Nature and Responses," Congressional Research Service, IF11864, last updated July 5, 2022).

[7] Natália Bueno, "Reconciliation in Mozambique: Was It Ever Achieved?" *Conflict, Security and Development*, Vol. 19, No. 5, 2019.

[8] Mozambique is suffering from the impacts of climate change. Almost every year, because of its long coastline, it is affected by tropical cyclones and storms, and recent years have shown an increased intensity in these weather events. Mozambique was ravaged by Tropical Cyclone Idai and Cyclone Kenneth in 2019, Tropical Storm Chalane in 2020, and Tropical Cyclone Eloise in 2021. Many people have been killed and displaced as a result. For example, with Tropical Cyclone Eloise, 43,327 people were displaced and 34,566 evacuated. Although experts note that this specific part of the world lacks the data needed for researchers to conclude that climate change was responsible for the occurrence of two cyclones in a row, they also note that storm surges and rainfall are more intense because of climate change. In addition, with Mozambique's economy largely depending on agriculture and fishing, climate is having a significant impact on the livelihood and food security of the country's rural population (International Organization for Migration, "Mozambique Tropical Cyclone Eloise Response: Situation Report #1, 25 January–12 February 2021," February 12, 2021; Mat Hope, "Cyclones in Mozambique May Reveal Humanitarian Challenges of Responding to a New Climate Reality," *The Lancet*, Vol. 3, No. 8, August 2019; Food and Agriculture Organization of the United Nations, "Economic and Policy Analysis of Climate Change: Mozambique," webpage, undated; and Lourenço Manuel, Emílio Tostão, Orcidia Vilanculos, Gaby Mandlhate, and Faaiqa Hartley, *Economic Implications of Climate Change in Mozambique*, Southern Africa—Towards Inclusive Economic Development, Working Paper No. 136, September 2020).

including interviews with experts, to better understand how the three great powers are likely to approach involvement in a conflict centered in Mozambique.[9]

We find that the most likely conflict scenario with great-power involvement through military means involves countering ASWJ, although humanitarian assistance to areas affected by cyclones and storms also would attract assistance from all three powers. Countering VEOs and supporting humanitarian operations would be the United States' primary motivations to become involved in Mozambique, but the interests of China and Russia are more diverse. Both have geopolitical and economic interests in the country, and they are interested in maintaining a presence there because of its natural resources and geographical location.

Overview of Local Political Dynamics

Mozambique's political scene is dominated by FRELIMO. The group has been in power since 1975, so Mozambique essentially has become a party state and developed a centralized system that cements the power of the party.[10] Although FRELIMO and President Filipe Nyusi (first elected president in 2015) have been capitalizing on the vast hydrocarbon resources politically and financially, the management of recent massive government debt scandals and the 2019 elections show that the governing party views itself as unrivaled.[11]

The Mozambican government's strategies to prepare for, counter, and mitigate the effects of ASWJ and the aftermath of the 2019 tropical cyclones have been unsuccessful because of the centralized but weak government, entrenched and normalized corruption, winner-takes-all system, and lack of military capabilities and training.[12] Furthermore, the natural gas reserves and the symbolic importance of Cabo Delgado and the Makonde River as the cradle of FRELIMO give the government a free hand to act in the northern region without respecting the rule of law or human rights standards; state actors deploy heavy-handed troops, impose curfews, and allow security personnel to exploit the situation to their advantage while banning reporters and researchers from the area.[13]

---

[9] See also the appendixes to Cohen, Treyger, et al., 2023.

[10] Pezu C. Mukwakwa, *Mozambique Conflict Insight*, Vol. 1, Addis Ababa, Ethiopia: Institute for Peace and Security Studies, April 2020.

[11] For example, in 2013–2016, state companies had taken out loans for public projects of more than $2 billion, and officials siphoned off significant amounts of the money. Upon discovery, the International Monetary Fund, the EU, and other international donors froze their direct contributions to the country's budget, which at the time were one-third of the budget (Benjamin Augé, *Mozambique: Security, Political and Geopolitical Challenges of the Gas Boom*, Paris: French Institute of International Relations, August 2020; and Ionel Zamfir, "Security Situation in Mozambique," European Parliamentary Research Service, July 2021).

[12] David M. Matsinhe and Estacio Valoi, *The Genesis of Insurgency in Northern Mozambique*, Pretoria, South Africa: Institute for Security Studies, Southern Africa Report No. 27, October 2019.

[13] The government of Mozambique reportedly suspended the Constitution of the Republic of Mozambique in Cabo Delgado extrajudicially, thus avoiding the need to declare an official state of emergency, which

Although the Mozambican government historically has been averse to foreign involvement in its internal security, the scale of the terrorism problem in northern Mozambique and the government's (misleading) recharacterization of ASWJ as caused and directed by outsiders have led to at least some recalibration of its approach.[14] In summer 2021, Rwanda, the Southern African Development Community (SADC), and the EU deployed troops to assist Mozambique in its fight against ASWJ in Cabo Delgado.[15] Nyusi has repeatedly set conditions on such support, stating in April 2021, "Those who arrive from abroad will not replace us, they will support us. This is . . . about sovereignty."[16]

The other most influential political actor in the country is RENAMO,[17] formerly FRELIMO's opponent during the civil war. Although RENAMO maintains footholds in some parts of the country, it received only 22 percent of the votes during the 2019 parliamentary elections, compared with FRELIMO's 77 percent.[18] RENAMO's political program is based on a demand for greater decentralization, greater provincial autonomy, and direct elections of governors, and the party continues to position itself as a force that counters the authoritarian FRELIMO.[19] Periodic tensions have reemerged among the two parties, particularly around the time of elections.[20] Large-scale escalations of violence have been avoided, but the tensions show that inter-party issues remain and could turn into violence. Furthermore, a faction known as the RENAMO Military Junta has splintered off RENAMO and claims to have 500 members (although some analysis suggests only 80). The group takes a

---

would imply that the government has lost control over the area and require it to give official information about the situation (Matsinhe and Valoi, 2019).

[14] Analysts and international organizations do not agree on the degree to which ASWJ in Mozambique is directed by or linked with ASWJ in Somalia (International Crisis Group, *Stemming the Insurrection in Mozambique's Cabo Delgado*, Brussels, Africa Report No. 303, June 11, 2021; and Cook, 2022).

[15] Helmoed-Römer Heitman and Jeremy Binnie, "SADC Mission in Mozambique Launched," Janes, August 12, 2021; and "Southern Africa: Mozambique Will Coordinate SADC Standby Force," *All Africa*, July 24, 2021.

[16] "UPDATE 1-Mozambique Seeks Targeted Foreign Support to Help Tackle Insurgency—President," Reuters, April 7, 2021; and Bill Corcoran, "Mozambique's Jihadists Gain Ground as Government Declines Help," *Irish Times*, December 31, 2020.

[17] In dealing with the Islamic insurgency in the northern provinces, RENAMO's leaders have shown interest in working with countries that have previously offered assistance to Mozambique, such as Portugal, the United States, Cuba, and Germany. At the same time, RENAMO deputy António Muchanga seems to be concerned that foreign partners prefer to support Mozambique by training local forces, which is time-consuming and would only prolong the violence in the north (Deutsche Welle, "Will France Station Forces in Cabo Delgado for Total to Return?—DW," Club of Mozambique, May 17, 2021).

[18] RENAMO was founded in 1976 as an anti-communist political group with the support of Rhodesia and South Africa. After the end of the civil war in 1992, it transformed into a political party (Daniel Mumbere, "Mozambique Polls: Key Stats from President Nyusi, Frelimo's Victory," Africanews, October 28, 2019; and Bueno, 2019).

[19] Mukwakwa, 2020.

[20] Bueno, 2019.

less conciliatory approach to its relations with FRELIMO and has called for RENAMO leader Ossufo Momade to step down.[21] It also seeks to nullify the 2019 peace deal to demilitarize, demobilize, and reintegrate RENAMO fighters—a process that has not been completed but that allowed RENAMO to uphold its bases and small weapons as an "insurance policy."[22] RENAMO combatants remain dissatisfied with being excluded from the full reintegration benefits and pensions to former combatants provided by the government, a proposal that has been denied by FRELIMO to show off its political power.[23] However, this movement may not have enough clout to become a powerful local actor, not only because of its reportedly small number of followers but also potentially because of the death of its leader in October 2021.[24]

Islamic militia group ASWJ—whose ideological and political identity remains unclear—has been a major source of violence in northern Mozambique since at least 2017.[25] However, analysis suggests that the first indications of the group's presence were observed by local imams in 2007, while other sources observe fighters from Tanzania, Uganda, Kenya, and the DRC.[26] Some commentators suggest that the causes of, or at least significant contributors to, the conflict in Mozambique are the material deprivation, poverty, and lack of prospects among the very young population of Mozambique's northern region; in addition, they argue that conflict is further fueled by "allegations of deeply entrenched corruption in the ruling party, poor governance, state absence and a general security vacuum," as well as ethnic rivalry.[27] Other observers suggest that preachers from Kenya and Tanzania have caused the radicalization of the local population.[28] Cabo Delgado is a politically and economically

---

[21] Bueno, 2019.

[22] Mukwakwa, 2020.

[23] Mukwakwa, 2020. The Mozambican civil war ended in 1992 with the signing of the Rome General Peace Agreement. Until 2013, Mozambique was regarded to have been carrying out a successful peace process, but incomplete demobilization and reintegration of former fighters, FRELIMO's unwillingness to share power and influence, and other issues may have motivated RENAMO to seek a better power position (Alex Vines, "Violence, Peacebuilding, and Elite Bargains in Mozambique Since Independence," in Terence McNamee and Monde Muyangwa, eds., *The State of Peacebuilding in Africa: Lessons Learned for Policymakers and Practitioners*, Cham, Switzerland: Palgrave Macmillan, 2021).

[24] Manuel Mucari, "Mozambique's Police Kill Leader of Armed Splinter Group of Main Opposition Party," Reuters, October 11, 2021. Since the completion of this research, Director of Operations of the Mozambican Armed Forces Chongo Vidigal claimed in February 2022 that the RENAMO Military Junta has selected a new leader but did not disclose the name of the person (AIM, "Mozambique: 'Renamo Military Junta' Has New Leader—AIM," Club of Mozambique, February 28, 2022).

[25] Dorina A. Bekoe, Stephanie M. Burchard, and Sarah A. Daly, *Extremism in Mozambique: Interpreting Group Tactics and the Role of the Government's Response in the Crisis in Cabo Delgado*, Alexandria, Va.: Institute for Defense Analyses, March 2020.

[26] Matsinhe and Valoi, 2019.

[27] Jakkie Cilliers, Liesl Louw-Vaudran, Timothy Walker, Willem Els, and Martin Ewi, "What Would It Take to Stabilise Cabo Delgado?" ReliefWeb, May 17, 2021.

[28] Eric Morier-Genoud, "The Jihadi Insurgency in Mozambique: Origins, Nature and Beginning," *Journal of Eastern African Studies*, Vol. 14, No. 3, 2020.

important region for FRELIMO: President Nyusi and the party itself can track their roots to Cabo Delgado province, while the party's popularity during the past two elections has hinged on the promise of using gas profits for economic development (and the province is rich in natural gas deposits). Despite that area's importance to the leading party, the Mozambican government has struggled to curb ASWJ's violent attacks in northern Mozambique, mostly because the Mozambican Army lacks the necessary capabilities and training. In 2020, Mozambique spent only an estimated 1.1 percent of its GDP on military expenditures.[29]

Other foreign international and state actors, as well as large energy companies, also have interests in Mozambique. Mozambique was considered a post–civil war success story, so international aid and financial organizations and foreign governments made significant investments to support its economy and political performance, which made its budget highly dependent on foreign contributions (up to 40 percent of the budget).[30] Yet, following the corruption scandal of 2016—when a secret debt scheme was discovered in which 12 percent of the country's GDP, guaranteed by the government, had been used for bribes—the International Monetary Fund and other foreign donors withdrew their budget support and other foreign investments were reduced, which led to increased inflation rates and currency depreciation.[31] Russia and China are historical partners of FRELIMO, and we discuss their objectives and presence in the country in the next section.

Notable other external actors in Mozambique include India, South Africa, Portugal, Italy, and France (mostly through the presence of the French energy company Total). Being an Indian Ocean Region power, India has strategic geopolitical interests in East Africa. For India, the Mozambique Channel holds strategic importance because of the natural gas and coal reserves and the offshore oil investments there; in addition, the channel is a potential maritime choke point in the Indian Ocean Region, which is India's primary area of interest as it looks to develop relations with key littoral nations of the ocean.[32] Although India's trade with Mozambique has been limited, New Delhi has sought to resurrect security relations. During the past decade or so, India has engaged in military and security presence in the region—for example, by reportedly providing training and equipment to Mozambique's intelligence service and reactivating an inactive joint defense working group.[33] The Indian

---

[29] Central Intelligence Agency, "Mozambique: Military and Security," *The World Factbook*, last updated June 29, 2021.

[30] Mukwakwa, 2020.

[31] See Edson Cortez, Aslak Orre, Baltazar Fael, Borges Nhamirre, Celeste Banze, Inocência Mapisse, Kim Harnack, and Torun Reite, *Costs and Consequences of the Hidden Debt Scandal of Mozambique*, Maputo, Mozambique: Centro de Integridade Pública, August 23, 2019; and Mukwakwa, 2020.

[32] Ministry of Defence (Navy) of India, *Ensuring Secure Seas: Indian Maritime Security Strategy*, New Delhi, Naval Strategic Publication 1.2, October 2015; Pramit Pal Chaudhuri, "India's 21st Century African Partner: Why Mozambique Was Modi's First Stop," *Hindustan Times*, July 7, 2016; and Abhishek Mishra, "Mozambique's Insurgency and India's Interest," Observer Research Foundation, April 6, 2021.

[33] Chaudhuri, 2016.

Navy also provided security for the African Union and World Economic Forum summits in Mozambique in 2003 and 2004, respectively.[34] Furthermore, India has security interests in the nearby Indian Ocean islands to support its maritime domain awareness. Moreover, India's relations with Mozambique improved under the leadership of Nyusi, who was a former pupil of a business school in India, and Prime Minister Agostinho do Rosário, who was ambassador to India.[35]

South Africa, the leading economic power in Southern Africa, has had long-standing economic and security interests in neighboring Mozambique. South Africa is Mozambique's main trading partner, but South Africa's role in the country may be declining as interest from the West and Asia rises, and South Africa's extractive industrial interests seem to be concentrated in the southern part of Mozambique.[36] Although South Africa has provided humanitarian assistance to the country following tropical cyclones, analysts note that it is not prepared or willing to directly and bilaterally engage in the security situation in Mozambique, at least partly because of financial constraints and the risk that the Islamic State or its supporters could seek retaliation by opening a fight inside South Africa's borders.[37] In fact, it had declined Maputo's request for bilateral military assistance on the basis that dealing with insurgency would be too big a mission for bilateral activity, but South Africa eventually did agree to send almost 1,500 military personnel to help Mozambique fight ASWJ for three months in 2021 as part of the SADC response.[38]

Portugal, a former colonial power, maintains close relations with Mozambique across many areas (including energy, tourism, medicine, public administration, infrastructure, and the preservation of Portuguese historical heritage) and upholds political dialogue through regular bilateral summits.[39] It has contributed to assistance and reconstruction funds and programs; has been an advocate for military assistance to Mozambique within the EU; and has sent troops to train Mozambican solders to increase their ability to fight the insurgency,

---

[34] Chaudhuri, 2016.

[35] Augé, 2020; and Permanent Mission of the Republic of Mozambique to the United Nations, "Filipe Jacinto Nyusi," webpage, Columbia University World Leaders Forum, September 2015.

[36] Bertelsmann Stiftung, *BTI 2020 Country Report Mozambique*, Gütersloh, 2020; and African Development Bank and African Development Fund, *Mozambique Country Strategy Paper 2018–2022: Supporting Mozambique Towards the High5S*, Abidjan, Côte d'Ivoire, June 2018.

[37] South Africa has extended Operation Cooper, which aims to combat maritime piracy. However, it is unlikely that South Africa will increase its naval or air operations, at least partly because of financial constraints and the risk of poor public support (Brenda Githing'u, "Will the South African Military Intervene in Mozambique?" *Terrorism Monitor*, Vol. 19, No. 8, April 23, 2021; and "South Africa Sends 1,500 Troops to Mozambique to Fight Jihadists," Africanews, July 29, 2021).

[38] "South African Military Deploys Troops to Pemba, Northern Mozambique," Africanews, August 5, 2021.

[39] Leighton G. Luke, "Mozambique Seeks Benefits from Links with Portugal," Future Directions International, July 10, 2019; and Government of the Portuguese Republic, "'Há uma nova dinâmica nas relações' entre Portugal e Moçambique" ["'There Is a New Dynamic in Relations' Between Portugal and Mozambique"], July 3, 2019.

share intelligence, and use drones for reconnaissance purposes.[40] Italy has been politically present in the country for nearly 30 years and had an important historic role in achieving peace: It sponsored the 1992 General Peace Agreement, signed in Rome, to end the civil war between FRELIMO and RENAMO.[41] Italy's Eni gas company has been gradually reducing its presence in the country, giving way to U.S.-based Exxon Mobil.[42]

France's interest in Mozambique stems partly from the proximity to France's territories in the southwest Indian Ocean (Réunion Island and Mayotte) and exclusive economic zone in the Mozambique Channel around the Scattered Islands.[43] Although France's economic relations with Mozambique are modest, the French oil company Total is a leading player in Mozambique's budding energy sector.[44] These strong energy interests have fueled speculations that Rwanda, one of the countries participating in the SADC anti-terrorism operation, may be operating on behalf of France; in particular, Rwanda's activities are concentrated near liquefied natural gas facilities on the Afungi Peninsula, the location of the Rovuma LNG project (a gas extraction and processing facility).[45]

Lastly, and particularly relevant for current and future U.S. military engagement, the military presence of SADC and EU military forces via the EU Training Mission Mozambique should also be mentioned. With coordination and command arrangements made to navigate Mozambique's requirement to be in charge of the coordination, SADC troops that were deployed to Mozambique in summer 2021 included troops from several African countries and were engaged in anti-terrorism operations in Cabo Delgado.[46] In summer 2021, the EU reportedly trained Mozambican marines and special operations forces.[47]

---

[40] Benjamin Fox, "EU Must Step Up Military Assistance to Mozambique, Says Portuguese Presidency," *EURACTIV*, February 1, 2021; and Catarina Demony and Emma Rumney, "Portugal to Send Another 60 Troops to Mozambique on Training Mission," Reuters, May 10, 2021.

[41] Daniela Sicurelli, "Italian Cooperation with Mozambique: Explaining the Emergence and Consolidation of a Normative Power," *Italian Political Science Review*, Vol. 50, No. 2, 2020.

[42] Augé, 2020.

[43] The Scattered Islands are part of the French Southern and Antarctic Lands. The French Armed Forces in the Southern Indian Ocean Zone, which operate in the nearby islands of Réunion and Mayotte, are mostly engaged in maritime safety and security, disaster risk management, and marine environment activities in the wider region. For example, France provided humanitarian support to Mozambique following Cyclone Idai in 2019 (Ministry of European and Foreign Affairs of France, "France in the South-West Indian Ocean," November 26, 2021).

[44] French Embassy in Maputo, "La France et le Mozambique—relations politiques et coopération militaire" ["France and Mozambique—Political Relations and Military Cooperation"], July 23, 2015.

[45] "Mocímboa da Praia: Turning Point or Stepping Stone to an Endless War?" 14 North, August 11, 2021.

[46] "Southern Africa: Mozambique Will Coordinate SADC Standby Force," 2021; Heitman and Binnie, 2021.

[47] "Southern Africa: Mozambique Will Coordinate SADC Standby Force," 2021.

Comparative Analysis of Great-Power Interests and Objectives, Posture and Access, and Capabilities

In this section, we provide an overview of the objectives, posture and access, and capabilities of the United States, China, and Russia in Mozambique.

Interests and Objectives

Like their interests in Nigeria, the United States', China's, and Russia's interests in Mozambique may be viewed through three common categories: strategic and geopolitical, security, and economic interests; however, the intensity and priority of these categories can vary across the three countries. The objectives of the three powers reflect their policies elsewhere in Africa. At the same time, Mozambique's energy discoveries, the emergence of a violent extremist group, and increased stability have amplified the three powers' interest in Mozambique. We observe that, while the United States' key motivation for potential future military engagement in Mozambique may be to help Mozambique counter VEOs, China's main interests are economic while Russia's are strategic.

United States' Interests and Objectives

The United States' objectives in Mozambique center on countering VEOs, assisting with development and humanitarian efforts, and pursuing economic interests (particularly in the energy sector).

From the security perspective, the United States highlights the need to counter violent extremist networks in Mozambique and the role of Mozambique and the broader East African coastline in illicit heroin-smuggling from Afghanistan, as well as in wildlife-trafficking. In addition, the United States recognizes the importance of the Mozambique Channel as a potential strategic choke point and sea line of communication for both commerce and military operations.[48] The channel offers a direct line between the Arabian Sea and the Gulf of Oman to the Cape of Good Hope, and the development of the large offshore gas reserve likely will increase maritime activity.[49] For the purposes of this report, we highlight that the U.S. government has declared its intent to support the Mozambican government in its counterterrorism and counterinsurgency efforts. Specifically, the United States seeks to be Mozambique's "security partner of choice" in the burgeoning counterterrorism campaign and the

---

[48] The U.S. Drug Enforcement Agency opened an office in Maputo in 2017. The office has working relationships with Mozambique's attorney general and National Criminal Investigations Service, which is the lead anti-drug law enforcement agency there (Bureau of International Narcotics and Law Enforcement Affairs, "Mozambique Summary," webpage, U.S. Department of State, undated; and Stephen J. Townsend, general, U.S. Army, "Africa: Securing U.S. Interests, Preserving Strategic Options," statement before the U.S. Senate Armed Services Committee, Washington, D.C., April 20, 2021).

[49] David Brewster, "The Mozambique Channel Is the Next Security Hotspot," *The Interpreter*, March 19, 2021; see also Ship Traffic, "Mozambique Channel Ships Marine Traffic Live Map," webpage, undated.

related socioeconomic development issues.[50] In particular, the United States has expressed concern over ASWJ's violence in Cabo Delgado province, noting that the violence could become a wider conflict that destabilizes Southern Africa and jeopardizes U.S. interests across the continent.[51] As the conflict has intensified, the U.S. government has devoted more attention and resources to Mozambique, even if the amount of these resources is small compared with other U.S. counter-VEO engagements in Africa. For instance, Nathan Sales, U.S. coordinator for counterterrorism, visited Mozambique in late 2020 to discuss ways that the United States could help Mozambique "contain, degrade, and defeat" ASWJ, and in March 2021, the U.S. Department of State designated ASWJ as a foreign terrorist organization.[52] Following ASWJ's declaration of allegiance to the Islamic State in 2019, the State Department also designated Abu Yasir Hassan, the leader of ASWJ, as a specially designated global terrorist.[53]

A second area of interest for the United States, and an area in which it has been more active, is development and humanitarian assistance.[54] In this capacity, the United States has sought to support implementing the 1992 peace agreement and its related objectives of fostering economic development, improving quality of life for the Mozambican people, and promoting good governance.[55] Since the decades of civil conflict that followed Mozambique's independence from Portugal drew to a close in 1992, the United States has provided support to the Mozambican peace process as a member of an international contact group, which monitors the peace process between FRELIMO and RENAMO and the implementation of the 2019 peace agreement, and advises on sustainable peace.[56]

The United States is Mozambique's largest single supplier of foreign aid—and the largest donor of humanitarian assistance—providing an average of $452 million in aid per year

---

[50] The U.S. embassy in Mozambique declared, "The United States is committed to supporting Mozambique with a multifaceted and holistic approach to counter and prevent the spread of terrorism and violent extremism. This approach addresses socioeconomic development issues as well as the security situation" (David Lewis, "U.S. Counterterrorism Chief Says Mozambique Militants Are Islamic State Affiliate," Reuters, December 9, 2020; and John Vandiver, "U.S. Special Operations Forces Train Mozambique Troops to Counter ISIS Threat," *Stars and Stripes*, March 16, 2021).

[51] Anita Powell, "US Offers Resources to Help 'Contain, Degrade, and Defeat' Mozambique Insurgency," Voice of America, December 8, 2020.

[52] U.S. Department of State, "State Department Terrorist Designations of ISIS Affiliates and Leaders in the Democratic Republic of the Congo and Mozambique," Office of the Spokesperson, March 10, 2021; and Powell, 2020.

[53] U.S. Department of State, 2021; Lewis, 2020.

[54] Nicolas Cook, *Mozambique: Politics, Economy, and U.S. Relations*, Washington, D.C.: Congressional Research Service, R45817, September 12, 2019.

[55] Bureau of African Affairs, "U.S. Relations with Mozambique: Bilateral Relations Fact Sheet," U.S. Department of State, last updated July 6, 2021b; and Cook, 2019.

[56] Other participants of the group are Botswana, China, the EU, Switzerland, and the United Kingdom (Ministry of Foreign Affairs of Norway, "The Peace Process in Mozambique," webpage, December 2, 2019; and AIM, "Nyusi Appoints 'Contact Group' for Peace Talks," Club of Mozambique, March 2, 2017).

between fiscal years 2016 and 2018.[57] Much of this aid has focused on bolstering democracy and strengthening governance in other ways. Another major focus of U.S. aid is the health sector, especially programs to combat AIDS, malaria, and other prolific diseases.[58] Additional priorities include education, food security, poverty alleviation, and job creation efforts, including the Basic Education Program.[59] The United States also has provided a great deal of humanitarian assistance, especially in the wake of two cyclones in March and April 2019 (Cyclones Idai and Kenneth) that had a sizable negative impact on Mozambique's infrastructure and economy.[60]

Third, the United States generates high levels of foreign direct investment in Mozambique, primarily stemming from U.S. energy companies. The three U.S. companies that invest the most in Mozambique are Anadarko Petroleum, Mozambique Leaf Tobacco Limitada, and Exxon Mobil.[61] Anadarko and Exxon Mobil's investments and activities are particularly significant, and their natural gas and liquefied natural gas efforts could raise Mozambique's GDP, but instability in the country has caused delays to several projects.[62]

In sum, the United States' objectives in Mozambique are to counter VEOs (specifically ASWJ); support the creation of sustainable peace and stability through improving governance, living, and economic conditions; provide humanitarian assistance; and pursue economic interests, especially in the natural gas and oil sector.

China's Interests and Objectives

Like its objectives elsewhere in Africa, China's main objectives in Mozambique are economic.[63] At the same time, Mozambique has geostrategic importance for China in its competition with India over influence in the southern Indian Ocean. As Chinese analysts point out, Africa's and China's economies are potentially quite complementary, given Africa's abundance of natural resources and need for financing and China's demand for natural resources and abundant foreign exchange reserves.[64] China's economic relations with Mozambique

---

[57] Cook, 2019, pp. 2, 13; and USAID, "U.S. Delivers Humanitarian Relief Supplies in Response to Insecurity in Mozambique," press release, May 6, 2021b.

[58] Two such assistance programs are the President's Malaria Initiative and the President's Emergency Plan for AIDS Relief (Bureau of African Affairs, 2021b).

[59] Bureau of African Affairs, 2021b.

[60] Cook, 2019.

[61] Bureau of African Affairs, 2021b.

[62] Bureau of African Affairs, 2021b. U.S. economic efforts in Mozambique are regulated by a U.S.-Mozambican Bilateral Investment Treaty and a Trade and Investment Framework Agreement, both of which have been in effect since 2005.

[63] Francisco Proença Garcia, "China's Economic Presence in Mozambique," *Estudos Internacionais Revista de Relações Internacionais da PUC Minas*, Vol. 8, No. 3, December 2020.

[64] Chinese sources also note Mozambique's large population and low labor costs as a possible competitive advantage. The two countries have signed a framework agreement to construct joint manufacturing facilities. They also have worked to establish industrial parks where Chinese companies can set up factories and

emerged in 2001 with the establishment of an Economic and Trade Joint Committee, which was followed in 2003 by the foundation of a Forum for Economic and Trade Cooperation between China and Portuguese-speaking countries.[65] In this sense, China's trade relationship with Mozambique is typical. Beijing is an important source of finance for the country (though by no means its only source), and Maputo provides Beijing with a market for manufactured goods and a variety of natural resources.[66] These include forestry products,[67] a large share of China's titanium ore, and graphite imports.[68] Recent, massive natural gas discoveries in northern Mozambique have also elicited great Chinese interest, both for imports and for investment, and China National Petroleum Corporation has a stake in the Rovuma LNG project, where it partners with U.S.-based ExxonMobil and Italy-based Eni.[69] China's interest in Mozambique's extractive industries suggests that it will continue to support the country via economic means at least.[70]

Following Mozambique's debt scandal and the consequent withdrawal of international funding, and because China's requirements likely are not always as demanding as those used by multinational creditors, China has emerged as Mozambique's largest bilateral creditor. In 2019, it was funding 37 percent of the bilateral foreign debt, and in 2020, Mozambique's debt to China was 20 percent of the country's total external debt.[71] Although China's rhetoric emphasizes its good will in providing these loans and construction projects, they are not charity. Beijing hopes to make money from its investments and has reason to fear that it

---

enjoy preferential trade policies (Stephen Ndegwa, "FOCAC at 20 Is Great, and Will Be Greater in the Next 20 Years," China Global Television Network, October 11, 2020; and Wang Hongyi [王洪一], "Sino African Industrial Parks: Progress, Problems, and Solutions" ["中非共建产业园: 历程、问题与解决思路"], Chinese Institute of International Studies [中国国际问题研究院], March 5, 2019).

[65] Garcia, 2020.

[66] Observatory of Economic Complexity, undated-a; and Observatory of Economic Complexity, "Mozambique," webpage, undated-b.

[67] Chinese loggers reportedly have been involved in timber-smuggling (Will Ross, "Mozambique's Debt Problem," BBC News, November 10, 2018).

[68] The 20 percent of China's titanium ore that Mozambique provided in 2019 was a drop from 41.4 percent in 2018 (Observatory of Economic Complexity, undated-a; Observatory of Economic Complexity, undated-b).

[69] "Debt Woe Continues for Mozambique," Macauhub, May 24, 2019; "Petro China and Mozambique Sign Cooperation Framework Agreement" ["中国石油与莫桑比克签署合作框架协议"], China Petroleum Enterprise [中国石油企业], May 2016; Africa Oil Week, "Understanding Chinese Investment in African Oil and Gas," October 7, 2019; and "China's CNPC Natural Gas Project in Mozambique Delayed," China-Lusophone Brief, April 8, 2020.

[70] For example, in 2021, China agreed to forgive debt of $375 million to help Mozambique fight the pandemic (Economist Intelligence Unit, "China Agrees to Write Off Some of Mozambique's Debts," March 24, 2021).

[71] Kim Harnack and Celeste Banze e Leila Constantino, "Dividas Contraidas Com A China Afectam Disponibilidade De Recursos No Orcamento Para Enfrentar a COVID-19" ["Debts Contracted with China Affect Availability of Resources in the Budget to Face COVID-19"], CIP Eleições, October 2020.

may fail to do so in Mozambique.[72] Maputo is among the most debt-distressed governments in Africa and has been forced to default on some of its loans; in addition, at least one high-profile infrastructure project—the Maputo-Katembe toll bridge—reportedly failed to meet revenue projections.[73] This has led some to question whether China could try to turn debt concessions into the long-term lease of Mozambique's national infrastructure as collateral or whether Chinese firms are being offered any concessionary access to natural resources in exchange for debt relief, as well as indignant assertions by the Mozambican authorities that such seizures are impossible.[74]

China's penchant for opacity in its debt relief deals may fuel worries despite assurances, but in Mozambique's case, Beijing may face resistance to attempts to seize either infrastructure or resource concessions as the result of secret or corrupt deals. In 2020, the Mozambican Constitutional Court invalidated $2 billion in secret Russian and Swiss loans made to build a fishery project that never materialized and became mired in corruption scandals.[75] Given Maputo's public assertion that there are no arrangements in its financing agreements that would allow Beijing to take control over its infrastructure, any such agreement likely would need to be secret and may be at risk of invalidation if China tried to collect. That being said, the high level of Mozambique's debt balance with China may render Mozambique vulnerable to becoming financially dependent on China and, as a result, increase China's political influence or give China more leverage to negotiate access to Mozambican ports or natural resources.[76] Furthermore, Chinese financing in Mozambique may have an outsized influence because it is concentrated in large, high-impact, and high-visibility infrastructure projects, many of which are located near the capital.[77]

It is important, however, to put the financial relationship into perspective. Beijing's investment in Pakistan, Angola, and other countries associated with its Belt and Road Initiative dwarfs its investment in Mozambique, and Beijing is hardly Maputo's only creditor.[78]

---

[72] Dong Feng, "China-Mozambique Financing Cooperation Is About Development," *Global Times*, November 9, 2020; and Alex Vines, "China's Southern Africa Debt Deals Reveal a Wider Plan," Chatham House, December 10, 2020b.

[73] "Debt Woe Continues for Mozambique," 2019.

[74] For an account of China's use of so-called debt-trap diplomacy, see Lee Jones and Shahar Hameiri, *Debunking the Myth of "Debt-Trap Diplomacy,"* London: Chatham House, August 19, 2020; Lusa, "Mozambique: No 'Indications' That China May Seize Assets Due to Debt—Government," Club of Mozambique, November 19, 2020; and Baker, 2019.

[75] Manuel Mucari, Emma Rumney, and Alexander Winning, "Mozambique Court Declares Void Two Loans in 'Hidden Debt' Scandal," Reuters, May 12, 2020.

[76] Similar concerns exist over the Port of Mombasa, Kenya (Harnack and Constantino, 2020).

[77] Examples include the new suspension bridge in Maputo, Mozambique's parliament building and several government ministries, and the national sports stadium, as well as some roads (Vines, 2020b; Lusa, 2020; Ross, 2018).

[78] Vines, 2020b; Lusa, 2020.

In addition to its economic interests, China hopes that Mozambique and other African states, a sizable voting bloc in the UN, will provide it with political support on the international stage; furthermore, China uses economic means to develop good elite-to-elite relations and disseminate its preferred narrative of win-win cooperation.[79] Thus, China seeks both to solicit support for its positions in international forums (such as the UN) and to help counteract narratives of debt-trap diplomacy and the threat posed by Beijing.[80] African states tend to support many Chinese priorities in international governance, including UN reform and efforts to make international financial and governance institutions more amenable to the interests of developing states.[81]

Mozambique was among the 53 countries that supported China's new national security law for Hong Kong at the UN Human Rights Council in 2020 and has supported China's Xinjiang policies.[82] The reportedly good government elite-to-elite relations between China and Mozambique may also serve as a means for China to disseminate rhetoric that portrays China's presence, business models, and models of governance as positive not only regionally but also across Africa and internationally.[83]

In terms of strategic and security interests, China's primary objective is protecting its citizens and their "legitimate interests" in Mozambique.[84] These can be threatened by natural disasters, public health crises, organized crime, and piracy.[85] Chinese analysts have expressed particular alarm at the spread of terrorism throughout Africa and have noted that the problem has become much more severe in northern Mozambique in recent years.[86] Beijing's preferred responses to this problem are greater trade and investment to spur economic development and thereby remove the root causes of terrorism, as well as greater regional cooperation

---

[79] Zhang, 2018.

[80] Feng, 2020; Zhang, 2018.

[81] Zhang, 2018.

[82] Dave Lawler, "The 53 Countries Supporting China's Crackdown on Hong Kong," Axios, July 2, 2020; and Catherine Putz, "2020 Edition: Which Countries Are for or Against China's Xinjiang Policies?" The Diplomat, October 9, 2020.

[83] Zeng, 2016; He Yin [和音], "Propelling and Improving Sino-African Cooperation" ["推动中非合作提质升级"], Qiushi [求是], January 11, 2021; Sun Yi [孙奕], "Xi Jinping Meets Mozambican President Nyusi" ["习近平会见莫桑比克总统纽西"], China Military Net [中国军网], September 1, 2018; and Baker, 2019.

[84] He Dan, 2021.

[85] He Dan, 2021; and Wei Hong [韦红] and Li Ciyuan [李次园], "The Development of the Indian Ocean Rim Alliance and China's Strategies for Engagement" ["环印度洋联盟的发展及中国的合作策略"], China Institute of International Studies [中国国际问题研究院], March 16, 2018.

[86] Ma Hanzhi [马汉智], "Africa's Serious Regional Security Problems Are Worthy of Note" ["非洲局部地区严峻安全形势值得关注"], China Institute of International Studies [中国国际问题研究院], August 27, 2020a.

among states in the region.[87] That being said, direct military action cannot be ruled out, especially if rapid evacuation is needed or if the UN sanctions a peacekeeping mission.[88]

China's government maintains strong relations with the FRELIMO-dominated government, so China likely would support that party in any future conflict in Mozambique. In the event of a major internal conflict, Beijing may prefer stability and a quick resolution to a protracted war and support FRELIMO as a proxy. Any successor government may not be as valuable a booster of China's preferred image of itself on the world stage, but it also would not be likely to stop trading with Beijing. A more hostile government might endanger Chinese investments or joint manufacturing facilities, but a protracted civil conflict is almost sure to negatively affect Chinese investments.

China's main strategic competitor in Mozambique is India. China may be interested in countering India's attempts to strengthen ties with Mozambique and use those ties to regularize its military presence in the southern Indian Ocean and its control of the Indian Ocean more broadly. Chinese scholars view such Indian policies as Project Mausam (a cultural and economic project aimed at connecting the countries of the Indian Ocean) and the Asia-Africa Growth Corridor as attempts by New Delhi to increase its capabilities in the region, possibly at China's expense.[89] Mozambique is a supporter and important target of these policies.[90] India has secured port use agreements in Maputo and a defense agreement with Mozambique, has built a coastal radar system in Madagascar, and has increased the frequency of its air and naval patrols near the Mozambique Channel.[91] India is known to be wary of China's Maritime Silk Road initiative in the Indian Ocean basin, and Beijing fears that New Delhi may seek to interfere with Chinese projects or relations in the region.[92] Nevertheless, some Chinese government–affiliated analysts have called for greater China-India cooperation to spur economic development in states across the Indian Ocean basin.[93]

---

[87] Ma, 2020a.

[88] In the past, the PLA has participated in civilian evacuations from Libya and Yemen following unrest there. The PLA is also a frequent contributor to UN peacekeeping missions across Africa (see Shannon Tiezzi, "Chinese Nationals Evacuate Yemen on PLA Navy Frigate," *The Diplomat*, March 30, 2015; and International Peace Institute, undated).

[89] Shi Hongyuan [时宏远], "The Modi Government's Indian Ocean Policy" ["莫迪政府的印度洋政策"], China Institute of International Relations [中国国际问题研究院], January 22, 2018; Lan Jianxue [蓝建学], "India's 'Link West' Policy: Origins, Progress, and Prospects" ["印度'西联'战略: 缘起、进展与前景"], China Institute of International Studies [中国国际问题研究院], May 31, 2019; and Sui Xinmin [随新民], "India's Strategic Culture and Patterns of Foreign Policy" ["印度的战略文化与国际行为模式"], China Institute of Strategic Studies [中国国际问题研究员], January 20, 2014.

[90] Lou Chunhao [楼春豪], "'The Asia-Africa Growth Corridor': Content, Motivations, and Prospects" ["'亚非增长走廊'倡议: 内涵、动因与前景"], China Institute of International Relations [中国国际问题研究院], January 22, 2018.

[91] Sui, 2014; Lan, 2019.

[92] Shi, 2018; Lan, 2019.

[93] Wei and Li, 2018; Lan, 2019.

Finally, it is important to put all of China's interests and objectives in Mozambique in perspective. Africa is very important to China's long-term economic and strategic plans, and Mozambique is important—but probably not nearly as important as other states on the continent. It is not one of China's three African "comprehensive strategic partners" (Egypt, Algeria, and South Africa).[94] On his first trip abroad, Xi Jinping visited Mozambique's northern and southern neighbors (Tanzania and South Africa) but not Mozambique.[95] And although Chinese trade with Mozambique includes some strategically important commodities (e.g., titanium), trade volumes (and strategic raw material import volumes) from other African nations are far greater, and Chinese companies have invested much more in such states as Angola and South Africa.[96] Furthermore, although Mozambique has many excellent natural harbors, other countries seem to be much more likely candidates for future PLA bases.[97]

Russia's Interests and Objectives

Russia's interests in Mozambique are both geopolitical and economic. Russia enjoys significant access to Mozambique's infrastructure and ports that may serve as potential rest stops or safe havens for Russian naval forces in West Africa, thus providing Russia with strategic-infrastructure access in Southeast Africa and the Indian Ocean.[98] Strong military relations also may facilitate future export of Russian weapons and military equipment, as well as repair and modernization services, to Mozambique. Russia has further sought to strengthen its military presence in the country by establishing a military defense attaché office at its embassy in Maputo in 2021.[99]

Moreover, Russia seeks to diversify its imports and exports to mitigate the impact of economic sanctions from Western countries, and it seeks to gain presence in Mozambique's energy sector to compensate for the increasing costs of Russian natural resources by accessing cheaper African alternatives. The intensification of Russia's relations with Mozambique can be traced back to 2013 (three years after the discovery of Mozambique's gas reserves), when

---

[94] Shannon Tiezzi, "FOCAC Turns 20: Deborah Brautigam on China-Africa Relations," *The Diplomat*, December 2, 2020.

[95] Ministry of Foreign Affairs of the People's Republic of China, "Xi Jinping Arrives in Dar es Salaam, Kicking Off His State Visit to Tanzania," March 25, 2013.

[96] Observatory of Economic Complexity, undated-a.

[97] Neither DoD's 2020 report on China's military developments (Office of the Secretary of Defense, 2020) nor the Janes report on possible PLA basing locations (Peltier, Nurkin, and O'Connor, 2020) mentions Mozambique as a likely basing site. It is impossible to say for certain whether the PLA has any intentions of building a future base in Mozambique, but the lack of any major intimation that this could be the case (as opposed to the frequent rumors about possible bases in many other countries in the Indian Ocean basin) suggests that, if the PLA has any such intentions, it is somehow hiding its interest there far better than elsewhere.

[98] See the later subsection on Russia's posture and access for a more detailed discussion of Russia's access to Mozambique's infrastructure.

[99] "Pri Posolstve Rosi V Mozambike Sozdali Apparat Voyennovo Attashe" ["Military Attaché Office Created at the Russian Embassy in Mozambique"], Interfax, March 18, 2021.

Russia's Minister of Foreign Affairs Sergey Lavrov visited the country to improve economic cooperation.[100] Some analysts also view Russia's strategy in Mozambique as an extension of its presence in natural resource–rich CAR or as a version of a concessions-for-protection policy.[101] (Russia is heavily present in CAR through its political and military support to President Faustin-Archange Touadéra and its efforts to reduce the long-standing French influence in the country.[102]) Moreover, Russia's image in Mozambique is enhanced by its historic support for Mozambique's revolution in 1975 and support to FRELIMO, its political patronage at the UN, and its willingness to build relations with the country's elites while disregarding accountability and transparency.[103]

Under the leadership of Vladimir Putin, Russia is interested in boosting its relations with Africa in general, and that includes Mozambique. Moscow is motivated by its own struggles with declining oil prices and sanctions and is particularly interested in Mozambique's hydrocarbon resources, chemical fertilizer production, and electricity.[104] Russia has showed an interest in improving its economic relations with Mozambique and backed its interest by writing off Mozambique's debt.[105] Mozambique used to be a close partner to the Soviet Union, yet the historical links have not translated into close economic cooperation today; according to Mozambique's Deputy Minister of Energy Augusto Fernando, cooperation between Mozambique and Russia is in an "embryonic" stage.[106] In fact, in terms of Russia's global trade volume, its trade with Mozambique ranked 116th in 2019.[107]

---

[100] During the visit, Lavrov discussed the possibility of increasing trade turnover and investments in geological survey, ferrous industry, petro-chemistry, agriculture, energy, and infrastructure projects, and he suggested cooperation in fishery, education, and personnel training (Ministry of Foreign Affairs of the Russian Federation, "Speech of and Answers to Questions of Mass Media by Russian Foreign Minister Sergey Lavrov During Joint Press Conference Summarizing the Results of Negotiations with Mozambique Foreign Minister Oldemiro Balói," February 12, 2013).

[101] Sergey Sukhankin, "The 'Hybrid' Role of Russian Mercenaries, PMCs and Irregulars in Moscow's Scramble for Africa," Jamestown Foundation, January 10, 2020a; and Cohen, Treyger, et al., 2023.

[102] Samuel Ramani, "Russia's Strategy in the Central African Republic," Royal United Services Institute, February 12, 2021.

[103] Dzvinka Kachur, "Russia's Resurgence in Africa: Zimbabwe and Mozambique," South African Institute of International Affairs, November 27, 2020.

[104] According to the Twitter account of Russia's embassy in Mozambique, Putin said, "Mozambique is our traditional partner on the African continent. There is a common interest in external intensification of political contacts, strengthening cooperation in such spheres as electricity, hydrocarbon extraction and chemical fertilizer production" (Rússia em Moçambique [@EmbRusMov], "#Putin: #Moçambique é o nosso parceiro tradicional no Continente Africano. Há interesse comum na ulterior intensificação . . . ," Twitter post, May 18, 2021.

[105] "Prezident Mozambika Zayavil O Novom Etape V Otnisheniyah S Rossiiyei" ["The President of Mozambique Announced a New Stage in Relations with Russia"], RBK, August 21, 2019.

[106] Agence Africaine de Presse, "Mozambique Eyeing Russian Investment in Hydrocarbons, Mining," Club of Mozambique, October 23, 2019.

[107] World Integrated Trade Solution, undated-b.

Russia is also trying to gain and maintain access to political decisionmakers. Although its ability to nurture close bilateral relations with Mozambique is limited by the availability of its own resources, Russia has conducted annual high-level meetings with Mozambique, maintains an embassy in the country, and has used its experience with elections to ensure support for President Nyusi.[108] Like it does elsewhere in Africa, Russia seeks to be viewed as Mozambique's friend; as a Russian ambassador said, Russia "provide[s] assistance to them [Mozambicans] without threatening their neighbors and rattling the saber, we only do what our partners in Mozambique ask for."[109] One of the means of maintaining access to Mozambique's political leadership through elite-to-elite support was Russia's support for the incumbent President Nyusi during the 2019 elections via the Association for Free Research and International Cooperation and the International Anticrisis Center, a Russian nongovernmental organization linked to Yevgeny Prigozhin (a Russian oligarch). Prior to the elections, the Association for Free Research and International Cooperation conducted a poll that suggested that Nyusi would win and published it on the website of the International Anticrisis Center, thus breaking Mozambican regulations that prohibit the publication of election polls during the campaign period.[110] Also, in 2019, Facebook took down a network of Prigozhin-linked Facebook pages that disseminated information slandering RENAMO.[111]

Mozambique seems to have welcomed better cooperation with Russia. In 2018, Mozambican Foreign Affairs Minister José Condungua Pacheco said, "there's room for Russia to become good partners with us" (in addition to China and South Africa).[112] However, Russia struggles to offer deals that work for Mozambique, and its economic and military presence remains limited. This is partly because of the limited capabilities and the appropriateness of what Moscow can offer to Mozambique. Its PMSCs reportedly did not fare well in Cabo Delgado; its economic and energy-sector offers come a little too late (the energy sector is already saturated by many other foreign players) and are a little too expensive (kickbacks to Russia

---

[108] In 2021, Russian Ambassador to Mozambique Alexander Surikov was reported to "make discreet approaches to [the] Mozambican administration in a bid to revive economic and security cooperation between the two countries" ("Moscow Seeks to Boost Contact with Nyusi," *Africa Intelligence*, April 7, 2021).

[109] "Russia Ready to Maintain Defense Cooperation with Mozambique, Says Ambassador," TASS, October 25, 2019.

[110] Kachur, 2020; and Anton Shekhovtsov, *Fake Election Observation as Russia's Tool of Election Interference: The Case of AFRIC*, Berlin: European Platform for Democratic Elections, April 2020.

[111] Kachur, 2020; Nathaniel Gleicher, "Removing More Coordinated Inauthentic Behavior from Russia," Meta, December 15, 2020; and Shelby Grossman, Daniel Bush, and Renee DiResta, *Evidence of Russia-Linked Influence Operations in Africa*, Stanford, Calif.: Freeman Spogli Institute for International Studies, October 29, 2019. The published information suggests that RENAMO had signed an agreement with China to dispose of radioactive waste in Mozambique and that members of RENAMO had attempted to remove urns from voting posts.

[112] "Mozambique Willing to Boost Cooperation with Russia, China," TASS, May 28, 2018.

may simply be too expensive for Mozambique); and working with Russian companies and getting international funding is difficult because of the international sanctions on Russia.[113]

Posture and Access

The military presence of all three great powers in Mozambique is limited or next to none. However, although U.S. military cooperation has been scant, Russia has been increasing its access to Mozambique's transport infrastructure via bilateral agreements, and China's naval ships have made goodwill visits to Maputo. Looking ahead, U.S. access may improve in the future as a result of slightly increased security cooperation with Mozambique.

United States' Posture and Access

The United States' posture and access in Mozambique and in the surrounding region is limited, and U.S. military experience in the country is low. The United States has only a light footprint in Southern Africa, and AFRICOM has reportedly struggled with resource gaps, as attention and resources flow to U.S. Indo-Pacific Command and U.S. European Command.[114] The U.S. military does not have any bases in Mozambique, and the United States' elite military-to-military relations are underdeveloped there. Mozambique is not a member of the National Guard's State Partnership Program, although neighboring South Africa and Botswana are (which could create the opportunity for future joint exercises or engagement).[115]

Historically, U.S. military engagement with Mozambique has been fairly scant, but security cooperation has increased in an effort to bolster Mozambique's counterterrorism capabilities against ASWJ. In November 2020, U.S. Naval Forces Africa conducted Exercise Cutlass Express in conjunction with U.S. Central Command's International Maritime Exercise, which together became the second-largest maritime exercise in the world.[116] In May 2021, U.S. and Mozambican military members engaged in a Joint Combined Exchange Training exercise, the first of its kind in 20 years.[117] The two-month-long exercise involved U.S. special operations forces (specifically, Army Green Berets) and Mozambican marines and focused on the development of "tactical skills, combat casualty care, marksmanship, and execut-

---

[113] Russian oil company Rosneft has sought cooperation opportunities with other actors in Mozambique. For example, in 2018, Rosneft and Exxon Mobil signed a contract with Mozambique for the exploration and extraction of hydrocarbons (Stanislav Ivanov, "Dzhihad Po Mozambiski" ["Jihad Mozambican Style"], *Voyenno-Promishlennii Kuryer* [*Military Industrial Courier*], May 4, 2020).

[114] Copp, 2019.

[115] South Africa and Botswana are members through the New York and North Carolina National Guards, respectively.

[116] Townsend, 2020, p. 11.

[117] U.S. Embassy in Mozambique, "U.S. Embassy and Ministry of Defense Commemorate Security Cooperation at Closing Ceremony of JCET Training Exercise," press release, May 5, 2021b.

ing a mission while avoiding damage to civilians and property."[118] As part of this exercise, the U.S. government also provided medical and communications equipment to Mozambican marines.[119] By February 2022, three Joint Combined Exchange Training exercises with Mozambique had taken place, reflecting sustained U.S. interest in countering VEOs in Mozambique.[120] This new security cooperation could lead to further military relations, provided there is interest from the U.S. and Mozambican governments. However, concerns about Mozambique's inability to maintain civilian control over security forces and reports about abuses committed by Mozambican forces may prevent more-substantial assistance.[121]

Prior to the renewed attention to the security situation in Cabo Delgado, U.S.-Mozambique security cooperation engagements were sparse, most likely because of the lack of capacity of Mozambique's armed forces, ongoing disarmament and reintegration processes, and a lack of interest on both sides. For example, in 2014, the U.S. military planned to send military advisers to help implement the cease-fire agreement between the FRELIMO and RENAMO factions, but this ended up not happening because RENAMO refused to disarm.[122] Additionally, the United States has donated military equipment to Mozambique in the past, though not in large quantities; for example, in 2017, the U.S. embassy donated $40,000 of boarding team equipment to the Mozambican Navy with the aim of strengthening Mozambique's maritime security capabilities.[123] Mozambican defense officials also make use of military training opportunities, such as by the African Contingency Operations Training and Assistance program—through which the U.S. military provides training to African peacekeepers—and the International Military Education and Training program coordinated by the Defense Attaché Office at the U.S. embassy in Maputo.[124] For example, in 2018, 56 Mozambicans participated in various foreign military training programs, and 22 participated in 2019.[125] These programs may be useful in establishing informal military relationships, but Mozambique seems to make use mostly of programs geared toward English-language acquisition or

---

[118] U.S. Embassy in Mozambique, 2021b.

[119] U.S. Embassy in Mozambique, "U.S. Government Provides Military Training to Mozambican Marines," press release, March 15, 2021a.

[120] U.S. Embassy in Mozambique, "U.S. Government Launches Third Military Exercise with Mozambican Armed Forces," press release, February 2, 2022.

[121] Bureau of Democracy, Human Rights, and Labor, *Mozambique 2020 Human Rights Report*, Washington, D.C.: U.S. Department of State, March 2021b.

[122] Cook, 2019.

[123] U.S. Embassy in Mozambique, "U.S. Embassy Donates Boarding Team Equipment to Mozambican Navy," press release, August 24, 2019.

[124] U.S. Embassy in Mozambique, "Sections & Offices," webpage, undated.

[125] DoD and U.S. Department of State, 2019.

in-country civil-military coordination in disaster relief rather than officer career courses or courses for more-specialized military skills.[126]

Beyond its involvement in DoD initiatives, Mozambique became a member of the State Department's Partnership for Regional East Africa Counterterrorism in 2018, through which the United States might fund law enforcement, justice, military, and civil society programs to "contain, disrupt, and marginalize terrorist networks in the region;" the partnership includes 13 African countries.[127]

Finally, although projecting power into Mozambique—as in much of the African continent—comes with a series of logistical challenges, the United States could leverage some of its existing bases to do so. The United States, after all, has bases in Djibouti and Diego Garcia in the Indian Ocean and reportedly has used the Seychelles for drone operations, which potentially could be leveraged during a Mozambique contingency; in addition, the United States could draw on its facilities and forces in Southern Europe.[128] The U.S. military also may need to expand the operations of the East Africa Response Force more to the south to cover Mozambique. As in the Nigeria scenario, if the United States decided to deploy troops to Mozambique, it could leverage its substantial recent deployment experience to locations across the world. In addition, given Mozambique's long coastline, the United States could rely on naval power as well.[179] Furthermore, the United States may also consider using the military bases of its allies and partners in the Indian Ocean, such as those of the French Armed Forces in the Southern Indian Ocean Zone; French military locations span several islands in or near the Mozambique Channel and the location beyond Madagascar.[130]

China's Posture and Access

China does not have any military presence in Mozambique or its neighboring countries, and it has not conducted any military exercises in Mozambique.[131] At the same time, as noted earlier, China seems to enjoy a strong elite-to-elite government relationship and is a significant investor in ports elsewhere in the region, which may create opportunities for more political influence and avenues for future posture and access, if necessary. Although China does not have a military base or, at least according to open-source materials, substantial military presence agreements in Mozambique, it has been reported that China is looking to establish an

---

[126] DoD and U.S. Department of State, 2019.

[127] Bureau of International Narcotics and Law Enforcement Affairs, "Partnership for Regional East Africa Counterterrorism (PREACT)," U.S. Department of State, February 14, 2019.

[128] U.S. Air Forces in Europe and Air Forces Africa, "U.S. Air Force MQ-9 Seychelles Crash," press release, December 13, 2011.

[129] Van Hooft, 2021.

[130] The French locations include the Scattered Islands, Mayotte, Tromelin, Réunion, the Crozet Islands, the Amsterdam and Saint-Paul Islands, and the Kerguelen Islands (Pierre Morcos, "France: A Bridge Between Europe and the Indo-Pacific?" Center for Strategic and International Studies, April 1, 2021).

[131] International Institute for Strategic Studies, undated.

additional foothold in East Africa (in addition to Djibouti). It is possible that China could build more military or dual-use facilities along the East African coast, including in Kenya or Tanzania.[132] China is investing in the development of ports in other East African countries, which could be used primarily to establish greater Chinese presence in the Indian Ocean, support commercial aims and China's access to Africa's resources and trade, and support an alternative shipping line to the Suez Canal between the Indian and Atlantic oceans, but such ports could also be used to project power into Mozambique.[133] Moreover, although the PLA is not engaged in a peacekeeping mission in Nigeria, it has significant peacekeeper presence distributed across several UN locations—bases that China could seek to use with the aim to pursue not only its economic but also its security interests.[134]

It does not seem that Mozambique has granted the PLA any significant access agreements, but the PLA may have other locations from which to operate in the region, if necessary. PLA Navy ships and replenishment vessels make regular visits to ports all along the East African coast in conjunction with their anti-piracy missions off the coast of Somalia.[135] The PLA Navy has demonstrated the ability to deploy flotillas of about a dozen ships or more into the Indian Ocean, including large amphibious assault vessels, and the size of the pier that China is constructing in Djibouti suggests that it may plan to dock aircraft carriers at the PLA facility there.[136] The Djibouti facility also hosts a small brigade of about 2,000 Chinese troops, and the PLA has demonstrated the ability to support at least 1,000–2,000 troops across the

---

[132] Using open sources, it is difficult to verify any specific Chinese plans for bases along the Southeast African coast. China's military access negotiations tend to be shrouded in secrecy. In Tanzania, at least, recent political developments may render a base there less likely, although it is difficult to say with certainty whether this will happen (Ryan D. Martinson, "China as an Atlantic Naval Power," *RUSI Journal*, Vol. 164, No. 7, 2019, p. 26; Peltier, Nurkin, and O'Connor, 2020; Chris Alden, "Beijing's Security Plans Beyond Djibouti and the Horn," Italian Institute for International Political Studies, September 27, 2018; and Fumbuka Ng'wanakilala, Brenda Goh, and Cate Cadell, "Tanzania's China-Backed $10 Billion Port Plan Stalls over Terms: Officials," Reuters, May 22, 2019).

[133] For example, China is a substantial investor in Bagamoyo Port of neighboring Tanzania. It has also invested in the Maputo airport. Although it is difficult to assess the PLA Navy's potential future access at Mozambican ports, PLA warships have made goodwill and replenishment visits to Maputo, and PLA medical teams have been allowed into Mozambique to provide aid (Ken Moriyasu, "China Looks to East Africa for Second Indian Ocean Foothold," *Nikkei Asia*, June 30, 2021; Gordon Pirie, "China Has Taken a Different Route to Involvement in African Aviation," The Conversation, September 1, 2019; Erickson and Strange, 2015, p. 11; and China Central Television, "After Completing Their Mission, China's First Group of Military Doctors Sent to Aid Mozambique Return Home" ["中国首批援助莫桑比克军事医疗专家组圆满结束任务回国"], January 15, 2018).

[134] Dyrenforth, 2021; Africa and special operations researcher, email exchange with the authors, December 2021.

[135] Erickson and Strange, 2015, p. 11.

[136] Engen Tham, Ben Blanchard, and Wang Jing, "Chinese Warships Enter East Indian Ocean amid Maldives Tensions," Reuters, February 20, 2018; and Sam LaGrone, "AFRICOM: Chinese Naval Base in Africa Set to Support Aircraft Carriers," *USNI News*, April 20, 2021.

continent on various peacekeeping missions.[137] Any new facilities farther to the east, in Pakistan or Sri Lanka, may also help provide logistical support for military operations in East African states.[138] The PLA's naval, amphibious, and expeditionary support capabilities have progressed in recent years, and the PLA is likely to continue to build its ability to support larger-scale operations in the Indian Ocean basin.

Lastly, China has been increasingly interested in developing military relations with Mozambique, which may increase Beijing's ability to lobby its interests. In 2016, China and Mozambique signed a military cooperation agreement establishing the basis for potential future cooperation, as well as for "technical assistance, including training, and supply of equipment and accessories, among others, worth about US 11.5 million."[139] Even before that, Mozambicans attended the Nanjing Military Academy.[140] Since the agreement was signed, China reportedly funded the renovation of some Mozambican armed forces facilities.[141]

Russia's Posture and Access

Russia does not have a bilateral or multinational military presence in Mozambique but enjoys significant access to local infrastructure, and Russian PMSCs have acquired recent experience in the country. Since 2009, Russia and Mozambique have signed a variety of diplomatic and military cooperation agreements that grant Russian officials with diplomatic passports 30-day visa-free entrance into the country, allow for the supply of military equipment and training, simplify the entrance of Russian military ships into Mozambique's ports and airports, and allow Russia to send cargo by air without customs procedures.[142] The 2018 memorandum of understanding on strengthening cooperation in the naval-military domain par-

---

[137] Jean-Pierre Cabestan, "China's Military Base in Djibouti: A Microcosm of China's Growing Competition with the United States and New Bipolarity," *Journal of Contemporary China*, Vol. 29, No. 125, 2020a; Jean-Pierre Cabestan, "China's Djibouti Naval Base Increasing Its Power," East Asia Forum, May 16, 2020b; and International Peace Institute, undated.

[138] Peltier, Nurkin, and O'Connor, 2020.

[139] Rádio Moçambique, "Mozambique and China Sign Military Cooperation Agreement," Club of Mozambique, December 20, 2016.

[140] Mozambique's government sources reported that, in 2015, 94 military personnel were being trained at the academy ("China quer reforçar apoio a Moçambique na formação militar" ["China Wants to Strengthen Support for Mozambique in Military Training"], *Observador*, July 11, 2017; and Government of Mozambique, "PR elogia Academia Militar de Nanjing," ["President of the Republic Praises Nanjing Military Academy"], May 18, 2016).

[141] Danilo Marcondes, "Brasil e Moçambique: construindo a cooperação em defesa" ["Brazil and Mozambique: Building Defense Cooperation"], in *Desafios para Moçambique 2019* [*Challenges for Mozambique 2019*], 2019.

[142] "Mezhdunarodniye Otnosheniya Rossii I Mozambika" ["International Relations Between Russia and Mozambique"], *Ria Novosti*, August 22, 2019; Evgeny Krutlkov, "Mozambik Zamanivayet Rossiiyu V Opastnii I Pribilnii Proyekt" ["Mozambique Lures Russia into a Dangerous and Profitable Project"], Vzglyad, August 21, 2019; Sergey Sukhankin, "Russia Prepared a Foothold in Mozambique; Risks and Opportunities," *Eurasia Daily Monitor*, Vol. 16, No. 142, October 15, 2019; and "Rossiya I Mozambik Zaklyuchili

ticularly establishes jump-points (or support bases) that are planned to serve as locations for replenishing supplies and rest stops for Russian crew without burdensome formalities.[143]

Russian vessels have been relatively common in Mozambique's ports, particularly over the past several years. In March 2017 and October 2018, for example, the Russian Northern Fleet's anti-submarine destroyer *Severomorsk* called at the Port of Maputo during its tour of African countries.[144] According to Russian sources, after leaving Mozambique's territorial waters, the destroyer's "crew trained to search, detect location and attack an enemy submarine."[145] Russian ambassador Surikov has denied allegations that, during the ship's port call at Pemba in 2018, it was used in anti-terrorist activities.[146] Russia also has officially denied the arrival of Russian PMSC Wagner Group to Mozambique in September 2019, shortly after President Nyusi's visit to Moscow, and the presence of any Russian military personnel in the country.[147] Russia does seem to have a "small group" of military experts in Mozambique, the main task of which, according to Surikov, "is to promote the implementation of the cooperation agreement;" according to media reports, however, these experts may be military advisers.[148] The presence of Wagner in the country has been widely reported in the media; the mercenaries reportedly were providing training and combat support to the Mozambican government troops in the campaigns against ASWJ in Cabo Delgado and reportedly were equipped with drones.[149] However, after experiencing difficulties working with the local partners and population, as well as the deaths of several Wagner operatives, Wagner reportedly left the country in March 2020, which may have been a factor hindering Russia's ability to establish closer relations with Mozambique's government.[150]

Russia's status with the Mozambican military sector is further reinforced by the fact that Mozambican citizens study in the educational institutions run by the Russian Ministry of Defense and Ministry of the Interior and that Russia has supplied Mozambique with military

---

Soglasheniye O Zashite Informacii" ["Russia and Mozambique Sign Agreement on Information Protection"], RIA Novosti, August 22, 2019.

[143] Krutlkov, 2019.

[144] Kachur, 2020.

[145] "Russia's Large Anti-Submarine Ship Ends Visit to Mozambique," TASS, October 17, 2018.

[146] Ministry of Foreign Affairs of the Russian Federation, "Interview of the Ambassador of Russia in Mozambique to the Portuguese News Agency," April 7, 2021.

[147] "V Kremle Opovergli Prisustviye Rossiiskih Voyennih V Mozambike" ["The Kremlin Denied the Presence of Russian Military in Mozambique"], Interfax, October 8, 2019.

[148] Nuno Rogeiro, "As Relações Entre a Rússia e Moçambique: Dos Acordos à Luta Contra o Terrorismo" ["Relations Between Russia and Mozambique: From Agreements to the Fight Against Terrorism"], Sicnoticias, April 9, 2021.

[149] Kachur, 2020.

[150] Media outlets also reported that the group included 200 soldiers, three attack helicopters, and crew (Sukhankin, 2019; Kachur, 2020; Africa and special operations researcher, interview with the authors, July 2021).

equipment (mainly transport helicopters) to support government forces fighting in the north of the country. However, Russia is not a regular arms supplier, and Mozambique's Minister of Foreign Affairs Pacheco said that the 2019 helicopter procurement was a "one-off support, which takes place within the framework of cooperation with Russia, is related to strengthening our ability to defend the people and maintain public order, security and tranquility."[151]

Like in the Nigeria scenario, because Russia's military is primarily designed for contingencies in or near Russia's territory, it has paid less attention to developing the ability to project larger-scale military forces to faraway regions. It therefore lacks the kind of naval and air assets that the United States could rely on to rapidly deploy forces to Mozambique.[152] However, Russia has long-range transport aircraft that could be used to support smaller deployments.[153] In fact, Wagner personnel reportedly arrived in Mozambique in 2019 in an Antonov An-124 airplane, allegedly owned by the Russian Air Force.[154]

Capabilities

Although all three great powers have limited military capabilities in Mozambique, both the United States and particularly Russia have been gaining recent military experience there.

United States' Capabilities

Given limited U.S. involvement in Mozambique until the uptick in counterterrorism-related engagement, the United States does not have any significant capabilities in Mozambique. As noted earlier, U.S. special operations forces have recently deployed to Mozambique to train Mozambican marines in counterterrorism operations. Indeed, the U.S. military presence across all of Africa is fairly limited; the only permanent U.S. base is located in Djibouti at Camp Lemonnier, more than 2,000 miles away from Mozambique, and there are a scattering of cooperative security locations elsewhere.[155] These forces and facilities could lend support to future operations in Mozambique, but a more substantial U.S. military deployment there likely would need to rely on the U.S. military bases in Europe.[156] Additionally, the New York and North Carolina National Guards deploy on a rotational basis to South Africa and Botswana and theoretically could provide support to operations in Mozambique, provided the appropriate legal agreements and authorities were in place.

---

[151] Adrian Frey, "Mozambique: Government Announces Military Equipment Reinforcement Supplied by Russia—Report," Club of Mozambique, October 4, 2019.

[152] Heerdt, 2020.

[153] Expert on the Russian military, interview with the authors, October 2021.

[154] Tim Lister and Sebastian Shukla, "Russian Mercenaries Fight Shadowy Battle in Gas-Rich Mozambique," CNN, November 29, 2019.

[155] Commander, Navy Installations Command, undated.

[156] Retired U.S. military officer previously stationed in Africa, interview with the authors, July 2021.

China's Capabilities

China does not have any military capabilities in Mozambique, and the Chinese PMSCs in the country are focused on protecting Chinese companies and civilians.[157] Despite this, if Maputo requested military aid, China's ability to provide the Mozambican military with weapons likely would be limited only by Beijing's willingness to foot the bill or Mozambique's ability to pay for military equipment. Moreover, we assess that China would be able to provide counterterrorism or other smaller-unit training, yet not to the scale of the training provided by the U.S. military in Iraq and Afghanistan.[158] China also would be able to provide considerable financial, diplomatic, and cyber or intelligence support to any proxy it chose, whether in a permissive or non-permissive environment.

China's ability to provide direct military support will be much more limited in a non-permissive environment. At present, it does not have any air bases within either strike or transport range of Mozambique, although that could change if it builds or gains access to a larger airstrip in Djibouti (its base there does not have an airstrip capable of supporting fixed-wing aircraft).[159] As noted earlier, China does have a demonstrated ability to operate at least one flotilla of between eight and 12 ships in the eastern Indian Ocean. With time, it likely will continue to increase the size, duration, and distance of its deployments, providing it with more naval firepower to support a proxy in either a permissive or non-permissive environment, although PLA Navy operations could be complicated by U.S. forces.[160]

Russia's Capabilities

Russia does not have a substantial official military presence in Mozambique, and, according to open-source reports, Russian PMSC Wagner has left the country. Military agreements allow Russia to have access to key infrastructure points in the country, so Russia could be able to send smaller numbers of military forces or PMSCs there; however, the reports on Wagner's experience in Mozambique suggest that the Russian military could have difficulties establishing good working relations with the local forces and local communities, accessing logistics support in the country's territory, and adjusting to the specifics of the local environment.[161] At the same time, Russia's ability to station military ships in Mozambique's ports

---

[157] China seems to have at least one PMSC, the China Overseas Security Group, in Mozambique (Sergey Sukhankin, "Chinese Private Security Contractors: New Trends and Future Prospects," *China Brief*, Vol. 20, No. 9, May 15, 2020c; and Legarda and Nouwens, 2018).

[158] However, the United States seems to be trying to move away from such surge missions to train large numbers of partner troops, focusing instead on smaller and more-persistent teams (see Kyle Rempfer, "Army SFAB Advisers Will Have to Share Some Friends with China," *Army Times*, October 13, 2020).

[159] Dutton, Kardon, and Kennedy, 2020, p. 31.

[160] Janes, 2021c; Tham, Blanchard, and Jing, 2018.

[161] Kachur, 2020; Sukhankin, 2019; and "De como os mercenários russos da Wagner perderam a guerra contra os terroristas no norte de Moçambique" ["How Wagner's Russian Mercenaries Lost the War Against Terrorists in Northern Mozambique"], *Carta de Moçambique*, April 20, 2020.

could allow Russia to support anti-terrorist operations by projecting ISR capabilities from the vessels. Russia's links with the military and security community are strengthened by the fact that Mozambicans train at the educational institutions run by the Russian Ministry of Defense and the Ministry of the Interior.[162]

Russia's capabilities, while limited, also extend to the diplomatic, political, and humanitarian areas. Russia's official statements maintain a narrative about the historical Soviet support for Mozambique during its war for independence and emphasize that Russian and Mozambican positions are largely aligned in international frameworks, including the UN.[163] Russia also could build on its experience with measures of information and political warfare in the country—particularly its meddling in Mozambican elections in 2019.[164] Furthermore, although Mozambique's arms imports are very low, Russia (and previously the Soviet Union) has been the most active arms supplier to Mozambique, only recently and sporadically joined by India, Ukraine, and China.[165]

How Might a Conflict Unfold?

Mozambique's ongoing security crisis in the northern part of the country from continued ASWJ violence—exacerbated by high levels of poverty and corruption, lack of government accountability, and the impact of recent natural disasters—may escalate low-level conflict to higher-intensity situations. The most likely conflict scenario that could lead to greater foreign engagement in support of Mozambique's security could include increased and sustained Islamic terrorism violence, potentially in combination with continued attacks on foreign workers and an increasingly dire situation with international narcotics-smuggling through Mozambique, which remains a long-standing concern for the United States. The fact that Mozambique hosts the largest exploitable gas reserves in Africa in one of its poorest regions may be another reason for increased international interest in getting involved to restore stability. Furthermore, the increased destabilization of the country from the violence in the north and the unresolved failures of the disarmament, demobilization, and reintegration

---

[162] Kachur, 2020.

[163] Embassy of the Russian Federation in the Republic of Mozambique, "О выступлении российского африканиста в Университете им. Ж.Чиссано" ["About the Speech of the Russian Africanist at the University J. Chissano"], 2020.

[164] See also the discussion in Cohen, Treyger, et al., 2023.

[165] Russia has been the largest arms supplier to Mozambique for the past 60 or so years and responded to Mozambique's arms sales request in 2019 by selling several transport helicopters, but in 2014 and 2016, China sold armored personnel carriers and all-purpose vehicles to Mozambique. The United Kingdom, Germany, Spain, and Ukraine sold light aircraft, patrol craft, armored personnel carriers, and transport aircraft to Mozambique between 2011 and 2014, and Portugal and India have delivered light aircraft and patrol craft as aid (SIPRI, undated-a, trade registers tool, data on the transfer of major weapons—specifically, deals with deliveries or orders made from 1991 to 2020).

process could lead to a struggle between RENAMO and its Military Junta faction, although we assess this as a less likely scenario for great-power engagement with military means.

Why Would the United States, China, and Russia Get Involved, and Whom Would Each Support?

Numerous countries and organizations in Africa and beyond have expressed concerns about the security situation in northern Mozambique and have offered assistance.[166] The most likely scenario that could involve the United States, China, and Russia could be one of intensified Islamic terrorism in northern Mozambique, especially if ASWJ gained a stronger international character, attacked the nationals of the three great powers, or affected the powers' economic interests. It is not likely, however, that the three powers would render substantial military or indirect support to local nongovernmental actors. Even if all or some of the great powers became involved in Mozambique, they likely would support the official government actor because of the character of the adversary. Our analysis shows that the United States' stakes in Mozambique are likely insufficient to devote a lot of resources to a conflict in this country. As in the Nigeria case, the United States is highly unlikely to involve itself in any Mozambique contingency through boots on the ground. But it could consider getting engaged for security and humanitarian reasons—such as supporting a stability and security mission led by European or regional forces—and its military forces could be used to evacuate U.S. citizens if they were endangered or to provide humanitarian support or food supplies.[167] Even if the United States wished to deploy a larger amount of and more heavily armed troops to conduct operations in Mozambique, doing so would prove to be logistically challenging.

Although China is an important economic actor for Mozambique and Mozambique's importance for China is marked by its location on the Indian Ocean, Mozambique is not among China's top economic or geopolitical interests. We assess that China does not have a strong motivation to become engaged in a conflict in Mozambique via military operations. If it were to become involved at all, China might consider some engagement to support stability as part of a larger objective to ensure the safety of Beijing's economic interests or to counterbalance what could be regarded as the potential for India to gain more influence on the coast of the southwestern Indian Ocean. Such purposes likely could be achieved by sending trainers, military equipment, and perhaps limited numbers of special operations personnel or security personnel without much direct PLA involvement. Larger-scale operations could occur if the security situation were to deteriorate and Chinese citizens required evacuation.

---

[166] See, for example, "Statement of H.E. Mr. Moussa Faki Mahamat, Chairperson of the African Union Commission, on the Terrorist Attacks in Mozambique," African Union, March 31, 2021; and Mfuneko Toyana, "European Union Agrees to Help Mozambique Tackle Insurgency: Statement," Reuters, October 14, 2020.

[167] Former U.S. government official and think-tank expert on Africa, interview with the authors, July 2021.

The PLA also could become more directly involved if the UN opened a formal peacekeeping operation in the country.[168]

Russia, however, has geopolitical interests in Mozambique (even if they may not be as strong as its interests in North Africa), specifically as a rest stop for Russia's naval forces and because of the considerable effort that Russia has invested into developing security and military ties. Moscow's interest in using Mozambican infrastructure for military purposes may be a good motivation for taking a practical stand in the Mozambican government's fight against ASWJ, despite the short-lived presence of Wagner in the country. Official Russian statements suggest that Russia likely would, at least officially, support a multinational anti-terrorism response under the auspices of the SADC and led by Mozambican security and defense forces. In fact, in 2021, Ambassador Surikov welcomed a coordinated response by the SADC while maintaining a policy of "African problems—African solutions."[169] In the tradition of Russian foreign policy toward Africa, it would be unlikely that Russian military forces would carry out a large deployment to Mozambique; rather, Moscow would use military advisers, potentially some smaller units, and PMSCs. The use of PMSCs, arms exports, and military equipment maintenance services in exchange for access to natural resources also could be part of the model. Some analysts also suggest that Russia could use methods it employed during the Syrian civil war—specifically, reinforcing a regional autocrat—to challenge or contest the U.S. role and influence and to become a political force in the region.[170] Russia could support the Mozambican government efforts by offering arms sales—which, however, could expose the country to the U.S. 2017 Countering America's Adversaries Through Sanctions Act.[171] Russia thus would seek to support its broader aim in Africa to offer an alternative partnership to that of the West. At the least, Russia could provide humanitarian aid, including food health care, bilaterally or via UN programs.

Hypothetically, however, provided that the United States continues training Mozambican forces or augments its presence in the country, U.S. forces could be exposed to Russian or Chinese forces or PMSCs. U.S. forces could face harassment activities from Russian or Chinese forces or PMSCs—as happened in Syria, Libya, and Djibouti[172]—or clash over access to airport infrastructure when delivering humanitarian aid or other assistance.[173] Furthermore, Russian or Chinese PMSCs might themselves become a source of repressive action and con-

---

[168] Former U.S. government official and think-tank expert on Africa, interview with the authors, July 2021.

[169] Ministry of Foreign Affairs of the Russian Federation, 2021.

[170] Benjamin Pearson, *Russia: Applying the Low Cost, High Return Syrian Strategy to Africa*, Maxwell Air Force Base, Ala.: Squadron Officer School, April 7, 2021.

[171] Pearson, 2021; Rogeiro, 2021.

[172] Idrees Ali and Phil Stewart, "U.S. Troops Injured in Russian Vehicle Collision in Syria, U.S. Officials Say," Reuters, August 26, 2020; Phil Stewart and Aidan Lewis, "Exclusive: U.S. Says Drone Shot Down by Russian Air Defenses Near Libyan Capital," Reuters, December 7, 2019; and "US Accuses China of Pointing Lasers at Pilots from Djibouti Base," BBC News, May 4, 2018.

[173] Retired U.S. military officer previously stationed in Africa, interview with the authors, July 2021.

tribute to human rights abuses, which may solicit a Western response.[174] Lastly, the interests of the three powers could converge in the Mozambique Channel, which is expected to become a new maritime security hotspot. All three countries and the United States' allies and partners, including India, may be interested in reducing the threat of smuggling and piracy affecting their interests in Mozambique's offshore gas fields and the Mozambique Channel. Yet the United States may experience similar issues in terms of harassment, difficulty negotiating port access, and difficulty ensuring safe air patrol operations.

Table 4.1 provides a summary of the interests and objectives, posture and access, and capabilities of the three great powers in Mozambique. In this table, by *external* reasons, we

TABLE 4.1

Key Characteristics of Possible Conflict Scenarios with Great-Power Involvement in Mozambique

	United States	China	Russia
Why would each power become involved?			
External reasons		Strategic and geopolitical (limited): • Counterbalance the influence of other powers (including India)	Strategic and geopolitical: • Pursue influence • Maintain or secure strategic access • Build status in the region
Internal reasons	Security and humanitarian: • Counter violent extremism (ASWJ) • Prevent and respond to humanitarian disasters	Economic: • Ensure access to hydrocarbons, timber, and critical infrastructure investments	Economic: • Ensure access to hydrocarbons
Whom might each power support?	• Government	• Government	• Government
What form would support likely take?	• Indirect overt support (e.g., training and working with partners and allies, such as Portugal, France, and the EU)	• Indirect overt and covert support, with a very low likelihood of limited overt military intervention	• Indirect overt and covert support, with a low likelihood of limited overt military intervention
What capabilities would each power bring?	• Training and advising • ISR • Airlift • Naval forces, potentially	• Training • Military equipment • Special operations forces • Financial support • Peacekeeping operations	• PMSCs • Training • Military equipment • ISR • Special operations support • Naval ships, if there is an overt military intervention

[174] Cohen, Treyger, et al., 2023.

mean objectives that pertain to broader geopolitical or other concerns beyond the borders of Mozambique; by *internal* reasons, we mean objectives that pertain to concerns that are largely focused within Mozambique.

What Factors Might Influence the Outcome of the Conflict?

An array of factors may affect the outcome of the conflict that we examined in the Mozambique scenario. Considering the low capability of Mozambican forces to fight ASWJ, the outcome of the conflict may be highly dependent on external assistance. The United States would not be the only external actor providing military assistance (after all, the SADC and the EU are already providing assistance to fight ASWJ); our focus in this section, however, is on the United States. The success of a potential U.S. engagement would depend on several factors, including issues related to U.S. strategy and policymaking (e.g., U.S. strategy toward Africa), political issues (e.g., the relations between the host country and the three great powers), operational and logistical issues (e.g., time and distance to deploy forces), and capacity issues (e.g., airspace deconfliction, use of drones). The great powers likely would intervene on the same side of the conflict and support the Mozambican government against ASWJ. Even so, it is likely that they would continue to seek influence and relations with Mozambique to pursue their interests in the country rather than focus on collaborating with each other. The United States most plausibly would want to counter VEOs to prevent ASWJ's spillover to other regions and its potential growth into a direct security threat to the United States. The United States also could conceivably consider cooperating with European or regional partners to expand its support. Thus, even though all three countries are notionally on the same side in this scenario, they would still be engaged in great-power competition.

A key factor affecting any U.S. decision to become more engaged in Mozambican security and the success of such a decision is the lack of (1) clear objectives regarding U.S. relations with the continent and Mozambique in particular and (2) defined policy toward China and Russia gaining more access and influence in the region.[175] As noted earlier, countering VEOs and countering drug-smuggling could be two likely key areas of interest for the United States in Mozambique and could result in some success, provided that any relevant plans receive clear strategic inputs and financial backing.

Second, the character and success of U.S. policies in an engagement in Mozambique also depend on the openness and interest of the Mozambican government. Here, the United States is at a disadvantage to China and Russia, whose actors are able to operate in ways that offer them more means of gaining influence with local leaders. Mozambique, and other countries that face immediate security concerns, may prefer cooperating with countries that respond to these immediate needs and offer assistance without necessarily demanding in return human

---

[175] Former U.S. government official and think-tank expert on Africa, interview with the authors, July 2021.

rights, accountability, and investment in economic development.[176] As a result, the U.S. military, including the Department of the Air Force, may not have priority over China or Russia for access to local airports.

Third, the United States would face significant time and distance challenges. Platforms used for deploying special operators or evacuating downed pilots—such as the CV-22 Osprey or the HH-60 Pave Hawk) have a range of only 500 nautical miles.[177] Intelligence platforms—such as the MQ-9 Reaper—have an extended range of 1,400 nautical miles.[178] Given that Mozambique is almost 4,000 nautical miles from key U.S. bases in Europe, U.S. Air Force assets would have to be based considerably closer to be relevant to the fight. Even some strategic assets—such as C-17 Globemaster cargo aircraft, which have a range of 2,400 nautical miles—would need to refuel in order to ferry cargo from Europe to Mozambique.[179]

Time and distance challenges pose problems even for U.S. bases in Africa. For example, Pemba, a coastal town in Cabo Delgado, is 1,876 miles from the only U.S. military base in Eastern Africa (Camp Lemonnier in Djibouti) and 2,761 miles from the U.S. drone base near Agadez, Nigeria. The distance to the most southern U.S. Air Force base in Europe is even larger—approximately 4,413 miles. These ranges are outside the range of rotary-wing aircraft, thus requiring access to fixed-wing airfields—infrastructure that remains underdeveloped in Africa.[180] Moreover, one study reports that, because of the time-distance issue, AFRICOM is often forced to rely on host-nation medical support.[181] With an increased number of U.S. forces on the ground, the airlift capacity of U.S. Transportation Command could experience additional stress. At the same time, the quality and accessibility of the local airfields and air traffic control may create further complications.[182] Lack of infrastructure (runways and fuel storage) and air traffic control–related issues are known problems for the African theater and are the reason that international civilian airports are often used for military and humanitarian assistance and disaster relief operations that involve fixed-wing aircraft. The use of civilian airports, however, creates additional deconfliction issues.[183] U.S. forces may therefore need to run some operations out of partner locations closer to the area of the mis-

---

[176] Former U.S. government official and think-tank expert on Africa, interview with the authors, July 2021.

[177] U.S. Air Force, "HH-60G Pave Hawk," webpage, undated-b; and Hurlburt Field, "CV-22 Osprey," webpage, U.S. Air Force, August 2020.

[178] U.S. Air Force, 2021.

[179] U.S. Air Force, "C-17 Globemaster III," webpage, undated-a.

[180] Logistics Cluster and World Food Programme, "Mozambique Aviation," Logistics Capacity Assessment, undated; Canso, "Aeroportos de Moçambique, E.P.," webpage, May 10, 2020; and Hattem, 2017.

[181] Brandon Carius, William T. Davis, Carlissa D. Linscomb, Mireya A. Escandon, Dylan Rodriguez, Nguvan Uhaa, Joseph K. Maddry, Kevin K. Chung, and Steve Schauer, "An Analysis of US Africa Command Area of Operations Military Medical Transportations, 2008–2018," *African Journal of Emergency Medicine*, Vol. 10, No. 1, March 2020.

[182] Retired U.S. military officer previously stationed in Africa, interview with the authors, July 2021.

[183] Former U.S. Department of State official, interview with the authors, July 2021.

sion. Furthermore, U.S. forces may face local sensitivities regarding the use of drones over certain territories.[184] That being said, any future U.S. military involvement in Mozambique and elsewhere in the region likely would be air-centric because of the scale of the continent and large distances required for forces to cover, the lack of surface land communications, and the few ports (compared with the continent's land mass).[185]

Next, the U.S. military may face issues of deconfliction when operating in the same location as personnel from China; Russia; and other actors from Rwanda, the SADC, or the EU. In Mozambique, the United States may need to compete with other forces for access to infrastructure—for example, for the same piece of tarmac for evacuation operations.[186]

The U.S. military also could face potential harassment from Russian and Chinese forces if these forces find themselves in operational entanglement. Precedents already exist from Syria, Libya, and Djibouti, as noted earlier.[187] The obscure status of Russian PMSCs is dangerous and creates uncertainty about their mission and whom they work for (a local actor or a Russian actor), and U.S. forces may have to deal with accidental friction or purposeful harassment.[188] The character and armament of Chinese PMSCs that are mostly unarmed currently do not pose such a threat, but this could change if these companies alter their modus operandi.

The United States, together with other allies and partners, could promote strengthening human rights, reducing corruption, increasing accountability, and incentivizing economic development in Mozambique.[189] Although these are all slow processes, they could have valuable stability and security results.

Lastly, the potential for cooperation with allied and partner countries cannot be overstressed, particularly if the United States chose to support future anti-piracy and security operations in the Mozambique Channel, an area of interest for not only the three great powers but also South Africa, France, and India.

---

[184] Former U.S. government official on Africa, interview with the authors, July 2021; retired U.S. military officer previously stationed in Africa, interview with the authors, July 2021.

[185] Africa and special operations researcher, interview with the authors, July 2021; retired U.S. military officer previously stationed in Africa, interview with the authors, July 2021.

[186] Africa and special operations researcher, interview with the authors, July 2021.

[187] Ali and Stewart, 2020; Stewart and Lewis, 2019; "US Accuses China of Pointing Lasers at Pilots from Djibouti Base," 2018.

[188] Africa and special operations researcher, interview with the authors, July 2021.

[189] Former U.S. Department of State official, interview with the authors, July 2021.

CHAPTER FIVE

Conclusion

In the era of renewed great-power competition, Africa—a continent where external powers have historically vied for primacy and become embroiled in conflicts—is yet again summoning more interest from the United States and its competitors China and Russia. Much of the strategic focus has been on the Indo-Pacific and, to a lesser extent, Europe, but competition in secondary theaters (including Africa) is intensifying as well. During the Cold War, competition erupted into numerous proxy wars and interventions, with the United States and its allies backing one side and the Soviet Union and its allies backing the other. Today, as our analysis suggests, even areas with the greatest involvement by all three great powers—and hence, areas of potentially more-intense competition—in very conflict-prone countries are unlikely to inaugurate a return to Cold War–style proxy wars or military interventions, but those areas may present different challenges. In this chapter, we synthesize the key lessons of the previous chapters and outline some of the key recommendations emerging from this project for the U.S. government, the joint force, and the Department of the Air Force on how to maximize their abilities to compete in Africa.

Findings

Potential for Competition in Africa Is Focused in the Largest Economies, Countries with Natural Resources, and Strategically Important Locations

Africa is home to a great many countries, and grasping its significance for great-power competition entails first understanding where on the continent the United States, China, and Russia are concentrating their influence-seeking efforts. As Chapter Two details, involvement by the three powers most visibly converges on Africa's largest economies: Four of the five focal countries—Nigeria, South Africa, Kenya, and Algeria—have the highest GDPs on the continent. The countries with the most competition potential are also rich in natural resources: Nigeria and Algeria are the top oil producers on the continent, South Africa is a leading platinum and gold producer, and all four countries possess other natural resources. Moreover, great powers prioritize countries in strategically important locations—such as Sudan, with its access to the Red Sea and the Gulf of Aden; the North African countries, with their access to the Mediterranean Sea; and Tanzania and Kenya, which are important for access to the Indian Ocean.

The United States Remains a Dominant Aid Donor and Military Actor in Africa, but China's and Russia's Influence-Seeking There Is Growing

The United States remains a leading military actor and aid provider to African countries. However, China's and, to a lesser extent, Russia's influence-seeking efforts have grown considerably on the continent. Chinese influence-seeking has been particularly active on the economic and diplomatic fronts: China's trade has grown over the past two decades, and China is now Africa's biggest trading partner of the three powers. China's aggressive investments in a variety of economic sectors are particularly significant. On the diplomatic front, China has made consistent efforts in developing elite-to-elite relations, and these efforts are reflected in its intense and regular pattern of high-level diplomatic visits. Moreover, China has expanded its presence in the media sector, especially in countries with the fastest-growing African entertainment and media markets. Although Chinese influence-seeking has not been as active in the military domain, Africa does host China's first overseas military base, and Chinese peacekeepers have been deployed to the continent. By contrast, Russia's most significant avenue of seeking influence has been in the military and security domain: Its arms imports dominate the African market, and it has aggressively pursued military agreements; Moscow signed at least 20 such agreements between 2015 and 2020, bringing the total to 33 as of 2020. Moreover, the activities of its PMSCs have expanded, and the companies have supported multiple parties across Africa. Russian involvement also has been reflected in the diplomatic domain, with increasing high-level visits to the continent over the past decade. At the same time, U.S. involvement in Africa has largely stagnated or even declined, particularly in the diplomatic and economic domains. For example, U.S. trade volumes with Africa declined since 2008, and U.S. high-level diplomatic visits to the region have declined since 2012.

Great Powers May Have Limited Motivations for Involvement in Military Conflicts in Africa

Although all three great powers have considerable interests in Africa and competition for influence there is becoming more significant, the nature of great-power interests is not likely to provide a sufficiently strong motivation for any of the powers to become involved in African conflicts—even in some of the countries where the potential for competition and opportunities for conflict are relatively high. For the United States, none of the interests that it has in Nigeria or Mozambique warrants substantial involvement in a conflict. The most-plausible motivations for involvement are connected to counterterrorism. Washington also has economic interests and humanitarian concerns. Yet all of these interests are unlikely to motivate a significant expenditure of resources to support a proxy in the scenarios that we considered.

At least in our two scenario countries—Nigeria and Mozambique—China and Russia also lack the kind of significant interests in Africa that might motivate them to expend resources on substantial support to parties in local conflicts. Like the United States, the two competitors are not at high risk of direct impact from violent extremist networks present in these countries, even if all three powers are concerned about international terrorism generally—and especially closer to their homelands. For China, its greatest motivation to become involved in a conflict would stem from its economic interests, particularly in maintaining stability around the Belt and Road Initiative. Russia's most-plausible motivations to engage in a conflict would be based on a combination of its strategic and economic interests—to maintain influence, ensure access to local political leadership, and support its interests in Africa's markets and natural resources.

Because of the relatively low willingness to engage substantially, the most-plausible forms of intervention in our scenario analyses entail indirect forms of support. The most-plausible conflict scenarios that we identified in Nigeria and Mozambique would entail counter-VEO engagements, training, non-combatant evacuations, support through PMSCs, or simply humanitarian assistance. Military engagements are most likely to involve small, specialized units or training teams. In the future, if U.S.-China and U.S.-Russia relations deteriorate further and increasingly become zero-sum, the powers' relations in Africa may follow the same trajectory. However, it is unlikely that, even then, the countries would engage in larger-scale military interventions; rather, they would focus on non-military competition, support for local actors, and small-scale engagements. The involvement of competing powers in the same conflict could, however, increase the likelihood that Chinese or Russian forces would harass U.S., partner, or allied forces and civilian personnel.

Great-Power Competition in Africa May Not Be a Zero-Sum Game

During the Cold War, many newly independent countries in Africa found themselves in the middle of the competition among the United States and its allies, the Soviet Union and its bloc, and Maoist China. In the era of renewed great-power contests, competition is intensifying in Africa, but it has not acquired an all-encompassing, zero-sum character comparable to that of the Cold War. Today, the United States, China, and Russia are leery of each other's presence and activities and would undermine competitors' influence when opportunities arise. Indeed, both Russia and China are interested in increasing their influence in Africa in order to boost their international status more broadly. Compared with the Cold War, great-power competition today lacks the same level of strong ideological motivation, and African countries have also changed, gained stronger and more-seasoned political leadership, and accumulated more influence and economic strength. However, competitors' presence is not viewed as an existential threat, and there are no concerns about a domino-style ideological contagion that characterized the Cold War. Moreover, both China and Russia are cautious about challenging the United States overtly in the context of conflicts: Instead of such challenges, Russia and, to a lesser extent, China seek to take advantage of openings to assume a larger role in particular countries.[1] That means that, at least in the near term and in the absence of other motivations, none of the great powers is likely to become involved in a far-away conflict primarily to hurt its competitors' interests or otherwise advance its standing in competition.

In the two case studies in Africa that we examined, we also found that, although all three great powers may have interests in these countries, their interests do not necessarily clash directly. Even if prospects for meaningful U.S.-China or U.S.-Russia cooperation in Nigeria or Mozambique are meager, there are precedents of cooperative action among commercial ventures.[2] Some suggestion of seeking cooperative approaches is also evident when it comes to security concerns; for example, the Chinese ambassador reportedly reached out to his U.S. counterparts following the kidnapping of Chinese nationals in Nigeria in 2018.[3] Competition may certainly become more acute in the future, but these examples suggest that, at least for the time being, great-power activities are not necessarily irreconcilable or mutually threatening.

In Some of the Most-Plausible Conflict Scenarios, the United States, China, and Russia Are More Likely to Support the Same Actors Rather Than Opposing Sides

Although we cannot generalize our findings regarding Nigeria and Mozambique to the rest of Africa, those scenarios indicate that the weakness of competition-related reasons for the great powers to become involved in African conflicts and the nature of the more likely roots of conflict mean that the United States, China, and Russia are unlikely to back opposing parties to a conflict simply to impose costs on their competitors. The Nigeria and Mozambique scenarios show that the interests that would likely play a bigger role in motivating great-power involvement tend to favor support for governments over non-state actors. All three powers at least rhetorically share a common interest in combating international terrorism and preventing the spillover of terrorism into areas closer to their respective homelands and perceived spheres of influence. Even if terrorism in most of Africa is too distant to present a realistic threat to China's and Russia's neighborhoods, the two countries are overwhelmingly likely to support governments against terrorist or violent extremist groups. Similarly, to varying degrees, all three powers share economic interests—which are best assured by the strongest local party, most likely to remain in control. Finally, to the extent that external reasons, such as strategic access or increasing influence, are motivating involvement, these interests too are best advanced by standing governments—as long as those governments are likely to remain

---

[1] For a more detailed discussion of how China and Russia are likely to approach proxy wars and limited conflicts, see Cohen, Treyger, et al., Appendixes B and C.

[2] Page, 2018; "China's CNPC Natural Gas Project in Mozambique Delayed," 2020; OpeOluwani Akintayo, "Lukoil to Buy Fresh Stake off Chevron's Oil Block in Nigeria," Sweet Crude Reports, December 7, 2019; and "Rosneft Signs Agreements on Offshore Gas Field Development with Mozambique," TASS, August 22, 2019.

[3] Page, 2018.

in control. In both Nigeria and Mozambique, this means that the United States, China, and Russia are much more likely to be fighting against the same adversaries.

Conflicts with Great-Power Involvement in Africa Are Likely to Involve Distinct Challenges of Deconfliction, Harassment, and Behind-the-Scenes Political Contests

Even if the three great powers become involved in conflicts in secondary theaters notionally on the same side, it does not mean that the three will cooperate with each other. It does, however, mean that great-power support to proxies in Africa likely will not resemble Cold War–style proxy wars or other forms of conflict. Instead, the dominant challenges that the United States is most likely to encounter will involve deconfliction, mutual harassment, and behind-the-scenes competition for political influence.

As demonstrated most recently by the interactions in Syria between the United States and Russia, deconflicting operations carry a host of operational challenges.[4] Even where deconfliction mechanisms are established—as between the United States and Russia in Syria—their effectiveness may be limited. There is a high likelihood that the U.S. military will face various frictions with Chinese and Russian forces or PMSCs—and perhaps even mutual harassment in situations of operational entanglement. Precedent exists where Russian or Chinese actors have harassed or inflicted harm on U.S. forces in Syria, Libya, and Djibouti.[5] Compounding these problems is the increasing involvement of PMSCs—leading to "double proxy wars," a term used by a Russian commentator to refer to conflicts in which the intervening state seeks to hide its support for a local proxy behind yet another actor.[6] The command and control aspects of Russian PMSCs in particular are unclear and may not respond to more-formal deconfliction frameworks between the United States and Russia. Thus, U.S. involvement in foreign conflicts alongside Russia does not rule out periods of low-level and covert direct kinetic conflict between the powers.[7] Moreover, deconfliction and harassment issues may complicate U.S. operations even where involvement is predominantly indirect; for example, frictions may arise when seeking access to civilian airfields.[8]

---

[4] Cohen, Kepe, et al., 2023.

[5] Ali and Stewart, 2020; Stewart and Lewis, 2019; "US Accuses China of Pointing Lasers at Pilots from Djibouti Base," 2018.

[6] Vasiliy Mikryukov, "Povoyte Za Menya" ["Fight for Me"], *Voyenno-Promishlennii Kuryer* [*Military Industrial Courier*], October 5, 2015.

[7] For example, Russian Wagner mercenaries attacked U.S. soldiers in Syria, although the connection to Moscow is unclear (Kimberly Marten, "The Puzzle of Russian Behavior in Deir Al-Zour," *War on the Rocks*, July 5, 2018; retired U.S. military officer previously stationed in Africa, interview with the authors, July 2021; and Cohen, Treyger, et al., Appendix C).

[8] Retired U.S. military officer previously stationed in Africa, interview with the authors, July 2021.

Recommendations

The insights that emerged from our analysis suggest several recommendations for how the United States may better prepare for the future competition with China and Russia in Africa and position itself to most effectively support military engagements there, if necessary. In this section, we provide recommendations for the U.S. government, the joint force, and the Department of the Air Force.

Recommendations for the U.S. Government

The United States' renewed focus on great-power competition has translated into prioritizing the Indo-Pacific and European theaters. But China and Russia have increasing global aspirations, and strategic competition is unlikely to be confined to those theaters. Africa is likely to only increase in importance for China and, to a lesser extent, Russia, and the U.S. government should avoid underestimating the continent's significance amid strategic planning for great-power competition. To this end, we make the following recommendations for the U.S. government.

Recognize That U.S. Interests in Africa Require a Long-Term Vision for the Region

The United States lacks a comprehensive long-term vision for Africa.[9] A comprehensive view of the aims that the United States wants to pursue in its relationship with Africa, irrespective of great-power competition with China and Russia, would help the United States adopt more-proactive policies rather than risk being mostly reactive to China's or Russia's actions. And articulating key objectives guiding U.S. relations with African countries, independent of competitive dynamics with China and Russia, might improve U.S. relations with African countries.[10]

Moreover, competition with China and Russia in Africa today is no longer the zero-sum game of the Cold War. A strategic vision for Africa requires an assessment of where and how Chinese and Russian influence most likely would undermine U.S. objectives and require countervailing actions. Chapter Two details where the potential for competition for influence is highest and, therefore, where the United States might pay particular attention. Even in countries where the potential for competition is most acute, however, aspects of China's

---

[9] Recent discussions about the necessity of an Africa strategy have suggested that there are potential benefits of not having a strategy. For instance, lacking a strategy may allow for a more malleable approach to the continent set by experts and practitioners as and when necessary, particularly considering Africa's vastness and the differences among African countries (Sam Wilkins, "Does America Need an Africa Strategy?" *War on the Rocks*, April 2, 2020).

[10] Some African countries perceive that, like during the Cold War, they will once again become a theater for great-power competition, yet none of the competing powers will really care about Africa's development. This perception can backfire for the United States, particularly when it comes to the ability to create more-positive relations with those African countries (Shurkin, 2018).

or Russia's involvement may not pose a direct threat to U.S. interests. For example, Chinese and Russian trade with Africa, particularly if it increases Africa's imports, may in fact benefit Africa's economy, and growing involvement by some Russian companies in African economies may not necessarily adversely affect the United States.[11]

Lastly, such a strategy could help guide U.S. decisionmakers in establishing a framework for either preventing the United States from being drawn into military confrontations with its great-power competitors or at least preparing for such future challenges. This framework should include preparing for operational harassment and planning for operational deconfliction. The plan also should focus on how to better collaborate with partners in countries where human rights abuses and lack of government accountability are intermingled with U.S. security interests. After all, U.S. forces in Africa currently are restricted from carrying out offensive strikes or accompanying the forces they train on operations.[12]

Maintain Long-Term Relations with Key African Partners

The United States has strong partnerships and good relations with many African states, but it risks appearing less active at maintaining those relationships compared with the increasing intensity of China's and, to a lesser extent, Russia's influence-seeking activities. As we observe in Chapter Two, the United States remains the top foreign aid donor in Africa, but its record of diplomatic engagements with the region has been lackluster, while China and even Russia have increased their diplomatic efforts. When it comes to maintaining the attention of African countries via high-level engagements, the United States appears to have fallen behind. The United States should identify key long-term strategic partners in Africa and sustain a level of diplomatic attention to maintain the health of existing partnerships, which may help minimize the influence that China or Russia might wield over these key actors.[13] Furthermore, during our research process, we identified a need to analyze the views of African leaders and populations on great-power dynamics in the region, but this topic was outside the scope of this study. Considering these views will not only help the U.S. government maintain good relations with African partners but also may provide it with innovative and tailored opportunities to develop stronger relations with its local partners.

---

[11] "Krupneishiye Rosiiskiye Proyekti V Afrike," 2019; Lukoil, undated-a; Lukoil, undated-b; Kolly and Cochrane, 2002.

[12] Katie Bo Williams, "AFRICOM Adds Logistics Hub in West Africa, Hinting at an Enduring US Presence," *Defense One*, February 20, 2019.

[13] Although the United States continues to be one of Africa's largest donors, our interviews with experts suggest that U.S. assistance programs often are less recognizable than those carried out by China, so the public might recognize China more as a key donor country. Thus, U.S.-supported programs likely should be publicized more. And, as noted earlier, the United States, together with other allies and partners, could promote strengthening human rights, reducing corruption, increasing accountability, and incentivizing economic development in Africa. Although these are all slow processes, they could promote stability and security (Devermont, 2020b; former U.S. Department of State official, interview with the authors, July 2021).

Recommendations for the Joint Force

Although our work suggests that it is unlikely both that the United States will engage in larger-scale military operations in Africa and that we will see a return to Cold War–style opposition between the United States and its competitors on the territories of third countries, the United States may still plausibly become involved in conflicts where China, Russia, or both are also involved, and the U.S. military needs to be prepared for a variety of engagements. With the following recommendations, we aim to provide the joint force with some strategic direction for such preparation informed by our analysis.

Maintain and Improve Access to Military or Dual-Use Infrastructure

The United States will face logistics, sustainment, and time and distance challenges in the conflict scenarios that we considered—but also in other parts of Africa. Many potential proxy conflict locations would be outside the operational range of a rotary-wing aircraft, thus requiring access to fixed-wing airstrips. Yet future U.S. military involvements in Africa likely will be air-centric because of the scale of the continent and large distances required for forces to cover, the lack of surface land communications, and the few ports (compared with the continent's land mass). The United States' ability to project power across Africa is limited by the lack of military infrastructure, as well as the overall state of civilian or dual-use port and airport infrastructure. Distributing or moving assets to and across the continent remains an expensive endeavor.[14] Although creating U.S. bases in Africa would improve U.S. posture, access, and readiness for operations there, those bases also would present new valuable targets for VEOs and even great-power competitors.[15] DoD may prefer the option of developing and maintaining access to a network of infrastructure owned and operated by host nations, partner and allied countries, or even large U.S. or multinational corporations as a means of ensuring a more flexible and resilient, even if less predictable and more in demand, resource. There are several activities that DoD can do to support that strategy. For instance, DoD should maintain access agreements and personal relations to be able to better coordinate the use of infrastructure and should continue the initiatives that are aimed at solving the air mobility issue, particularly in sub-Saharan Africa—such as helping improve partner infrastructure, equipment and maintenance capabilities, and knowledge.[16] Moreover, to improve the impact of such assistance activities, DoD may encourage regional state partners

---

[14] Brig Gen Leonard J. Kosinski of AFRICOM summarized the problem of moving equipment and materials to West Africa in 2019 as "expensive, ad hoc, and it's not efficient" (Jacqueline Feldscher, "French, U.S. Special Forces Agree to Beef Up Partnership in Africa," *Defense One*, July 9, 2021).

[15] Sudarsan Raghavan and Craig Whitlock, "A City in Niger Worries a New U.S. Drone Base Will Make It a 'Magnet' for Terrorists," *Washington Post*, November 24, 2017.

[16] Ryan McCaughan, "Air Mobility Challenges in Sub-Saharan Africa," *Journal of European, Middle Eastern, and African Affairs*, Vol. 1, No. 1, Spring 2019; and Marta Kepe, Richard Flint, and Julia Muravska, *Future Collaboration Opportunities for Light and Medium Multirole Helicopters in Europe*, Santa Monica, Calif., and Cambridge, United Kingdom: RAND Corporation, RR-3034-EDA, 2019.

to collaborate in expanding their aircraft fleets and increasing efficiencies to their sustainment and maintenance.

Maintain Working Relations with Allies and Partners

The United States has benefited from the capabilities, infrastructure access, and political relationships of its allies and partners, and the United States has in turn supported those allies and partners. Because its European allies and other partners have a significant presence across Africa, the United States could seek opportunities for cooperation in areas of mutual interest—for example, in development and humanitarian assistance and in programs aimed at supporting democratic elections, good governance, and accountability. Such cooperation may offer an additional boost to the United States' political leverage and military capabilities. In fact, the presence of allied and partner military forces, and their diplomatic and economic potential and power in the continent, may serve as a significant advantage to the United States over China and Russia. After all, France was the largest European troop contributor to Africa in 2020, while Italy, Turkey, the United Kingdom, and Portugal also each had more than 200 troops on the continent.[17] Thus, the United States could build on the example of its partnership with France, with which it signed a bilateral agreement to strengthen collaboration between their special operations forces on counterterrorism operations in the Sahel.[18] Despite France's intentions to scale down its military operations in West Africa, its political and military networks—and, according to our interviewees, influence in some aspects of airport infrastructure—are likely to continue. In addition to partnering with France, the United States may collaborate with the Nordic countries that, at least prior to the 2022 Russian invasion of Ukraine, showed the intention to assume a bigger role in the region: In 2021, Sweden took over the command of Task Force Takuba in Mali from France, and Finland announced its intention to increase its participation in crisis management in Africa.[19] In Nigeria, the United States may consider working more closely with the United Kingdom, which provides training to Nigerian troops.[20] In Mozambique, the United States may consider collaborating with the SADC mission and the EU mission, both established in 2021, as well as France, considering the proximity of Mozambique to the French territories in the Indian Ocean.

Most of the research and analysis on the U.S. competition with China and Russia in Africa is undertaken though the lens of great-power competition. As a result, existing literature pays

---

[17] The troop presence for these countries was mostly as part of their participation in different EU or UN missions (International Institute for Strategic Studies, undated).

[18] Feldscher, 2021.

[19] Former U.S. government official and think-tank expert on Africa, interview with the authors, July 2021; Swedish Armed Forces Headquarters, "Swedish Senior Position in Task Force Takuba," September 16, 2021; and "Finland Wants to Increase Crisis Management Role in Africa," Yle News, March 17, 2021. Note, however, that Task Force Takuba ceased its operations in Mali in 2022 following two military coups in the country, and the new leadership established close ties with Moscow ("EU's Takuba Force Quits Junta-Controlled Mali," France 24, July 1, 2022).

[20] Campaign Against Arms Trade, "Country Profiles: Nigeria," November 13, 2020.

little attention to the potential that resides in the United States' ability to leverage the influence and capabilities of its allies and partners, some of which may have more-established experience or presence in some regions of Africa or across some of the four influence-seeking domains (diplomacy, information, military, and economics). The experiences of allied and partner countries may be specifically pertinent to the United States' preparation for future military operations. Allies and partners have gathered significant experience not only in working with African countries but also in facing Russian PMSCs—for example, through the tensions and clashes during their deployments to UN and EU missions in CAR and through the proxy influence campaigns against France and other Western countries (such as the EU's mission in Mali).[21] Therefore, we recommend that DoD analyze the potential benefits of working with the United States' key allies and partners and seek to integrate cooperation with allies and partners in future policy development toward Africa.

Recommendations for the Department of the Air Force

The United States is unlikely to deploy larger ground-force units to Africa in the future. In view of this, the Department of the Air Force is likely to play a key role in U.S. involvement in potential future conflicts. The following recommendations provide suggestions for how the Department of the Air Force can prepare for these roles.

Prepare for Increased and Potentially Shifting Demand for U.S. Air Force Assets

Airpower is likely to remain a key asset in countering VEOs in Africa. The role of the U.S. Air Force will continue and potentially even increase, as very few African countries have meaningful air assets. Air campaigns fit with the overall U.S. policy of indirect military engagement and limited-objective campaigns in Africa, offering the ability to carry out limited-liability, limited-objective campaigns against VEOs in complex security environments.[22]

In the future, the Department of the Air Force will need to not only continue to resource this counter-VEO requirement but also ensure that these assets can meet the demands of great-power competition. As explored in the Nigeria and Mozambique analyses, countering terrorism is one of the more plausible scenarios for the United States to militarily bump against China or Russia. If this occurs, the United States will need to ensure that the assets that it deploys to counter VEOs can simultaneously monitor; deconflict; and, if necessary, defend themselves against rival great powers.

---

[21] For example, in order to manage escalation in a security situation in 2021, the UN Multidimensional Integrated Stabilization Mission in CAR had to force the heavily armed Wagner Group to return to its base (Forku, 2021; and "Germany, France Warn Mali over Russian Mercenary Deal," EURACTIV, September 16, 2021).

[22] Adam R. Grissom and Karl P. Mueller, "Airpower in Counter-Terrorist Operations: Balancing Objectives and Risks," *The Future of Air Power*, SEGMA conference proceedings, November 2017.

Consequently, if the United States decides to take a more active military role in Africa (such as we identify in the Nigeria and Mozambique scenarios), the U.S. Air Force may need to prepare for assisting the movement of troops not only from outside Africa to the continent but also within the continent, often in the conditions of challenging ground infrastructure. Therefore, the United States will need to ensure that the necessary capabilities are available in existing regional hubs or potentially even create new hubs. For example, the West African Logistics Network at the Kotoka Airport in Ghana, where the 405th Army Field Support Brigade provides traffic and cargo management, is designed to support 300 soldiers for up to 30 days.[23]

The U.S. Air Force may expect an increased demand for its airborne ISR assets and its air mobility support, air defense, vertical lift, aerial firepower, and precision-strike capabilities, and that demand may come from more locations across the continent. Given that many of the more plausible scenarios we identified revolve around counterterrorism, this might drive continued demand for platforms—such as the MQ-9As—that have been critical to the global war on terrorism but that might not be as important in great-power conflicts that are fought at a higher end of warfare. Thus, the Department of the Air Force should be judicious before divesting from these assets, even as it moves to focus on great-power competition.

Prepare for Multifaceted Operational Challenges, Including Deconfliction and Harassment, in Future Conflicts That May Involve China and Russia

In a future conflict in Africa, the U.S. military likely could face deconfliction issues with forces from China, Russia, or both. Similar issues were experienced, for example, in Djibouti, where U.S. and PLA forces needed to deconflict with each other and with civilian users for access to airspace and the civilian airstrip. These issues may repeat themselves in other countries, particularly ones with underdeveloped airport infrastructure and airspace management traditions. To solve this issue, the Department of the Air Force may consider training airspace managers and helping develop airstrips in locations that it deems strategically important. It may also leverage allied and partner resources in the region, particularly of the allies that are widely present or have long-standing relations with African militaries, as France does.

The African theater of operations may be a rather congested and even political theater with numerous actors and different interests and a theater that requires more-efficient, rapid, and robust command and control. There may be fog and friction (i.e., uncertainty and unexpected events that make easy tasks more difficult) between the forces on the ground and air assets in unconventional operations that involve special operations forces and between U.S. forces and the forces of different partners. As a result, it is imperative to be able to communicate and to share data not only among different U.S. forces but also with partners and

---

[23] 405th Army Field Support Brigade, 2018.

allies.[24] Moreover, recent examples show that the United States is likely to be the provider of command and control capabilities—thus requiring the U.S. Air Force to continue investing in its ability to ensure communications and data exchange with other U.S. military service representatives and local, regional, European, and other partners in Africa.

Final Thoughts

Our analysis suggests that, at least in the countries that we considered in our scenario analyses, Cold War–style proxy warfare or limited conflicts in which African actors firmly align with the United States, Russia, or China are unlikely. However, both China and Russia are increasingly growing their influence in Africa, as their geopolitical and economic interests are expanding. Although, at present, the United States, China, and Russia do not have the expedient motivation to engage in a proxy conflict with each other, these interests could serve as a motivation or a pretext for such engagements in the future. Even in the most-plausible scenarios for conflicts where the three great powers could become engaged, the powers are likely to support the same actor in a fight against VEOs and likely would face each other in incidents of harassment or situations that would require deconfliction.

China's and Russia's influence in Africa is only growing, while that of the United States has been stagnating in many respects. There are several steps that the U.S. government, the joint force, and the Department of the Air Force could take to not only maintain but also improve the United States' position in Africa and to prepare for competition and potential great-power proxy conflict in Africa. These steps are largely centered on developing a clear strategic vision for U.S.-Africa relations across the diplomatic, informational, military, and economic domains; cultivating relations with African partners and partners from non-African countries that are present in the region; ensuring the availability of and access to personnel, equipment, and infrastructure resources; and preparing for multifaceted operational challenges.

---

[24] Damon Matlock, Jonathan Gaustad, Jason Scott, and Danielle J. Bales, "Command and Control in Africa: Three Case Studies Before and After Tactical C2," *Air & Space Power Journal*, July–August 2014.

Details on the Competition-Potential and Conflict-Potential Indices

This appendix presents more-detailed information about the competition-potential index and the conflict-potential index discussed in Chapter Two.

Competition Potential

Table A.1 summarizes the data and sources used to measure each of the three great powers' involvement or influence-seeking in each country, across each of the four instruments of national power (diplomacy, information, military, economics). Binary variables—such as the existence of an embassy in a country—were assigned a value of 1 if the variable was present or 0 if it was absent.

To synthesize this broad set of variables, we constructed metrics, or *indices*, measuring great-power involvement in each of four domains (i.e., diplomacy, information, military, and economics) and combined them into an overall index for competition potential.[1] Next, we describe how we constructed the five indices for competition potential—that is, for each domain and overall.

Standardizing Variables

Each variable was standardized—that is, converted into z-scores for each country and great-power pair in the region for any given variable—as follows:

$$Z_{ij} = \frac{x_{ij} - \mu}{\sigma}.$$

That is, for each country and great-power pair ij, a z-score for a given variable x measures standard deviations (σ) above or below a mean value (μ) of x across all countries i in the region for

---

[1] For a similar approach, see Daniel Kaufmann, Aart Kraay, and Massimo Mastruzzi, "Governance Matters VIII: Aggregate and Individual Governance Indicators, 1996–2008," World Bank Policy Research Working Paper No. 4978, June 29, 2009, pp. 7–19.

TABLE A.1

Measuring Influence-Seeking and Potential for Competition: Summary of Variables

Variable	Description	Sources
Diplomacy		
Foreign aid and assistance	Total aid or assistance reported to the country for the most recent year available ($)	
	• U.S.: 2019 disbursements of total foreign assistance, including military and economic assistance	ForeignAssistance.gov, 2022; USAID, 2021a.
	• China: Official Development Assistance for the latest year available between 2000 and 2014	AidData, "China's Global Development Footprint," webpage, undated.
	• Russia: Official Development Assistance (total net) for the latest year available between 2012 and 2019	Organisation for Economic Co-operation and Development, undated.
High-level visits	Total visits by heads of state, top foreign policy officials, and top military officials (for the U.S.) between 2006 and 2020 (aggregated number of visits)	
	• U.S.: Visits by the President, Secretary of State, and Secretary of Defense	Office of the Historian, "Travels Abroad of the Secretary of State," webpage, U.S. Department of State, undated-b; and DoD, "Releases," webpage, undated.
	• China: Visits by the President, Prime Minister, and Minister of Foreign Affairs	Ministry of Foreign Affairs of the People's Republic of China, "Top Stories," webpage, undated-b; we supplemented that search by searching Chinese and regional news sources.
	• Russia: Visits by the President, Prime Minister, and Minister of Foreign Affairs	Ministry of Foreign Affairs of the Russian Federation, "Russia in International Relations," webpage, undated; and President of Russia, "Events," webpage, undated.
Embassy	Existence of an embassy in the country (binary)	
	• Verified for each country and great-power pair individually using official state information • For Africa, looked at resident embassies	U.S. Department of State, "Websites of U.S. Embassies, Consulates, and Diplomatic Missions," webpage, undated; Ministry of Foreign Affairs of the People's Republic of China, "Chinese Embassies," webpage, undated-a; Ministry of Foreign Affairs of the Russian Federation, undated; and the website of the Russian embassy in each country.

Table A.1—Continued

Variable	Description	Sources
Visa-free travel	Visa-free travel from each great power to and from the country (two binary variables)	
	• Verified for each country and great-power pair individually using official state information	U.S. Department of State, undated; Ministry of Foreign Affairs of the People's Republic of China, undated-a; Ministry of Foreign Affairs of the Russian Federation, undated; and the website of the Russian embassy in each country.

Information

State-sponsored media	Presence of each great power's state-sponsored media (binary)	
	• U.S.: Presence of Voice of America bureaus, Middle East Broadcasting Networks bureaus, transmitters, FM frequencies, or contracts with local radio or television affiliates that retranslate	Voice of America, undated; and U.S. Agency for Global Media, "Middle East Broadcasting Networks," webpage, undated.
	• China: Presence of the China Global Television Network (i.e., China Central Television's international division), China Radio International, China Daily, or Xinhua bureaus	China Global Television Network [القناة العربية للتبشك تلفزيون الصين الدولية], "Who We Are" ["من نحن"], webpage, undated; China Central Television, "List of Overseas Bureaus," webpage, undated; China Culture, "Xinhua News Agency," webpage, undated; Wasserman and Madrid-Morales, 2018; and Leslie, 2016; we supplemented these sources with media reports.
	• Russia: Presence of cooperation agreements signed by state-controlled media (RT, Sputnik, or TASS) with local media outlets and news agencies	Bugayova and Barros, 2020; we supplemented this source with news sources.

Military

Involvement in post–Cold War conflicts	Participation in intra- or inter-state conflicts in the country between 1991 and 2021 (binary)	
	• Based on data on actors in conflicts between 1991 and 2021	Uppsala Conflict Data Program, undated (data are from 1975 to 2020)—in particular, the External Support Dataset provides data on the existence, type, and provider of external support for all warring parties (actors) coded as active in Uppsala Conflict Data Program data, on an annual basis for 1989–2011, for Africa (see Högbladh, Pettersson, and Themnér, 2011)—and Dangerous Companions Project, undated.[a] We supplemented these sources with media reports.

Table A.1—Continued

Variable	Description	Sources
Arms exports	Volume of exports to the country based on SIPRI's trend-indicator value of exports • U.S.: 2014–2019 • China: 2014–2018 • Russia: 2014–2018	SIPRI, undated-a; and SIPRI, "SIPRI Arms Transfers Database—Methodology," webpage, undated-b.[b]
Presence of military forces and bases	Each great power's force presence in the country between 2014 and 2020 (number of person-years)	International Institute for Strategic Studies, *The Military Balance*, London, Vols. 114–120, 2014–2020.
Military agreements	Presence of active military or defense cooperation agreements (binary)[c]	Brandon J. Kinne, "Defense Cooperation Agreement Dataset," *Journal of Conflict Resolution*, Vol. 64, No. 4, 2020; Office of Treaty Affairs, "Treaties in Force: A List of Treaties and Other International Agreements of the United States in Force on January 1, 2020," U.S. Department of State, 2021; Government of the Russian Federation, "Mezhdunorodniye Dogovori Roisiiskoi Federacii" ["International Agreements of the Russian Federation"], database, undated; Jakob Hedenskog, "Russia Is Stepping Up Its Military Cooperation in Africa," Swedish Defence Research Agency, December 2018; and Shinn, 2020.
Military exercises	Total number of exercises performed with the country between 2014 and 2020	International Institute for Strategic Studies, 2014–2020.
PMSCs	Presence of PMSCs in the country (binary) • U.S.: Compiled based on the websites of major PMSCs • China and Russia: Compiled for each country and great-power pair based on various research, investigative, and media sources	 Aning, Jaye, and Atuobi, 2008; and the websites of Constellis, Continuity Global Solutions, DynCorp, ISC Security, MPRI, and Reed International. Arduino, 2020; Paul Nantulya, "Chinese Security Contractors in Africa," Carnegie Endowment for International Peace, October 8, 2020; Legarda and Nouwens, 2018; R. Kim Cragin and Lachlan MacKenzie, "Russia's Escalating Use of Private Military Companies in Africa," Institute for National Strategic Studies, November 24, 2020; "V Afrike Obyavilis Noviye Naemniki Vmesto CHVK Vagnera" ["New Mercenaries Have Appeared in Africa Instead of OMC Wagner"], Lenta.ru, April 10, 2020; Gostev, 2019; Brian Katz, Seth G. Jones, Catrina Doxsee, and Nicholas Harrington, "Moscow's Mercenary Wars: The Expansion of Russian Private Military Companies," Center for Strategic and International Studies, September 2020; and Sukhankin, 2020c. We supplemented these sources by reviewing some shorter Chinese publications and Russian media reports.

Table A.1—Continued

Variable	Description	Sources
Military access	Access to the country (standing agreement or access granted in practice) (binary)	
	• U.S.: Presence of U.S. military installations or publicly known cooperative security locations	Townsend, 2020; Teil, 2018; Madelene Lindström, "The United States—From Counter-Terrorism to Great Power Competition in Africa?" Swedish Defence Research Institute, FOI Memo 6817, August 2019; and Lostumbo et al., 2013. We supplemented these sources by reviewing media reports.
	• China: Port visits by the PLA Navy[d]	DoD, *Assessment on U.S. Defense Implications of China's Expanding Global Access*, Washington, D.C., December 2018b.
	• Russia: Access to ports or air bases	We identified naval port calls and access to ports by searching English- and Russian-language press for each country.

Economics

Trade volume	Trade volume ($)	
	• World Bank's World Integrated Trade Solution, merchandise trade, for 2018, which was the most recent common year available	World Integrated Trade Solution, undated-a, data set on U.S., Chinese, and Russian trade activity in Africa, 2000–2018.
Investment	Foreign direct investment position (U.S. and Russia), foreign investments (China) ($)	U.S. Bureau of Economic Analysis, "U.S. Direct Investment Position Abroad on a Historical-Cost Basis," 2019; American Enterprise Institute and Heritage Foundation, undated (aggregate data for 2005–2020); and International Monetary Fund, "Coordinated Direct Investment Survey," webpage, undated (data for most recent year available, either 2018 or 2019).
Critical infrastructure	Presence of major Russian companies in critical infrastructure sectors (binary)	
	• Russia only: Investigated for each country individually through news reports and public corporate information, focusing on key Russian companies operating in the relevant sectors (energy, raw materials, transport, financial services, communications)	We reviewed news and research reports on Russian companies in Africa and supplemented that research by reviewing the websites of key Russian companies—notably, Rosatom, Lukoil, Gazprom, Transneft, Alrosa, Rusal, Norilsk Nickel, Severstal, Nordgold, Ferrum Mining, and Uralkali. In addition, we reviewed news sources in English, Russian, and French.

[a] The Dangerous Companions Project captures data on international support for non-state armed groups that are "engaged in violent conflict against one or more governments within or outside the state(s) they live." This support

takes many forms, such as funds, safe havens, sanctuary, arms, logistics, and transportation of such resources as well as diplomatic support from states, diaspora groups, non-governmental organizations (NGO), inter-governmental organizations (IGO), non-state armed groups, and foreign political parties (Dangerous Companions Project, undated).

Table A.1—Continued

Variable	Description	Sources

b SIPRI's trend-indicator value is

    based on the known unit production costs of a core set of weapons and is intended to represent the transfer of military resources rather than the financial value of the transfer. . . . SIPRI calculates the volume of transfers to, from and between all parties using the [trend-indicator-value] and the number of weapon systems or subsystems delivered in a given year. This data is intended to provide a common unit to allow the measurement [of] trends in the flow of arms to particular countries and regions over time (SIPRI, undated-b).

c To determine what counts as a military agreement, we sought to follow the Correlates of War Project's Defense Cooperation Agreement Dataset, which defines *bilateral defense cooperation agreements* as "treaties that coordinate and institutionalize routine, day-to-day defense co-operation between signatories" (Kinne, 2020). Where we sought to identify such agreements outside this data set, we excluded agreements limited to arms sales and matters pertaining more to law enforcement than military cooperation.

d PLA Navy visits were coded in bands from 0 to 4, where 0 = no visits to the country; 1 = 1 to 5 visits; 2 = 6 to 10 visits; 3 = 11 to 15 visits; and 4 = 15+ visits.

that great power *j*. For example, the *z*-scores for trade between Kenya and China indicate how much trade there is between those countries, relative to China's trade with all other countries in Africa. We then converted the *z*-scores into percentiles, for easier interpretation.

Although our selection of data sources and variables was driven in part by the need to minimize missing data, some missingness is inevitable. Missing data were handled as follows: In the few cases when it was highly likely, based on other sources, that the value should be zero—for example, because we located no references to China or Russia sending foreign aid to a particular country—the missing value was treated as zero.[2] In all other cases, missing values remained missing, and the observation was excluded from generating the *z*-score for observations on that variable.

Constructing the Influence-Seeking Indices

All standardized variables capturing influence-seeking activities in *each domain* (diplomacy, information, military, and economics) for each of the three great powers were then aggregated into an influence-seeking index, and each variable was accorded an equal weight, subject to some exceptions. That is, the *z*-scores were multiplied by the reciprocal of the number of variables in each dimension and summed for each country and great-power pair.[3] For example, each of the four variables in the diplomatic domain was weighted equally—as one-fourth—in the index that captures relative diplomatic involvement for each power in each country.

---

[2] For example, we treated Chinese foreign aid to Eswatini as a zero because Eswatini recognizes Taiwan and maintains no official relations with Beijing.

[3] In the diplomatic dimension, we counted (1) the visa-free travel from each competing power to each country and (2) the visa-free travel in the reverse direction together as one variable. That is, the two sets of *z*-scores were weighted as one. For Russia, its direct investment position and critical infrastructure investments were also weighted together as a single variable. This is because both U.S. and Chinese direct investment data include critical infrastructure, whereas Russia's official direct investment position data are less reliable or complete.

All standardized variables *across the four domains* were also combined into an index that captures overall influence-seeking *for each great power*, also weighting each variable equally.

Missing data for any variables for any country and great-power pair reduced the number of variables employed to construct the weighted index for that pair. For example, if foreign aid data from China were missing for a given country, the index was produced by averaging z-scores for the three nonmissing variables (i.e., high-level visits, presence of an embassy, visa-free travel) equally. However, for the countries for which foreign aid was present, all four z-scores were averaged.[4]

We chose to weight *each variable* equally—rather than *each of the four domains* equally—for the following reasons: Overall, we do not have strong theoretical reasons to prejudge that any single variable matters more than any other in creating the potential for competition. That is, we want to avoid assumptions that, for example, the volume of trade matters more or less than the volume of diplomatic visits or military exercises in shaping the intensity of strategic competition in the future. Thus, we do not weight the diplomacy, information, military, and economics categories equally, as this would, in effect, suggest that each military variable is less informative about great-power interests than the single variable in the informational domain is. Therefore, our overall index is most influenced by military variables (of which we had seven) and least influenced by informational variables (of which we had only one). The emphasis on military or security forms of influence-seeking is partly a function of data availability, reflecting the fact that we were able to gather more-quantifiable information about the military domain than about the informational domain. However, given that the focus of this study is ultimately on the potential for involvement in conflicts, an index that is more influenced by military factors also appears justifiable. The analysis of each of the four domains separately helps ensure that we do not simply neglect countries where the potential for economic or informational competition, for example, is relatively high but military competition is low.

Constructing the Competition-Potential Indices

For *each domain*, the index that captures the potential for competition in each country was calculated by summing the influence-seeking indices for involvement in that domain for each of the three great powers. For example, in Table A.2, the diplomatic influence-seeking indices for the three great powers add up to produce a competition-potential index of 2.05 for Kenya in the diplomatic domain.

Tables A.2 through A.5 report results for each of the four domains, respectively. Specifically, the tables show the influence-seeking indices for each African country and great-power pair, as well as the competition-potential index for each African country in that domain. The countries are sorted from highest to lowest potential for competition.

---

[4] Although this introduces a degree of non-comparability in the indices for each domain and great power, we concluded that this solution was preferable to the alternatives, such as imputing values, assigning zero to the missing cell, or not using otherwise informative data because such information was not available for every single country in a region.

Summing the overall influence-seeking indices for *all three powers* across *all four domains* produces the overall competition-potential index for each country in the region. We do not list these scores separately in this appendix, but the results are shown in Figure 2.5.

TABLE A.2

Diplomatic Influence-Seeking and Competition Potential in Africa

Country	Influence-Seeking Index, by Great Power			Competition-Potential Index
	United States	China	Russia	
Kenya	0.80	0.66	0.60	2.05
Ethiopia	0.76	0.56	0.68	1.99
South Africa	0.70	0.58	0.68	1.96
Tanzania	0.72	0.65	0.55	1.92
Mozambique	0.57	0.58	0.75	1.91
Uganda	0.66	0.57	0.62	1.85
Zimbabwe	0.52	0.64	0.64	1.80
Nigeria	0.72	0.54	0.53	1.79
Tunisia	0.68	0.48	0.60	1.76
Namibia	0.43	0.71	0.61	1.74
Senegal	0.59	0.58	0.53	1.70
DRC	0.67	0.45	0.57	1.69
Morocco	0.54	0.47	0.67	1.68
Rwanda	0.52	0.60	0.55	1.68
Zambia	0.57	0.53	0.56	1.67
Madagascar	0.45	0.48	0.70	1.63
Somalia	0.65	0.48	0.48	1.61
Angola	0.44	0.56	0.57	1.58
Sierra Leone	0.42	0.67	0.47	1.56
Guinea	0.34	0.53	0.64	1.51
Sudan	0.46	0.40	0.63	1.49
Gabon	0.41	0.53	0.53	1.47
Algeria	0.51	0.36	0.59	1.46
Mauritania	0.43	0.49	0.53	1.46
Côte d'Ivoire	0.61	0.42	0.41	1.45
Libya	0.50	0.36	0.57	1.44

Table A.2—Continued

Country	Influence-Seeking Index, by Great Power			Competition-Potential Index
	United States	China	Russia	
Ghana	0.52	0.44	0.44	1.40
Guinea Bissau	0.42	0.48	0.49	1.39
Djibouti	0.50	0.48	0.39	1.37
Mali	0.41	0.44	0.51	1.36
Botswana	0.43	0.42	0.49	1.34
CAR	0.46	0.39	0.49	1.33
South Sudan	0.48	0.37	0.49	1.33
Chad	0.43	0.43	0.45	1.31
Malawi	0.56	0.52	0.23	1.31
Congo	0.34	0.48	0.49	1.30
Togo	0.42	0.53	0.32	1.27
Benin	0.45	0.42	0.40	1.26
Cameroon	0.38	0.48	0.41	1.26
Niger	0.41	0.56	0.27	1.24
Burundi	0.35	0.41	0.47	1.23
Liberia	0.56	0.44	0.22	1.22
Eritrea	0.33	0.39	0.47	1.19
Equatorial Guinea	0.41	0.44	0.32	1.18
Lesotho	0.43	0.39	0.33	1.14
Gambia	0.42	0.41	0.32	1.14
Burkina Faso	0.45	0.36	0.28	1.09
Eswatini	0.43	0.23	0.30	0.95

TABLE A.3

Informational Influence-Seeking and Competition Potential in Africa

Country	Influence-Seeking Index, by Great Power			Competition-Potential Index
	United States	China	Russia	
South Africa	0.61	0.93	0.99	2.54
Ghana	0.61	0.93	0.35	1.89
Kenya	0.61	0.93	0.35	1.89
Nigeria	0.61	0.93	0.35	1.89
Senegal	0.61	0.93	0.35	1.89
Togo	0.61	0.93	0.35	1.89
Uganda	0.61	0.93	0.35	1.89
Algeria	0.61	0.26	0.99	1.86
DRC	0.61	0.26	0.99	1.86
Côte d'Ivoire	0.61	0.26	0.99	1.86
Eritrea	0.61	0.26	0.99	1.86
Morocco	0.61	0.26	0.99	1.86
Zambia	0.00	0.93	0.35	1.28
Zimbabwe	0.00	0.93	0.35	1.28
Congo	0.00	0.26	0.99	1.25
Angola	0.61	0.26	0.35	1.22
Benin	0.61	0.26	0.35	1.22
Botswana	0.61	0.26	0.35	1.22
Burkina Faso	0.61	0.26	0.35	1.22
Burundi	0.61	0.26	0.35	1.22
Cameroon	0.61	0.26	0.35	1.22
CAR	0.61	0.26	0.35	1.22
Chad	0.61	0.26	0.35	1.22
Djibouti	0.61	0.26	0.35	1.22
Equatorial Guinea	0.61	0.26	0.35	1.22
Eswatini	0.61	0.26	0.35	1.22
Ethiopia	0.61	0.26	0.35	1.22
Gabon	0.61	0.26	0.35	1.22
Gambia	0.61	0.26	0.35	1.22

Table A.3—Continued

Country	Influence-Seeking Index, by Great Power			Competition-Potential Index
	United States	China	Russia	
Guinea	0.61	0.26	0.35	1.22
Guinea Bissau	0.61	0.26	0.35	1.22
Lesotho	0.61	0.26	0.35	1.22
Liberia	0.61	0.26	0.35	1.22
Libya	0.61	0.26	0.35	1.22
Madagascar	0.61	0.26	0.35	1.22
Malawi	0.61	0.26	0.35	1.22
Mali	0.61	0.26	0.35	1.22
Mauritania	0.61	0.26	0.35	1.22
Mozambique	0.61	0.26	0.35	1.22
Namibia	0.61	0.26	0.35	1.22
Niger	0.61	0.26	0.35	1.22
Rwanda	0.61	0.26	0.35	1.22
Sierra Leone	0.61	0.26	0.35	1.22
Somalia	0.61	0.26	0.35	1.22
South Sudan	0.61	0.26	0.35	1.22
Tanzania	0.61	0.26	0.35	1.22
Tunisia	0.61	0.26	0.35	1.22
Sudan	0.00	0.26	0.35	0.61

TABLE A.4

Military Influence-Seeking and Competition Potential in Africa

Country	Influence-Seeking Index, by Great Power			Competition-Potential Index
	United States	China	Russia	
Sudan	0.61	0.84	0.82	2.27
Nigeria	0.55	0.77	0.62	1.93
South Africa	0.47	0.70	0.70	1.87
Senegal	0.71	0.53	0.51	1.75
Angola	0.56	0.55	0.64	1.75
Mozambique	0.49	0.61	0.60	1.71
Tanzania	0.45	0.72	0.50	1.68
Mali	0.55	0.59	0.52	1.66
Algeria	0.46	0.70	0.50	1.66
Kenya	0.70	0.53	0.42	1.64
DRC	0.54	0.49	0.60	1.63
Gabon	0.49	0.62	0.51	1.62
Morocco	0.60	0.60	0.41	1.62
Cameroon	0.64	0.55	0.42	1.61
Somalia	0.67	0.51	0.42	1.60
Niger	0.75	0.40	0.42	1.57
Djibouti	0.57	0.67	0.32	1.55
Chad	0.61	0.42	0.51	1.54
Libya	0.49	0.42	0.60	1.51
CAR	0.40	0.42	0.65	1.46
Guinea	0.34	0.51	0.60	1.46
Uganda	0.63	0.42	0.42	1.46
Congo	0.43	0.51	0.51	1.45
Côte d'Ivoire	0.47	0.42	0.56	1.45
Ghana	0.60	0.42	0.42	1.44
Zimbabwe	0.39	0.51	0.51	1.42
South Sudan	0.39	0.51	0.50	1.40
Liberia	0.56	0.38	0.44	1.38
Ethiopia	0.42	0.52	0.42	1.36

Table A.4—Continued

Country	Influence-Seeking Index, by Great Power			Competition-Potential Index
	United States	China	Russia	
Sierra Leone	0.43	0.42	0.51	1.35
Madagascar	0.33	0.42	0.60	1.35
Tunisia	0.56	0.32	0.42	1.30
Rwanda	0.45	0.32	0.52	1.29
Mauritania	0.61	0.35	0.32	1.27
Namibia	0.32	0.53	0.42	1.26
Zambia	0.40	0.45	0.42	1.26
Burundi	0.53	0.32	0.42	1.26
Gambia	0.32	0.42	0.51	1.25
Burkina Faso	0.48	0.32	0.42	1.22
Benin	0.48	0.32	0.42	1.22
Guinea Bissau	0.42	0.32	0.42	1.15
Botswana	0.49	0.32	0.32	1.13
Eritrea	0.29	0.42	0.42	1.13
Togo	0.48	0.32	0.32	1.12
Equatorial Guinea	0.43	0.32	0.32	1.07
Malawi	0.41	0.32	0.32	1.04
Lesotho	0.29	0.32	0.42	1.03
Eswatini	0.29	0.32	0.32	0.93

TABLE A.5

Economic Influence-Seeking and Competition Potential in Africa

Country	Influence-Seeking Index, by Great Power			Competition-Potential Index
	United States	China	Russia	
Algeria	0.94	0.88	0.93	2.75
South Africa	1.00	0.90	0.79	2.69
Nigeria	1.00	0.97	0.69	2.66
Angola	0.61	0.99	0.50	2.10
Morocco	0.69	0.43	0.92	2.03
Ghana	0.64	0.73	0.54	1.91
Kenya	0.47	0.74	0.58	1.79
Tanzania	0.55	0.65	0.55	1.75
Ethiopia	0.49	0.72	0.51	1.72
DRC	0.37	0.79	0.49	1.64
Libya	0.59	0.48	0.57	1.63
Congo	0.41	0.70	0.49	1.60
Zambia	0.38	0.73	0.49	1.60
Guinea	0.39	0.63	0.52	1.54
Mozambique	0.43	0.56	0.51	1.50
Sudan	0.35	0.48	0.62	1.46
Côte d'Ivoire	0.48	0.42	0.55	1.46
Cameroon	0.38	0.56	0.51	1.45
Senegal	0.38	0.42	0.64	1.44
Zimbabwe	0.36	0.53	0.50	1.39
Uganda	0.36	0.48	0.50	1.35
Tunisia	0.48	0.31	0.53	1.32
Gabon	0.40	0.39	0.52	1.30
Burkina Faso	0.35	0.27	0.64	1.26
Madagascar	0.43	0.33	0.49	1.25
Sierra Leone	0.36	0.40	0.48	1.24
South Sudan	0.35	0.41	0.48	1.24
Namibia	0.38	0.35	0.49	1.22
Equatorial Guinea	0.51	0.39	0.31	1.22

Table A.5—Continued

Country	Influence-Seeking Index, by Great Power			Competition-Potential Index
	United States	China	Russia	
Liberia	0.39	0.33	0.48	1.19
Botswana	0.39	0.30	0.49	1.18
Chad	0.39	0.46	0.31	1.16
Rwanda	0.35	0.29	0.49	1.14
Niger	0.35	0.47	0.31	1.13
Gambia	0.35	0.27	0.48	1.11
Togo	0.40	0.33	0.37	1.10
CAR	0.35	0.26	0.48	1.09
Benin	0.37	0.37	0.32	1.05
Djibouti	0.36	0.34	0.33	1.03
Mauritania	0.36	0.33	0.32	1.02
Mali	0.35	0.32	0.32	1.00
Malawi	0.36	0.28	0.34	0.98
Lesotho	0.38	0.27	0.31	0.96
Eritrea	0.35	0.28	0.32	0.94
Somalia	0.35	0.28	0.32	0.94
Guinea Bissau	0.35	0.27	0.31	0.93
Burundi	0.35	0.26	0.32	0.93
Eswatini	0.35	0.22	0.31	0.88

Internal Conflict Potential

Our assessment of the potential for internal conflict erupting in each of the countries relative to the rest of the region relied on Uppsala University's ViEWS model and data. In particular, we used a country-level predicted probability that at least one of the three conflict outcomes (armed conflict involving states and rebel groups, armed conflict between non-state actors, and violence against civilians) would occur in a country-month for the forthcoming 36 months (starting with April 2021). Because our main interest is in identifying which countries are at relatively greater risk of conflict than others—rather than by *how much* one country's risk is greater than another's—we converted predicted probabilities into ordinal rankings. To do so, we averaged the monthly predicted probabilities of at least one of the conflict outcomes occurring in each country over the available 36 months. Table A.6 presents those averaged probabilities of conflict and the corresponding rank for each country, which we used to generate Figure 2.8 in Chapter Two.

TABLE A.6
Conflict Potential

Country	Overall Conflict-Potential Ranking	Probability of Conflict
Nigeria	1	0.96
DRC	2	0.95
Somalia	3	0.90
Mali	4	0.76
Cameroon	5	0.71
Burkina Faso	6	0.67
South Sudan	7	0.67
Mozambique	8	0.61
Sudan	9	0.59
Ethiopia	10	0.57
CAR	11	0.51
Libya	12	0.49
Niger	13	0.44
Chad	14	0.28
Kenya	15	0.24
Burundi	16	0.22
Uganda	17	0.19
South Africa	18	0.15
Tunisia	19	0.14
Tanzania	20	0.14
Côte d'Ivoire	21	0.12
Ghana	22	0.11
Angola	23	0.11
Zimbabwe	24	0.11
Congo	25	0.10
Algeria	26	0.10

Table A.6—Continued

Country	Overall Conflict-Potential Ranking	Probability of Conflict
Malawi	27	0.10
Djibouti	28	0.09
Rwanda	29	0.08
Benin	30	0.08
Morocco	31	0.08
Guinea	32	0.08
Mauritania	33	0.08
Madagascar	34	0.08
Equatorial Guinea	35	0.07
Togo	36	0.07
Zambia	37	0.07
Senegal	38	0.07
Eritrea	39	0.07
Sierra Leone	40	0.07
Guinea-Bissau	41	0.06
Eswatini	42	0.06
Liberia	43	0.06
Gabon	44	0.05
Botswana	45	0.05
Namibia	46	0.04
Lesotho	47	0.04
Gambia	48	0.03

SOURCE: ViEWS: The Violence Early-Warning System, undated (data from 2021). We are grateful to the ViEWS team for providing the underlying data.

Abbreviations

AFRICOM	U.S. Africa Command
ASWJ	Ansar al-Sunna Wa Jamma
CAR	Central African Republic
COVID-19	coronavirus disease 2019
DoD	U.S. Department of Defense
DRC	Democratic Republic of the Congo
EU	European Union
FRELIMO	Frente de Libertação de Moçambique
GDP	gross domestic product
ISR	intelligence, surveillance, and reconnaissance
ISWAP	Islamic State – West Africa Province
NATO	North Atlantic Treaty Organization
PLA	People's Liberation Army
PMSC	private military and security company
RENAMO	Resistência Nacional Moçambicana
SADC	Southern African Development Community
SIPRI	Stockholm International Peace Research Institute
UAE	United Arab Emirates
UN	United Nations
USAID	U.S. Agency for International Development
VEO	violent extremist organization
ViEWS	Violence Early-Warning System

References

Unless otherwise indicated, the authors of this report provided the translations of bibliographic details for the non-English sources included in this report. To support conventions for alphabetizing, sources in Chinese are introduced with and organized according to their English translations. The original rendering in Chinese appears in brackets after the English translation.

"350,000 Killed, 3M Displaced in Nigeria, Boko Haram Conflict," *The Star Democrat*, July 4, 2021.

405th Army Field Support Brigade, "405th Army Field Support Brigade LOGCAP Mission on the African Continent Reaches Another Milestone," press release, December 13, 2018.

Adeniyi, Adesoji, "Peacekeeping Contributor Profile: Nigeria," Providing for Peacekeeping, April 24, 2015.

Africa Center for Strategic Studies, "Russian Disinformation Campaigns Target Africa: An Interview with Shelby Grossman," February 18, 2020.

Africa Oil Week, "Understanding Chinese Investment in African Oil and Gas," October 7, 2019.

African Development Bank and African Development Fund, *Mozambique Country Strategy Paper 2018–2022: Supporting Mozambique Towards the High5S*, Abidjan, Côte d'Ivoire, June 2018.

African Union, *African Trade Statistics: 2020 Yearbook*, Addis Ababa, August 2020.

"African Union Prioritizes Russia's Role in Ensuring Stability in Africa," TASS, May 5, 2021.

AFRICOM—*See* U.S. Africa Command.

Agence Africaine de Presse, "Mozambique Eyeing Russian Investment in Hydrocarbons, Mining," Club of Mozambique, October 23, 2019.

Agubamah, Edgar, "Nigeria-Russia Relations: After and Now," *European Scientific Journal*, Vol. 10, No. 14, May 2014, pp. 193–204.

AidData, "China's Global Development Footprint," webpage, undated. As of August 27, 2021: https://www.aiddata.org/china-official-finance

AIM, "Nyusi Appoints 'Contact Group' for Peace Talks," Club of Mozambique, March 2, 2017.

———, "Mozambique: 'Renamo Military Junta' Has New Leader—AIM," Club of Mozambique, February 28, 2022.

Akintayo, OpeOluwani, "Lukoil to Buy Fresh Stake off Chevron's Oil Block in Nigeria," Sweet Crude Reports, December 7, 2019.

Alden, Chris, "Beijing's Security Plans Beyond Djibouti and the Horn," Italian Institute for International Political Studies, September 27, 2018.

Ali, Idrees, "U.S. Special Forces Rescue American Held in Nigeria: Officials," Reuters, October 31, 2020.

Ali, Idrees, and Phil Stewart, "U.S. Troops Injured in Russian Vehicle Collision in Syria, U.S. Officials Say," Reuters, August 26, 2020.

Allison, Simon, "Russia in Africa: Soft Power Comes with Hard Edges," *Mail & Guardian*, October 24, 2019.

American Enterprise Institute and Heritage Foundation, "China Global Investment Tracker," webpage, undated. As of June 3, 2021:
https://www.aei.org/china-global-investment-tracker

Amnesty International, "Nigeria: At Least 150 Peaceful Pro-Biafra Activists Killed in Chilling Crackdown," November 24, 2016.

———, "Niger Delta Negligence," webpage, March 2018. As of June 31, 2021:
https://www.amnesty.org/en/latest/news/2018/03/niger-delta-oil-spills-decoders

Anderson, Gail, "Shell to Divest Its Entire Nigeria Joint Venture Portfolio," Wood Mackenzie, August 16, 2021.

Aning, Kwesi, Thomas Jaye, and Samuel Atuobi, "The Role of Private Military Companies in US-Africa Policy," *Review of African Political Economy*, Vol. 35, No. 118, 2008, pp. 613–628.

Arduino, Alessandro, "China's Private Security Companies: The Evolution of a New Security Actor," in Nadège Rolland, ed., *Securing the Belt and Road Initiative: China's Evolving Military Engagement Along the Silk Roads*, Seattle, Wash.: National Bureau of Asian Research, Special Report No. 80, September 2019, pp. 91–103.

———, *The Footprint of Chinese Private Security Companies in Africa*, Washington, D.C.: Johns Hopkins University, Working Paper No. 35, 2020.

Arnold, Thomas D., "The Geoeconomic Dimensions of Russian Private Military and Security Companies," *Military Review*, November–December 2019, pp. 6–18.

Associated Press, "China's Africa Outreach Poses Growing Threat, US General Warns," Voice of America, May 6, 2021.

Asymmetric Warfare Group and U.S. Army Training and Doctrine Command, *Russian Private Military Companies: Their Use and How to Consider Them in Operations, Competition, and Conflict*, Baltimore, Md.: Johns Hopkins Applied Physics Laboratory, April 2020.

Augé, Benjamin, *Mozambique: Security, Political and Geopolitical Challenges of the Gas Boom*, Paris: French Institute of International Relations, August 2020.

Ayemoba, Andrea, "Ghana's Entertainment and Media Revenue to More Than Double over the Next Five Years—PWC Report," Africa Business Communities, September 21, 2017.

Baez Ramirez, Javier Eduardo, German Daniel Caruso, Chiyu Niu, and Cara Ann Myers, *Mozambique Poverty Assessment: Strong but Not Broadly Shared Growth*, Washington, D.C.: World Bank, October 2018.

Baker, Lauren, "Bridging Perceptions: China in Mozambique," Marco Polo, August 27, 2019.

Barraza, Alfredo, "USACE Establishes Permanent Presence in Africa to Support Key Missions," U.S. Army, March 2, 2021.

Basu, Zachary, "More Countries Join Condemnation of China over Xinjiang Abuses," Axios, October 8, 2020.

Bekoe, Dorina A., Stephanie M. Burchard, and Sarah A. Daly, *Extremism in Mozambique: Interpreting Group Tactics and the Role of the Government's Response in the Crisis in Cabo Delgado*, Alexandria, Va.: Institute for Defense Analyses, March 2020.

Bertelsmann Stiftung, *BTI 2020 Country Report Mozambique*, Gütersloh, 2020.

Besaw, Clayton, Matthew Frank, Eric Keels, Jay Benson, John Filitz, and Jonathan Powell, *Annual Risk of Coup Report*, Broomfield, Colo.: One Earth Future, April 2019.

Besenyő, János, "The Africa Policy of Russia," *Terrorism and Political Violence*, Vol. 31, No. 1, 2019, pp. 132–153.

Biden, Joseph R., Jr., *Interim National Security Strategic Guidance*, Washington, D.C.: White House, March 2021.

Blanchard, Ben, "Stranded Chinese Workers in Iraq Being Evacuated," Reuters, June 27, 2014.

Blanchard, Christopher M., "Libya and U.S. Policy," Congressional Research Service, IF11556, last updated September 2, 2021.

Blinken, Antony J., "Secretary Antony J. Blinken Opening Remarks at D-ISIS Meeting Opening Session," remarks in Rome, U.S. Department of State, June 28, 2021.

"Boko Haram 'Plot to Attack UK and US Embassies Foiled,'" BBC News, April 12, 2017.

Bourdillon, Yves, "La Russie Pousse Ses Pions En Afrique Via Ses Mercenaires" ["Russia Pushes Its Pawns in Africa via Its Mercenaries"], *Les Echos*, December 13, 2021.

Brewster, David, "The Mozambique Channel Is the Next Security Hotspot," *The Interpreter*, March 19, 2021.

Brishpolets, Ksenija, "Strategicheskiye Interesy Rossii V Afrike" ["Russian Strategic Interests in Africa"], *Mezhdunarodnaya Analitika [International Analytics]*, No. 1-2, 2019.

Brown, Seyom, "Purposes and Pitfalls of War by Proxy: A Systemic Analysis," *Small Wars and Insurgencies*, Vol. 27, No. 2, 2016, pp. 243–257.

Bueno, Natália, "Reconciliation in Mozambique: Was It Ever Achieved?" *Conflict, Security and Development*, Vol. 19, No. 5, 2019, pp. 427–452.

Bugayova, Nataliya, and George Barros, "The Kremlin's Expanding Media Conglomerate," Institute for the Study of War, January 15, 2020.

Bugayova, Nataliya, and Darina Regio, *The Kremlin's Campaign in Africa: Assessment Update*, Washington, D.C.: Institute for the Study of War, August 2019.

Bukkvoll, Tor, and Åse G. Østensen, "The Emergence of Russian Private Military Companies: A New Tool of Clandestine Warfare," *Special Operations Journal*, Vol. 6, No. 1, 2020, pp. 1–17.

Bureau of African Affairs, "Our Mission," webpage, U.S. Department of State, undated. As of March 22, 2022:
https://www.state.gov/bureaus-offices/under-secretary-for-political-affairs/
bureau-of-african-affairs

———, "U.S. Relations with South Africa: Bilateral Relations Fact Sheet," U.S. Department of State, last updated January 14, 2020a.

———, "U.S. Relations with Kenya: Bilateral Relations Fact Sheet," U.S. Department of State, last updated August 21, 2020b.

———, "U.S. Relations with Nigeria: Bilateral Relations Fact Sheet," U.S. Department of State, last updated April 29, 2021a.

———, "U.S. Relations with Mozambique: Bilateral Relations Fact Sheet," U.S. Department of State, last updated July 6, 2021b.

Bureau of Democracy, Human Rights, and Labor, "About the Leahy Law: Fact Sheet," U.S. Department of State, January 20, 2021a.

———, *Mozambique 2020 Human Rights Report*, Washington, D.C.: U.S. Department of State, March 2021b.

Bureau of International Narcotics and Law Enforcement Affairs, "Mozambique Summary," webpage, U.S. Department of State, undated. As of March 22, 2022: https://www.state.gov/bureau-of-international-narcotics-and-law-enforcement-affairs-work-by-country/mozambique-summary

———, "Partnership for Regional East Africa Counterterrorism (PREACT)," U.S. Department of State, February 14, 2019.

Bureau of Political-Military Affairs, "U.S. Security Cooperation with Nigeria: Fact Sheet," U.S. Department of State, last updated March 19, 2021.

Burgess, Stephen, "Military Intervention in Africa: French and US Approaches Compared," *Journal of European, Middle Eastern, and African Affairs*, Vol. 1, No. 1, Spring 2019, pp. 69–89.

Cabestan, Jean-Pierre, "China's Military Base in Djibouti: A Microcosm of China's Growing Competition with the United States and New Bipolarity," *Journal of Contemporary China*, Vol. 29, No. 125, 2020a, pp. 731–747.

———, "China's Djibouti Naval Base Increasing Its Power," East Asia Forum, May 16, 2020b.

Campaign Against Arms Trade, "Country Profiles: Nigeria," November 13, 2020. As of May 21, 2022: https://caat.org.uk/data/countries/nigeria

Campbell, John, "Nigeria Turns to Russia, Czech Republic, and Belarus for Military Training and Materiel," Council on Foreign Relations, October 29, 2014.

———, "Cutting U.S. Military Support for France in West Africa Would Be a Mistake," Council on Foreign Relations, January 28, 2020.

———, "Yoruba Debate 'Restructuring' of Nigeria or 'Autonomy,'" Council on Foreign Relations, April 16, 2021.

Campbell, John, and Nolan Quinn, "What's Behind Growing Separatism in Nigeria?" Council on Foreign Relations, August 3, 2021.

Canso, "Aeroportos de Moçambique, E.P.," webpage, May 10, 2020. As of May 13, 2022: https://canso.org/member/aeroportos-de-mocambique-e-p/

Carius, Brandon, William T. Davis, Carlissa D. Linscomb, Mireya A. Escandon, Dylan Rodriguez, Nguvan Uhaa, Joseph K. Maddry, Kevin K. Chung, and Steve Schauer, "An Analysis of US Africa Command Area of Operations Military Medical Transportations, 2008–2018," *African Journal of Emergency Medicine*, Vol. 10, No. 1, March 2020, pp. 13–16.

Carsten, Paul, "ISWAP Militant Group Says Nigeria's Boko Haram Leader Is Dead," Reuters, June 7, 2021.

Center for Preventive Action, "Instability in Libya," Council on Foreign Relations, May 12, 2022.

Central Intelligence Agency, "Mozambique: Military and Security," *The World Factbook*, last updated June 29, 2021. As of August 29, 2021: https://www.cia.gov/the-world-factbook/countries/mozambique/#military-and-security

Chaudhuri, Pramit Pal, "India's 21st Century African Partner: Why Mozambique Was Modi's First Stop," *Hindustan Times*, July 7, 2016.

Chen Xulong [陈须隆], "Proposals for U.N. Reform" ["联合国改革的出路"], China Institute of International Studies [中国国际问题研究院], October 28, 2015.

China Central Television, "List of Overseas Bureaus," webpage, undated. As of September 1, 2021:
http://cctvenchiridion.cctv.com/special/C19918/24/index

———, "After Completing Their Mission, China's First Group of Military Doctors Sent to Aid Mozambique Return Home" ["中国首批援助莫桑比克军事医疗专家组圆满结束任务回国"], January 15, 2018.

China Culture, "Xinhua News Agency," webpage, undated. As of September 1, 2021:
http://en.chinaculture.org/library/2008-02/06/content_126954.htm

China Global Television Network [القناة العربية لشبكة تلفزيون الصين الدولية], "Who We Are" ["من نحن"], webpage, undated. As of April 14, 2022:
https://arabic.cgtn.com

China Media Project, "Telling China's Story Well," April 16, 2021.

"China quer reforçar apoio a Moçambique na formação militar" ["China Wants to Strengthen Support for Mozambique in Military Training"], *Observador*, July 11, 2017.

"China's CNPC Natural Gas Project in Mozambique Delayed," *China-Lusophone Brief*, April 8, 2020.

Chindea, Irina A., Elina Treyger, Raphael S. Cohen, Christian Curriden, Kurt Klein, Carlos Sanchez, Holly Gramkow, and Khrystyna Holynska, *Great-Power Competition and Conflict in Latin America*, Santa Monica, Calif.: RAND Corporation, RR-A969-4, 2023. As of April 1, 2023:
https://www.rand.org/pubs/research_reports/RRA969-4.html

Chkoniya, Lora, Gabriel Kotchofa, and Dmitry Ezhov, "Kompetencii Afriki. Chto Afrika Mozhet Predlozhit Rosii I Miru?" ["Africa's Competence. What Can Africa Offer Russia and the World?"], in Andrey Kortunov, Nataliya Zaiser, Elena Kharitonova, Lora Chkoniya, Gabriel Kotchofa, and Dmitry Ezhov, *Afrika-Rosiiya+: Dostizheniya, Problemi, Perspektivi [Africa-Russia+: Achievements, Problems, Prospects]*, Moscow: Russian International Affairs Council, Report No. 53, 2020, pp. 11–25.

Cilliers, Jakkie, Liesl Louw-Vaudran, Timothy Walker, Willem Els, and Martin Ewi, "What Would It Take to Stabilise Cabo Delgado?" ReliefWeb, May 17, 2021.

Cohen, Raphael S., Marta Kepe, Nathan Beauchamp-Mustafaga, Asha Clark, Kit Conn, Michelle Grisé, Roby Valiaveedu, and Nathan Vest, *Evaluating the Prospects for Great Power Cooperation in the Global Commons*, Santa Monica, Calif.: RAND Corporation, RR-A597-4, 2023. As of March 24, 2023:
https://www.rand.org/pubs/research_reports/RRA597-4.html

Cohen, Raphael S., Elina Treyger, Irina A. Chindea, Christian Curriden, Kristen Gunness, Khrystyna Holynska, Marta Kepe, Kurt Klein, Ashley L. Rhoades, and Nathan Vest, *Great-Power Competition and Conflict in the 21st Century Outside the Indo-Pacific and Europe*, Santa Monica, Calif.: RAND Corporation, RR-A969-1, 2023. As of April 1, 2023:
https://www.rand.org/pubs/research_reports/RRA969-1.html

Commander, Navy Installations Command, "Welcome to Camp Lemonnier, Djibouti," webpage, undated. As of June 14, 2021:
https://www.cnic.navy.mil/regions/cnreurafcent/installations/camp_lemonnier_djibouti.html

Commonwealth Initiative for Freedom of Religion or Belief, "CIFORB Country Profile: Nigeria," University of Birmingham, undated.

Cook, Nicolas, *Mozambique: Politics, Economy, and U.S. Relations*, Washington, D.C.: Congressional Research Service, R45817, September 12, 2019.

———, "Insurgency in Northern Mozambique: Nature and Responses," Congressional Research Service, IF11864, last updated July 5, 2022.

Copp, Tara, "Understaffed AFRICOM Cutting Hundreds More Troops," *Military Times*, February 20, 2019.

Corcoran, Bill, "Mozambique's Jihadists Gain Ground as Government Declines Help," *Irish Times*, December 31, 2020.

Cortez, Edson, Aslak Orre, Baltazar Fael, Borges Nhamirre, Celeste Banze, Inocência Mapisse, Kim Harnack, and Torun Reite, *Costs and Consequences of the Hidden Debt Scandal of Mozambique*, Maputo, Mozambique: Centro de Integridade Pública, August 23, 2019.

Cragin, R. Kim, and Lachlan MacKenzie, "Russia's Escalating Use of Private Military Companies in Africa," Institute for National Strategic Studies, November 24, 2020.

Daly, Samuel Fury Childs, "Unfinished Business: Biafran Activism in Nigeria Today," *Georgetown Journal of International Affairs*, April 7, 2021.

Dangerous Companions Project, homepage, undated. As of June 12, 2022: https://www.armedgroups.net

"De como os mercenários russos da Wagner perderam a guerra contra os terroristas no norte de Moçambique" ["How Wagner's Russian Mercenaries Lost the War Against Terrorists in Northern Mozambique"], *Carta de Moçambique*, April 20, 2020.

"Debt Woe Continues for Mozambique," Macauhub, May 24, 2019.

DeCapua, Joe, "Analysts Weigh Nigeria-Russia Arms Deal," Voice of America, December 10, 2014.

Deloitte, *So, Nigeria Is the Largest Economy in Africa. Now What?* Johannesburg, South Africa, 2014.

Demony, Catarina, and Emma Rumney, "Portugal to Send Another 60 Troops to Mozambique on Training Mission," Reuters, May 10, 2021.

Deutsch, Karl W., "External Involvement in Internal Wars," in Harry Eckstein, ed., *Internal War: Problems and Approaches*, New York: Free Press of Glencoe, 1964, pp. 100–110.

Deutsche Welle, "Will France Station Forces in Cabo Delgado for Total to Return?—DW," Club of Mozambique, May 17, 2021.

Devermont, Judd, "The World Is Coming to Sub-Saharan Africa. Where Is the United States?" Center for Strategic and International Studies, August 24, 2018.

———, director, Africa Program, Center for Strategic and International Studies, "China's Strategic Aims in Africa," testimony before the U.S.-China Economic and Security Review Commission, Washington, D.C., May 8, 2020a.

———, "A New U.S. Policy Framework for the African Century," Center for Strategic and International Studies, August 7, 2020b.

Devermont, Judd, Marielle Harris, and Alison Albelda, "Personal Ties, Measuring Chinese and U.S. Engagement with African Security Chiefs," Center for Strategic and International Studies, August 2021.

DoD—*See* U.S. Department of Defense.

Duke, Otu Offiong, "The Role of Military Logistics Supports in Safeguarding National Security in Nigeria," *International Journal of Trend in Scientific Research and Development*, Vol. 3, No. 5, August 2019, pp. 830–843.

Dutton, Peter A., Isaac B. Kardon, and Conor M. Kennedy, *Djibouti: China's First Overseas Strategic Strongpoint*, Newport, R.I.: U.S. Naval War College, China Maritime Report No. 6, 2020.

DynCorp International, "DynCorp International Wins $20 Million AFRICAP Task Order in Liberia," press release, January 2010.

Dyrenforth, Thomas, "Beijing's Blue Helmets: What to Make of China's Role in UN Peacekeeping in Africa," Modern War Institute at West Point, August 18, 2021.

Echeverria-Estrada, Carlos, and Jeanne Batalova, "Sub-Saharan African Immigrants in the United States," Migration Policy Institute, November 6, 2019.

Economist Intelligence Unit, "China Offers Help Against Boko Haram," May 9, 2014.

———, "China Agrees to Write Off Some of Mozambique's Debts," March 24, 2021.

Egbejule, Michael, and Adeyemi Adepetun, "IYC Laments Alleged Marginalisation of Ijaw in Political Appointments," *The Guardian*, October 11, 2021.

Egwu, Patrick, "50 Years On, Biafra's Pain Is Still Fresh," *Foreign Policy*, June 11, 2020.

Eisenman, Joshua, "Comrades-in-Arms: The Chinese Communist Party's Relations with African Political Organisations in the Mao Era, 1949–76," *Cold War History*, Vol. 18, No. 4, 2018, pp. 429–445.

Embassy of the Russian Federation in Nigeria, "Rossiya-Nigeriya" ["Russia-Nigeria"], undated.

Embassy of the Russian Federation in the Republic of Mozambique, "О выступлении российского африканиста в Университете им. Ж.Чиссано" ["About the Speech of the Russian Africanist at the University J. Chissano"], 2020.

Erickson, Andrew S., and Austin M. Strange, "China's Blue Soft Power," *Naval War College Review*, Vol. 68, No. 1, Winter 2015.

Esri, Garmin, and CIA—*See* Esri, Garmin International Inc., and U.S. Central Intelligence Agency (*The World Factbook*).

Esri, Garmin International Inc., and U.S. Central Intelligence Agency (*The World Factbook*), "World Countries," ArcGIS, map package, last updated 2019. As of December 5, 2019: https://www.arcgis.com/home/item.html?id=d974d9c6bc924ae0a2ffea0a46d71e3d

"Ethnicity in Nigeria," PBS NewsHour, April 5, 2007.

Eurasian Economic Commission, "EEC and African Union Commission Signed Memorandum of Understanding," press release, October 24, 2019.

European External Action Service, "Political and Strategic Environment of CSDP Missions in the Central African Republic (CAR)," November 22, 2021.

"EU's Takuba Force Quits Junta-Controlled Mali," France 24, July 1, 2022.

Executive Research Associates, *China in Africa: A Strategic Overview*, Craighall, South Africa, October 2009.

Fagbadebo, Omololu, "Corruption, Governance and Political Instability in Nigeria: A Dysfunctional Conundrum," *Current Research in Education and Social Studies*, Vol. 1, November 2019, pp. 55–68.

Famutimi, Temitayo, "U.S. Donates 24 Armored Personnel Carriers to Nigeria," U.S. Africa Command, January 11, 2016.

Felbab-Brown, Vanda, "Militias (and Militancy) in Nigeria's North-East: Not Going Away," Brookings Institution, April 14, 2020.

Feldscher, Jacqueline, "French, U.S. Special Forces Agree to Beef Up Partnership in Africa," *Defense One*, July 9, 2021.

Feng, Dong, "China-Mozambique Financing Cooperation Is About Development," *Global Times*, November 9, 2020.

Fernandes, Sofia, "China and Angola: A Strategic Partnership?" in Marcus Power and Ana Cristina Alves, eds., *China & Angola: A Marriage of Convenience?* Oxford, United Kingdom: Pambazuka, 2012, pp. 68–84.

"Finland Wants to Increase Crisis Management Role in Africa," Yle News, March 17, 2021.

Fokina, Alexandra, and Ekaterina Pervysheva, "Bratya Po Oruzhiyu. Rossiya Pitayetsya Vosstonovit Vliyaniye V Afrike. Pochemu Eyo Presledyyt Neydachi?" ["Brothers in Arms: Russia Is Trying to Restore Influence in Africa. Why Does It Fail?"], Lenta Ru, November 21, 2020.

Food and Agriculture Organization of the United Nations, "Economic and Policy Analysis of Climate Change: Mozambique," webpage, undated. As of August 30, 2021: http://www.fao.org/in-action/epic/countries/moz/en/

ForeignAssistance.gov, "Data," webpage, last updated April 22, 2022. As of May 20, 2022: https://foreignassistance.gov/data

Forku, Rodrigue, "Tensions High Between UN Forces, Russian Mercenaries in C. African Republic," Anadolu Agency, July 12, 2021.

Foucher, Vincent, "The Islamic State Franchises in Africa: Lessons from Lake Chad," International Crisis Group, October 29, 2020.

Fox, Benjamin, "EU Must Step Up Military Assistance to Mozambique, Says Portuguese Presidency," *EURACTIV*, February 1, 2021.

French Embassy in Maputo, "La France et le Mozambique—relations politiques et coopération militaire" ["France and Mozambique—Political Relations and Military Cooperation"], July 23, 2015.

Frey, Adrian, "Mozambique: Government Announces Military Equipment Reinforcement Supplied by Russia—Report," Club of Mozambique, October 4, 2019.

Gänsler, Katrin, "Nigeria Looks Back on 20 Years of Sharia Law in the North," Deutsche Welle, October 27, 2019.

Garamone, Jim, "Commander Says Africa Is Too Important for Americans to Ignore," *DoD News*, April 21, 2021.

Garcia, Francisco Proença, "China's Economic Presence in Mozambique," *Estudos Internacionais Revista de Relações Internacionais da PUC Minas*, Vol. 8, No. 3, December 2020, pp. 110–127.

Gbadamosi, Nosmot, "Violence Spreads in the Sahel," *Foreign Policy*, December 15, 2021.

Gehrold, Stefan, and Lena Tietze, "Far from Altruistic: China's Presence in Senegal," *KAS International Reports*, Vol. 11, November 2011, pp. 90–118.

"Germany, France Warn Mali over Russian Mercenary Deal," EURACTIV, September 16, 2021.

Giroux, Jennifer, "Africa's Growing Strategic Relevance," *CSS Analyses in Security Policy*, Vol. 3, No. 38, July 2008.

Githing'u, Brenda, "Will the South African Military Intervene in Mozambique?" *Terrorism Monitor*, Vol. 19, No. 8, April 23, 2021.

Gleicher, Nathaniel, "Removing More Coordinated Inauthentic Behavior from Russia," Meta, December 15, 2020.

Goodman, Peter S., and Stanley Reed, "With Suez Canal Blocked, Shippers Begin End Run Around a Trade Artery," *New York Times*, March 29, 2021.

Goodrich, Grace, "Top 10: Africa's Leading Oil Producers in 2021," Energy Capital & Power, June 16, 2021.

Goodwin, Jeff, "Why We Were Surprised (Again) by the Arab Spring," *Swiss Political Science Review*, Vol. 17, No. 4, 2011, pp. 452–456.

Gostev, Aleksandr, "'Dikiye Gysi' Ili 'Psi Voiny'? Rossiskiye Nayomniki V AFrike: Kto, Gde Pochem" ["'Wild Geese' or 'Dogs of War'? Russian Mercenaries in Africa: Who, Where, How Much"], Radio Liberty Russia, January 11, 2019.

Government of Mozambique, "PR elogia Academia Militar de Nanjing," ["President of the Republic Praises Nanjing Military Academy"], May 18, 2016.

Government of the Portuguese Republic, "'Há uma nova dinâmica nas relações' entre Portugal e Moçambique" ["'There Is a New Dynamic in Relations' Between Portugal and Mozambique"], July 3, 2019.

Government of the Russian Federation, "Mezhdunorodnıye Dogovorı Roisiiskoi Federacıı" ["International Agreements of the Russian Federation"], database, undated. As of February 1, 2021:
http://publication.pravo.gov.ru/SignatoryAuthority/international

Gowan, Richard, "China's Pragmatic Approach to UN Peacekeeping," Brookings Institution, September 14, 2020.

Gramer, Robbie, "U.S. Congress Moves to Restrain Pentagon over Africa Drawdown Plans," *Foreign Policy*, March 4, 2020.

———, "U.S. Lawmakers Hold Up Major Proposed Arms Sale to Nigeria," *Foreign Policy*, July 27, 2021.

Green, Will, Leyton Nelson, and Brittney Washington, *China's Engagement with Africa: Foundations for an Alternative Governance Regime*, Washington, D.C.: U.S.-China Economic and Security Review Commission, May 1, 2020.

Grissom, Adam R., and Karl P. Mueller, "Airpower in Counter-Terrorist Operations: Balancing Objectives and Risks," *The Future of Air Power*, SEGMA conference proceedings, November 2017.

Grossman, Shelby, Daniel Bush, and Renee DiResta, *Evidence of Russia-Linked Influence Operations in Africa*, Stanford, Calif.: Freeman Spogli Institute for International Studies, October 29, 2019.

Gunness, Kristen, "The PLA's Expeditionary Force: Current Capabilities and Future Trends," in Joel Wuthnow, Arthur S. Ding, Phillip C. Saunders, Andrew Scobell, and Andrew N. D. Yang, eds., *The PLA Beyond Borders: Chinese Military Operations in Regional and Global Context*, Washington, D.C.: National Defense University Press, 2021, pp. 23–72.

Hamasi, Linnet, "Kenya-US Relations Under Joe Biden's Presidency: Prospects and Challenges," *Kujenga Amani*, February 10, 2021.

Harchaoui, Jalel, "The Pendulum: How Russia Sways Its Way to More Influence in Libya," *War on the Rocks*, January 7, 2021.

Harnack, Kim, and Celeste Banze e Leila Constantino, "Dividas Contraidas Com A China Afectam Disponibilidade De Recursos No Orcamento Para Enfrentar a COVID-19" ["Debts Contracted with China Affect Availability of Resources in the Budget to Face COVID-19"], CIP Eleições, October 2020.

Harris, Grant T., "Why Africa Matters to US National Security," Atlantic Council, May 25, 2017.

Hattem, Julian, "Why Is African Air Travel So Terrible?" Bloomberg, November 21, 2017.

Haynes, Sam, "The Countries to Watch for a Coup: Political Risk Outlook 2019," Verisk Maplecroft, February 5, 2019.

He Dan [何丹], "China Shows Greater Care in Protecting Overseas Interests" ["中国海外利益保护更加温暖人心"], China Institute of International Studies, May 19, 2021.

He Yin [和音], "Propelling and Improving Sino-African Cooperation" ["推动中非合作提质升级"], Qiushi [求是], January 11, 2021.

Hedenskog, Jakob, "Russia Is Stepping Up Its Military Cooperation in Africa," Swedish Defence Research Agency, December 2018.

Heerdt, William, "Russian Hard Power Projection: A Brief Synopsis," Center for Strategic and International Studies, March 25, 2020.

Hegre, Håvard, Curtis Bell, Michael Colaresi, Mihai Croicu, Frederick Hoyles, Remco Jansen, Maxine Ria Leis, Angelica Lindqvist-McGowan, David Randahl, Espen Geelmuyden Rød, and Paola Vesco, "ViEWS2020: Revising and Evaluating the ViEWS Political Violence Early-Warning System," *Journal of Peace Research*, Vol. 58, No. 3, 2021, pp. 599–611.

Heitman, Helmoed-Römer, and Jeremy Binnie, "SADC Mission in Mozambique Launched," Janes, August 12, 2021.

Hicks, Marcus, Kyle Atwell, and Dan Collini, "Great-Power Competition Is Coming to Africa," *Foreign Affairs*, March 4, 2021.

Högbladh, Stina, Thérése Pettersson, and Lotta Themnér, "External Support in Armed Conflict 1975–2009, Presenting New Data," paper presented at the 52nd Annual International Studies Association Convention, Montreal, Canada, March 16–19, 2011.

Hope, Mat, "Cyclones in Mozambique May Reveal Humanitarian Challenges of Responding to a New Climate Reality," *The Lancet*, Vol. 3, No. 8, August 2019, pp. 338–339.

Huang Yupei [黄玉沛], "China-Africa Economic Cooperation Zones: Challenges and Means for Deepening Cooperation" ["中非经贸合作区建设: 挑战与深化路径"], China Institute of International Studies [中国国际问题研究院], July 25, 2018.

———, "Building a Sino-African 'Digital Silk Road': Opportunities, Challenges, and Options for Moving Forward" ["中非共建'数字丝绸之路': 机遇、挑战与路径选择"], China Institute of International Studies [中国国际问题研究院], August 23, 2019.

Hull, Andrew, and David Markov, "Chinese Arms Sales to Africa," *IDA Research Notes*, Summer 2012, pp. 25–31.

Human Rights Watch, "Nigeria," in *World Report 2020: Events of 2019*, New York, 2020.

Hurlburt Field, "CV-22 Osprey," webpage, U.S. Air Force, August 2020. As of December 13, 2021:
https://www.hurlburt.af.mil/About-Us/Fact-Sheets/Fact-Sheets/Article/1058084/cv-22-osprey

Hursh, John, "Tanzania Pushes Back on Chinese Port Project," *Maritime Executive*, December 2, 2019.

Husted, Tomás F., "Boko Haram and the Islamic State's West Africa Province," Congressional Research Service, IF10173, last updated March 26, 2021.

Husted, Tomás F., and Lauren Ploch Blanchard, *Nigeria: Current Issues and U.S. Policy*, Washington, D.C.: Congressional Research Service, RL33964, September 18, 2020.

"Ijaw Leaders Plan Secession from Nigeria, Meet British Government with Demands," Sahara Reporters, July 6, 2021.

International Crisis Group, *Stemming the Insurrection in Mozambique's Cabo Delgado*, Brussels, Africa Report No. 303, June 11, 2021.

International Institute for Strategic Studies, Military Balance Plus, online database, undated. As of August 27, 2021:
https://www.iiss.org/publications/the-military-balance-plus

———, *The Military Balance*, London, Vols. 114–120, 2014–2020.

International Monetary Fund, "Coordinated Direct Investment Survey," webpage, undated. As of August 31, 2021:
https://data.imf.org/?sk=40313609-F037-48C1-84B1-E1F1CE54D6D5

International Organization for Migration, "Mozambique Tropical Cyclone Eloise Response: Situation Report #1, 25 January–12 February 2021," February 12, 2021.

International Peace Institute, Peacekeeping Database, online database, undated. As of July 6, 2021:
https://www.ipinst.org/providing-for-peacekeeping-database

International Telecommunication Union, "Statistics," webpage, undated. As of May 20, 2022:
https://www.itu.int/en/ITU-D/Statistics/Pages/stat/default.aspx

Ivanov, Stanislav, "Dzhihad Po Mozambiski" ["Jihad Mozambican Style"], *Voyenno-Promishlennii Kuryer* [*Military Industrial Courier*], May 4, 2020.

Jacobs, Andrew, "Pursuing Soft Power, China Puts Stamp on Africa's News," *New York Times*, August 16, 2012.

Janes, "Nigeria: Army," *World Armies*, last updated February 28, 2021a. As of June 4, 2021:
https://customer.janes.com/Janes/Display/JWARA213-JWAR

———, "Nigeria: Air Force," *Sentinel Security Assessment: West Africa*, March 9, 2021b. As of July 9, 2021:
https://customer.janes.com/Janes/Display/JWAFA196-WAFR

———, "China: Navy," *Sentinel Security Assessment: China and Northeast Asia*, May 24, 2021c. As of July 7, 2021:
https://customer.janes.com/Janes/Display/JWNA0034-CNA

———, "XAC Y-20 Kunpeng," *All the World's Aircraft: Development and Production*, December 16, 2021d. As of June 8, 2021:
https://customer.janes.com/Janes/Display/JAWAA998-JAWA

Jiang Zemin, "Report at the 16th Party Congress," China Internet Information Center, November 17, 2002.

Johns Hopkins China-Africa Research Initiative, "Data: China-Africa Trade," webpage, undated. As of August 31, 2021:
http://www.sais-cari.org/data-china-africa-trade

Jones, Lee, and Shahar Hameiri, *Debunking the Myth of "Debt-Trap Diplomacy,"* London: Chatham House, August 19, 2020.

Kachur, Dzvinka, "Russia's Resurgence in Africa: Zimbabwe and Mozambique," South African Institute of International Affairs, November 27, 2020.

Kanet, Roger E., "The Superpower Quest for Empire: The Cold War and Soviet Support for 'Wars of National Liberation,'" *Cold War History*, Vol. 6, No. 3, 2006, pp. 331–352.

Katz, Brian, Seth G. Jones, Catrina Doxsee, and Nicholas Harrington, "Moscow's Mercenary Wars: The Expansion of Russian Private Military Companies," Center for Strategic and International Studies, September 2020.

Kaufmann, Daniel, Aart Kraay, and Massimo Mastruzzi, "Governance Matters VIII: Aggregate and Individual Governance Indicators, 1996–2008," World Bank Policy Research Working Paper No. 4978, June 29, 2009.

Keating, Christopher, "Nearly 600 Connecticut National Guard Troops Headed to Africa in Global War on Terrorism; Largest Deployment Since 2009," *Hartford Courant*, March 10, 2021.

Kelly, Fergus, "AFRICOM Shifts Strategy from Degrading to Containing West Africa Insurgents, OIG Report Says," *Defense Post*, February 12, 2020.

Kepe, Marta, Richard Flint, and Julia Muravska, *Future Collaboration Opportunities for Light and Medium Multirole Helicopters in Europe*, Santa Monica, Calif., and Cambridge, United Kingdom: RAND Corporation, RR-3034-EDA, 2019. As of May 21, 2022:
https://www.rand.org/pubs/research_reports/RR3034.html

Kinne, Brandon J., "Defense Cooperation Agreement Dataset," *Journal of Conflict Resolution*, Vol. 64, No. 4, 2020, pp. 729–755.

Klinger, Julie Michelle, "China, Africa, and the Rest: Recent Trends in Space Science, Technology, and Satellite Development," Washington, D.C.: SAIS China-Africa Research Initiative, Policy Brief No. 45, May 2020.

Klobucista, Claire, "Nigeria's Battle with Boko Haram," Council on Foreign Relations, Backgrounder, August 8, 2018.

Klomegah, Kester Kenn, "Russia's Strategy to Enter the African Market," *Modern Diplomacy*, May 21, 2021.

Kolly, Etienne, and Justin Michael Cochrane, "To Deal or Not to Deal, That Is the Question . . . ," IHS Markit, July 9, 2002.

"Kompetencii Rossii Dlya Afriki" ["Russian Competences for Africa"], Roscongress, October 23, 2019.

Kondratenko, Tatiana, "Russian Arms Exports to Africa: Moscow's Long-Term Strategy," Deutsche Welle, May 29, 2020.

Korinek, Jane, and Isabelle Ramdoo, "Local Content Policies in Mineral-Exporting Countries: The Case of Mozambique," Organisation for Economic Co-operation and Development, Trade Policy Paper No. 209, December 2017.

"Krupneishiye Rosiiskiye Proyekti V Afrike" ["The Largest Russian Projects in Africa"], October 23, 2019.

Krutlkov, Evgeny, "Mozambik Zamanivayet Rossiiyu V Opastnii I Pribilnii Proyekt" ["Mozambique Lures Russia into a Dangerous and Profitable Project"], Vzglyad, August 21, 2019.

LaGrone, Sam, "AFRICOM: Chinese Naval Base in Africa Set to Support Aircraft Carriers," *USNI News*, April 20, 2021.

Lan Jianxue [蓝建学], "India's 'Link West' Policy: Origins, Progress, and Prospects" ["印度 '西联'战略: 缘起、进展与前景"], China Institute of International Studies [中国国际问题研究院], May 31, 2019.

Larson, Deborah Welch, *Anatomy of Mistrust: U.S.-Soviet Relations During the Cold War*, Ithaca, N.Y.: Cornell University Press, 1997.

Lawler, Dave, "The 53 Countries Supporting China's Crackdown on Hong Kong," Axios, July 2, 2020.

Legarda, Helena, and Meia Nouwens, "Guardians of the Belt and Road: The Internationalization of China's Private Security Companies," Mercator Institute for China Studies, August 16, 2018.

Leslie, Michael, "The Dragon Shapes Its Image: A Study of Chinese Media Influence Strategies in Africa," *African Studies Quarterly*, Vol. 16, No. 3 4, December 2016, pp. 161–174.

Lewis, David, "U.S. Counterterrorism Chief Says Mozambique Militants Are Islamic State Affiliate," Reuters, December 9, 2020.

Lichtenbaum, Annika, "U.S. Military Operational Activity in the Sahel," *Lawfare*, January 25, 2019.

Lim, Louisa, and Julia Bergin, *The China Story: Reshaping the World's Media*, Brussels: International Federation of Journalists, June 2020.

Lindström, Madelene, "The United States—From Counter-Terrorism to Great Power Competition in Africa?" Swedish Defence Research Institute, FOI Memo 6817, August 2019.

Lister, Tim, "The March 2021 Palma Attack and the Evolving Jihadi Terror Threat to Mozambique," *CTC Sentinel*, Vol. 14, No. 4, April/May 2021.

Lister, Tim, and Sebastian Shukla, "Russian Mercenaries Fight Shadowy Battle in Gas-Rich Mozambique," CNN, November 29, 2019.

Liu Xuanzun, "Nigeria Received China-Made Armed Reconnaissance Drones: Reports," *Global Times*, November 11, 2020.

Logistics Cluster and World Food Programme, "Mozambique Aviation," Logistics Capacity Assessment, undated. As of June 10, 2021:
https://dlca.logcluster.org/display/public/DLCA/2.2+Mozambique+Aviation

Lopez, C. Todd, "U.S. to Resume Small, Persistent Presence in Somalia," U.S. Department of Defense, May 16, 2022.

Loshkaryov, Ivan, "Russia's Policy in a Dynamic Africa: Searching for a Strategy," Russian International Affairs Council, October 9, 2019.

Lostumbo, Michael J., Michael J. McNerney, Eric Peltz, Derek Eaton, David R. Frelinger, Victoria A. Greenfield, John Halliday, Patrick Mills, Bruce R. Nardulli, Stacie L. Pettyjohn, Jerry M. Sollinger, and Stephen M. Worman, *Overseas Basing of U.S. Military Forces: An Assessment of Relative Costs and Strategic Benefits*, Santa Monica, Calif.: RAND Corporation, RR-201-OSD, 2013. As of June 9, 2021:
http://www.rand.org/pubs/research_reports/RR201.html

Lou Chunhao [楼春豪], "'The Asia-Africa Growth Corridor': Content, Motivations, and Prospects" ["'亚非增长走廊'倡议: 内涵、动因与前景"], China Institute of International Studies [中国国际问题研究院], January 22, 2018.

Luke, Leighton G., "Mozambique Seeks Benefits from Links with Portugal," Future Directions International, July 10, 2019.

Lukoil, "Ghana," webpage, undated-a. As of August 27, 2021:
https://upstreamwest.lukoil.com/en/Activities/Ghana

———, "Nigeria," webpage, undated-b. As of August 27, 2021:
https://upstreamwest.lukoil.com/en/Activities/Nigeria

Lusa, "Mozambique: No 'Indications' That China May Seize Assets Due to Debt—Government," Club of Mozambique, November 19, 2020.

Lynch, Colum, "China's Arms Exports Flooding Sub-Saharan Africa," Washington Post, August 25, 2012.

Ma Hanzhi [马汉智], "Africa's Serious Regional Security Problems Are Worthy of Note" ["非洲局部地区严峻安全形势值得关注"], China Institute of International Studies [中国国际问题研究院], August 27, 2020a.

———, "Africa Continental Free Trade Agreement Is Worth Looking Forward To" ["非洲自贸区故事值得期待"], China Institute of International Studies [中国国际问题研究院], December 29, 2020b.

Mackinnon, Amy, "With Base in Sudan, Russia Expands Its Military Reach in Africa," Foreign Policy, December 14, 2020.

Mackinnon, Amy, Robbie Gramer, and Jack Detsch, "Russia's Dreams of a Red Sea Naval Base Are Scuttled—for Now," Foreign Policy, July 15, 2022.

Malsin, Jared, "Russia Reinforces Foothold in Libya as Militia Leader Retreats," Wall Street Journal, June 29, 2020.

Manuel, Lourenço, Emílio Tostão, Orcidia Vilanculos, Gaby Mandlhate, and Faaiqa Hartley, Economic Implications of Climate Change in Mozambique, Southern Africa—Towards Inclusive Economic Development, Working Paper No. 136, September 2020.

Manyuan, Dong [董漫远], "The Influence and Outlook for ISIS's Rise" ["'伊斯兰国'崛起的影响及前景"], China Institute of International Studies [中国国际问题研究院], October 14, 2014.

———, "The Interregional Influence and Course of the Libyan Proxy War" ["利比亚代理人战争的跨地区影响及走向"], China Institute of International Studies [中国国际问题研究院], July 23, 2020.

Marcondes, Danilo, "Brasil e Moçambique: construindo a cooperação em defesa" ["Brazil and Mozambique: Building Defense Cooperation"], in Desafios para Moçambique 2019 [Challenges for Mozambique 2019], 2019, pp. 377–392.

Marinho, Jorge, "China in Africa (2019): Facebook and Twitter as Part of Public Diplomacy," CPD Blog, University of Southern California Center on Public Diplomacy, August 14, 2020. As of June 10, 2021:
https://uscpublicdiplomacy.org/blog/china-africa-2019-facebook-twitter-part-public-diplomacy

Marten, Kimberly, "The Puzzle of Russian Behavior in Deir Al-Zour," War on the Rocks, July 5, 2018.

Martinson, Ryan D., "China as an Atlantic Naval Power," RUSI Journal, Vol. 164, No. 7, 2019, pp. 18–31.

Matlock, Damon, Jonathan Gaustad, Jason Scott, and Danielle J. Bales, "Command and Control in Africa: Three Case Studies Before and After Tactical C2," *Air & Space Power Journal*, July–August 2014, pp. 119–138.

Matsinhe, David M., and Estacio Valoi, *The Genesis of Insurgency in Northern Mozambique*, Pretoria, South Africa: Institute for Security Studies, Southern Africa Report No. 27, October 2019.

Mazarr, Michael J., Jonathan Blake, Abigail Casey, Tim McDonald, Stephanie Pezard, and Michael Spirtas, *Understanding the Emerging Era of International Competition: Theoretical and Historical Perspectives*, Santa Monica, Calif.: RAND Corporation, RR-2726-AF, 2018. As of June 8, 2021:
https://www.rand.org/pubs/research_reports/RR2423.html

McBain, Will, "Skepticism Follows Russia-Nigeria Deal Announcements," *African Business*, December 9, 2019.

McCaughan, Ryan, "Air Mobility Challenges in Sub-Saharan Africa," *Journal of European, Middle Eastern, and African Affairs*, Vol. 1, No. 1, Spring 2019, pp. 90–102.

Mehta, Aaron, "Two US Airmen Injured by Chinese Lasers in Djibouti, DOD Says," *Defense News*, May 3, 2018.

"Mezhdunarodniye Otnosheniya Rossii I Mozambika" ["International Relations Between Russia and Mozambique"], *Ria Novosti*, August 22, 2019.

Mikryukov, Vasiliy, "Povoyte Za Menya" ["Fight for Me"], *Voyenno-Promishlennii Kuryer [Military Industrial Courier]*, October 5, 2015.

Mining Africa, "These Are the Top Mining Countries of Africa," webpage, undated. As of May 20, 2022:
https://miningafrica.net/mining-countries-africa

Ministry of Defence (Navy) of India, *Ensuring Secure Seas: Indian Maritime Security Strategy*, New Delhi, Naval Strategic Publication 1.2, October 2015.

Ministry of European and Foreign Affairs of France, "France in the South-West Indian Ocean," November 26, 2021.

Ministry of Foreign Affairs of Norway, "The Peace Process in Mozambique," webpage, December 2, 2019. As of May 16, 2022:
https://www.regjeringen.no/en/topics/foreign-affairs/peace-and-reconciliation-efforts/norways_engagement/mozsambique_peace/id2541641/

Ministry of Foreign Affairs of the People's Republic of China, "Chinese Embassies," webpage, undated-a. As of April 14, 2022:
https://www.fmprc.gov.cn/mfa_eng/wjb_663304/zwjg_665342/2490_665344/

———, "Top Stories," webpage, undated-b. As of April 14, 2022:
https://www.fmprc.gov.cn/mfa_eng

———, "Xi Jinping Arrives in Dar es Salaam, Kicking Off His State Visit to Tanzania," March 25, 2013.

Ministry of Foreign Affairs of the Russian Federation, "Russia in International Relations," webpage, undated. As of April 14, 2022:
https://www.mid.ru/en/maps/ru/

———, "Speech of and Answers to Questions of Mass Media by Russian Foreign Minister Sergey Lavrov During Joint Press Conference Summarizing the Results of Negotiations with Mozambique Foreign Minister Oldemiro Balói," February 12, 2013.

———, "Foreign Policy Concept of the Russian Federation," Moscow, December 1, 2016.

———, "Agreement Between the Government of the Russian Federation and the Government of the Federal Republic of Nigeria on Military Cooperation," August 22, 2017.

———, "Interview of the Ambassador of Russia in Mozambique to the Portuguese News Agency," April 7, 2021.

Miroshnichenko, Kristina, and Irina Mandrykina, "Rossiya–Afrika: Stariye Druzya I Perspektivniye Partneri" ["Russia–Africa: Old Friends and Promising Partners"], TASS, February 4, 2021.

Mishra, Abhishek, "Mozambique's Insurgency and India's Interest," Observer Research Foundation, April 6, 2021.

"Mocímboa da Praia: Turning Point or Stepping Stone to an Endless War?" 14 North, August 11, 2021.

Morcos, Pierre, "France: A Bridge Between Europe and the Indo-Pacific?" Center for Strategic and International Studies, April 1, 2021.

Morier-Genoud, Eric, "The Jihadi Insurgency in Mozambique: Origins, Nature and Beginning," *Journal of Eastern African Studies*, Vol. 14, No. 3, 2020, pp. 396–412.

Moriyasu, Ken, "China Looks to East Africa for Second Indian Ocean Foothold," *Nikkei Asia*, June 30, 2021.

"Moscow Seeks to Boost Contact with Nyusi," *Africa Intelligence*, April 7, 2021.

"Moskva Zakluchila Soglasheniye Flota V Sudane" ["Moscow Signed an Agreement on the Base of the Russian Fleet in Sudan"], RBK, December 8, 2020.

Moyer, J. D., D. K. Bohl, and S. Turner, "Diplometrics Diplomatic Representation," data set, Frederick S. Pardee Center for International Futures, 2016.

"Mozambique Willing to Boost Cooperation with Russia, China," TASS, May 28, 2018.

Mucari, Manuel, "Mozambique's Police Kill Leader of Armed Splinter Group of Main Opposition Party," Reuters, October 11, 2021.

Mucari, Manuel, Emma Rumney, and Alexander Winning, "Mozambique Court Declares Void Two Loans in 'Hidden Debt' Scandal," Reuters, May 12, 2020.

Mukwakwa, Pezu C., *Mozambique Conflict Insight*, Vol. 1, Addis Ababa, Ethiopia: Institute for Peace and Security Studies, April 2020.

Mumbere, Daniel, "Mozambique Polls: Key Stats from President Nyusi, Frelimo's Victory," Africanews, October 28, 2019.

Mumford, Andrew, *Proxy Warfare*, Cambridge, United Kingdom: John Wiley & Sons, 2013.

Mwakideu, Chrispin, "Experts Warn of China's Growing Media Influence in Africa," Deutsche Welle, January 29, 2021.

Myers, Meghann, "US Troops Now 'Commuting to Work' to Help Somalia Fight Al-Shabab," *Military Times*, April 27, 2021.

Mzyece Mjumo, and Mzukisi Qobo, "US-China Tension Creates Opportunities Africa Must Seize," Africa Report, June 22, 2020.

Nantulya, Paul, "Chinese Security Contractors in Africa," Carnegie Endowment for International Peace, October 8, 2020.

Ndegwa, Stephen, "FOCAC at 20 Is Great, and Will Be Greater in the Next 20 Years," China Global Television Network, October 11, 2020.

Neelov, Vladimir, *Chastniya Voyenniye Kompanyi Rossii: Opit I Perspektivi Ispolzovaniya* [*Private Military Companies in Russia: Experience and Prospects for Use*], St. Petersburg: Center for Strategic Assessments and Forecasts, 2013.

Ng'wanakilala, Fumbuka, Brenda Goh, and Cate Cadell, "Tanzania's China-Backed $10 Billion Port Plan Stalls over Terms: Official," Reuters, May 22, 2019.

Niaga, Thiam, and Tim Cocks, "China Opens Embassy After Burkina Faso Severs Ties with Taiwan," Reuters, July 12, 2018.

"Nigeria Ends US Mission to Counter Boko Haram," *Defense News*, December 1, 2014.

"Nigeria, Russia in Rail, Steel, Defence Deals," Agence de Presse Africaine, October 24, 2019.

"Nigeria's Nigcomsat to Receive $550 Million Investment from China Great Wall Industry Corporation," Spacewatch Africa, April 2018.

Obasi, Nnamdi, "Nigeria: How to Solve a Problem Like Biafra," International Crisis Group, May 29, 2017.

Observatory of Economic Complexity, "China," webpage, undated-a. As of July 9, 2021:
https://oec.world/en/profile/country/chn?depthSelector2=HS6Depth

———, "Mozambique," webpage, undated-b. As of July 9, 2021:
https://oec.world/en/profile/country/moz?depthSelector1=HS6Depth

———, "Nigeria," webpage, undated-c. As of July 9, 2021:
https://oec.world/en/profile/country/nga

———, "Russia/Nigeria Trade," webpage, undated-d. As of July 9, 2021:
https://oec.world/en/profile/bilateral-country/rus/partner/nga

Office of Counterterrorism, "Pan Sahel Initiative," U.S. Department of State Archives, November 7, 2002. As of March 22, 2022:
https://2001-2009.state.gov/s/ct/rls/other/14987.htm

Office of the Historian, "Milestones: 1969–1976—The Angola Crisis 1974–75," U.S. Department of State, undated-a. As of March 25, 2022:
https://history.state.gov/milestones/1969-1976/angola

———, "Travels Abroad of the Secretary of State," webpage, U.S. Department of State, undated-b. As of May 21, 2022:
https://history.state.gov/departmenthistory/travels/secretary

Office of the Secretary of Defense, *Military and Security Developments Involving the People's Republic of China 2020: Annual Report to Congress*, Washington, D.C., 2020.

Office of the Secretary of the Interior, "Final List of Critical Minerals 2018," *Federal Register*, Vol. 83, No. 97, May 18, 2018, pp. 23295–23296.

Office of the United States Trade Representative, "Nigeria," webpage, undated-a. As of July 8, 2021:
https://ustr.gov/countries-regions/africa/nigeria

———, "The People's Republic of China," webpage, undated-b. As of August 10, 2021:
https://ustr.gov/countries-regions/china-mongolia-taiwan/peoples-republic-china

Office of Treaty Affairs, "Treaties in Force: A List of Treaties and Other International Agreements of the United States in Force on January 1, 2020," U.S. Department of State, 2021.

Oghuvbu, Ejiroghene Augustine, and Blessing Oluwatobi Oghuvbu, "Corruption and the Lingering of Insecurity Challenges in Nigeria," *Journal of Public Administration, Finance and Law*, No. 18, 2020, pp. 88–99.

Ogunmodede, Chris Olaoluwa, "Biden's 'Low Bar' for Improving Ties with Nigeria," *World Politics Review*, January 26, 2021.

Oil and Gas 360, "US Slashes Nigerian Oil Imports by 11.67m Barrels," August 23, 2020.

Oil Capital, "Западная Африка—наиболее перспективный район для инвестиций ЛУКОЙЛа" ["West Africa—The Most Promising Region for LUKOIL Investments"], October 18, 2019.

Oladipo, Doyinsola, and Andrea Shalal, "Biden Revives Trump's Africa Business Initiative; Focus on Energy, Health," Reuters, July 27, 2021.

Oladipo, Doyinsola, and Mike Stone, "Proposed U.S. Arms Sale to Nigeria on 'Hold' over Human Rights Concerns—Sources," Reuters, July 30, 2021.

Olander, Eric, "China's StarTimes Is Now One of Africa's Most Important Media Companies," *Medium*, August 26, 2017.

———, "Tanzania's Relationship Status with China: It's Complicated," *China in Africa Podcast*, January 29, 2021.

Ollivant, Douglas A., and Erica Gaston, "The Problem with the Narrative of 'Proxy War' in Iraq," *War on the Rocks*, May 31, 2019.

Omotuyi, Sunday, "Russo/Nigerian Relations in the Context of Counterinsurgency in Nigeria," *Jadavpur Journal of International Relations*, Vol. 23, No. 1, 2019, pp. 48–68.

Onuah, Felix, and Alexis Akwagyiram, "Nigeria Urges U.S. to Move Africa Command Headquarters to Continent," Reuters, April 27, 2021.

Organisation for Economic Co-operation and Development, "Aid (ODA) Disbursements to Countries and Regions [DAC2a]," webpage, undated. As of August 27, 2021: https://stats.oecd.org/Index.aspx?DataSetCode=Table2A#

Page, Matthew T., *The Intersection of China's Commercial Interests and Nigeria's Conflict Landscape*, Washington, D.C.: United States Institute of Peace, September 1, 2018.

Palik, Júlia, Siri Aas Rustad, and Fredrik Methi, *Conflict Trends in Africa, 1989–2019*, Oslo: Peace Research Institute Oslo, 2020.

Panin, Nikita, "Vozmozhen Li Afrikanskii Gambit Vo Vneshnei Politike Rosii?" ["Is the African Gambit Possible in Russian Foreign Policy?"], Russian International Affairs Council, April 23, 2021.

Parkinson, Joe, Nicholas Bariyo, and Josh Chin, "Huawei Technicians Helped African Governments Spy on Political Opponents," *Wall Street Journal*, August 15, 2019.

Paulinus, Aidoghie, "Atomic Partnership with Russia'll Propel Nigeria's Economy—Sherbashin Russian Envoy," *The Sun*, March 14, 2021.

Pawlyk, Oriana, "US Begins Drone Operations out of New Niger Air Base," Military.com, November 1, 2019.

Pearson, Benjamin, *Russia: Applying the Low Cost, High Return Syrian Strategy to Africa*, Maxwell Air Force Base, Ala.: Squadron Officer School, April 7, 2021.

Peltier, Chad, Tate Nurkin, and Sean O'Connor, *China's Logistics Capabilities for Expeditionary Operations*, Coulsdon, United Kingdom: Janes, 2020.

Permanent Mission of the Republic of Mozambique to the United Nations, "Filipe Jacinto Nyusi," webpage, Columbia University World Leaders Forum, September 2015. As of August 5, 2022:
https://worldleaders.columbia.edu/directory/filipe-jacinto-nyusi

Petersohn, Ulrich, "Everything in (Dis)Order? Private Military and Security Contractors and International Order," *Journal of Future Conflict*, 2020.

"Petro China and Mozambique Sign Cooperation Framework Agreement" ["中国石油与莫桑比克签署合作框架协议"], *China Petroleum Enterprise* [中国石油企业], May 2016.

Petrov, Alexander, "Tam Horosho, No Nam Tuda Ne Nado" ["It's Good There, but We Don't Need to Go There"], Versia, June 17, 2021.

Pildegovičs, Tomass, Kristina VanSant, and Monika Hanley, eds., *Russia's Activities in Africa's Information Environment—Case Studies: Mali and Central African Republic*, Riga, Latvia: NATO Strategic Communications Centre of Excellence, 2021.

Pincombe, Morgan, *Casting a Neocolonial Net: China's Exploitative Fishing in the Gulf of Guinea*, Williamsburg, Va.: Project on International Peace and Security, Brief No. 13.5, May 2021.

Pirie, Gordon, "China Has Taken a Different Route to Involvement in African Aviation," The Conversation, September 1, 2019.

Powell, Anita, "US Offers Resources to Help 'Contain, Degrade, and Defeat' Mozambique Insurgency," Voice of America, December 8, 2020.

President of Russia, "Events," webpage, undated. As of April 14, 2022:
http://en.kremlin.ru/events/president/news

———, "Top-Level Russian-Nigerian Talks Were Held in the Kremlin," March 6, 2001.

"Prezident Mozambika Zayavil O Novom Etape V Otnisheniyah S Rossiiyei" ["The President of Mozambique Announced a New Stage in Relations with Russia"], RBK, August 21, 2019.

"Pri Posolstve Rosi V Mozambike Sozdali Apparat Voyennovo Attashe" ["Military Attaché Office Created at the Russian Embassy in Mozambique"], Interfax, March 18, 2021.

Pudovkin, Evgeniy, "CAR Pered Viborami Okazalas Na Grani Politicheskovo Kollapsa" ["Before the Elections CAR Found Itself on the Verge of Political Collapse"], RBK, December 23, 2020.

Putz, Catherine, "2020 Edition: Which Countries Are for or Against China's Xinjiang Policies?" *The Diplomat*, October 9, 2020.

Rádio Moçambique, "Mozambique and China Sign Military Cooperation Agreement," Club of Mozambique, December 20, 2016.

Raghavan, Sudarsan, and Craig Whitlock, "A City in Niger Worries a New U.S. Drone Base Will Make It a 'Magnet' for Terrorists," *Washington Post*, November 24, 2017.

Railway Pro, "TMH Signed Agreements to Develop Nigerian Railway Industry," October 24, 2019.

Ramani, Samuel, "Russia Takes Its Syrian Model of Counterinsurgency to Africa," Royal United Services Institute, September 9, 2020.

———, "Russia's Strategy in the Central African Republic," Royal United Services Institute, February 12, 2021.

Raval, Anjli, and Neil Munshi, "Nigeria Set to Sell Down Stake in Oil Ventures to Boost Finances," *Financial Times*, March 20, 2019.

Reho, Samantha, "Senior African Military Intelligence Directors Discuss Lake Chad Region Threat Environment," U.S. Africa Command, August 14, 2019.

Rempfer, Kyle, "Army SFAB Advisers Will Have to Share Some Friends with China," *Army Times*, October 13, 2020.

Reporters Without Borders, "World Press Freedom Index," webpage, undated. As of May 20, 2022:
https://rsf.org/en/ranking

Rhoades, Ashley L., Elina Treyger, Nathan Vest, Christian Curriden, Brad A. Bemish, Irina A. Chindea, Raphael S. Cohen, Jessica Giffin, and Kurt Klein, *Great-Power Competition and Conflict in the Middle East*, Santa Monica, Calif.: RAND Corporation, RR-A969-3, 2023. As of April 1, 2023:
https://www.rand.org/pubs/research_reports/RRA969-3.html

Rodriguez, David M., general, U.S. Army, "United States Africa Command 2016 Posture Statement," statement before the U.S. Senate Armed Services Committee, March 8, 2016.

Rogeiro, Nuno, "As Relações Entre a Rússia e Moçambique: Dos Acordos à Luta Contra o Terrorismo" ["Relations Between Russia and Mozambique: From Agreements to the Fight Against Terrorism"], Sicnoticias, April 9, 2021.

"Roscosmos to Deploy GLONASS Monitoring Stations in Five Countries," TASS, September 16, 2021.

"Rosneft Signs Agreements on Offshore Gas Field Development with Mozambique," TASS, August 22, 2019.

Ross, Will, "Mozambique's Debt Problem," BBC News, November 10, 2018.

"Rossiya I Mozambik Zaklyuchili Soglasheniye O Zashite Informacii" ["Russia and Mozambique Sign Agreement on Information Protection"], RIA Novosti, August 22, 2019.

"Rossiya, SSHA Ili Kotai—Kto Pobedit V Afrikanskoi Kosmicheskoi Gonke," FAN, June 27, 2020.

Rossotrudnichestvo, "Zarubezhniye Predstavitelstva" ["Overseas Representations"], webpage, undated. As of March 24, 2022:
https://rs.gov.ru/ru/contacts

Ruan Zongze [阮宗泽], "Winning the Next 10 Years: China's Multi-Strongpoint Diplomacy" ["赢得下一个十年: 中国塑造多支点外交"], China Institute of International Studies [中国国际问题研究院], July 23, 2013.

RUDN University, "Studencheskii Konkurs 'Miss Afrika'" ["Student Competition 'Miss Africa'"], webpage, undated. As of June 10, 2021:
https://www.rudn.ru/media/events/studencheskiy-konkurs-miss-afrika

Rudolph, Josh, and Thomas Morley, *Covert Foreign Money: Financial Loopholes Exploited by Authoritarians to Fund Political Interference in Democracies*, Washington, D.C.: Alliance for Securing Democracy, August 2020.

Rússia em Moçambique [@EmbRusMov], "#Putin: #Moçambique é o nosso parceiro tradicional no Continente Africano. Há interesse comum na ulterior intensificação . . . ," Twitter post, May 18, 2021. As of March 21, 2022:
https://twitter.com/EmbRusMoz/status/1394650177688985605

"Russia in Africa: What's Behind Moscow's Push into the Continent?" BBC News, May 7, 2020.

"Russia May Create Glonass Ground Stations in Africa and Asia-Pacific Region," TASS, June 18, 2019.

"Russia Ready to Maintain Defense Cooperation with Mozambique, Says Ambassador," TASS, October 25, 2019.

"Rússia renuncia ao dólar e se flexibiliza na exportação de armas para contrariar sanções" ["Russia Renounces the Dollar and Becomes More Flexible in Arms Exports to Counter Sanctions"], Sputnik, July 21, 2021.

"Russia to Deploy Space Monitoring Stations in South Africa, Mexico and Chile," Space in Africa, March 7, 2019.

Russian Federation, *Military Doctrine of the Russian Federation*, Moscow, December 25, 2014.

————, *Maritime Doctrine of the Russian Federation for the Period up to 2020*, Moscow, July 2015.

"Russia's Large Anti-Submarine Ship Ends Visit to Mozambique," TASS, October 17, 2018.

Salehyan, Idean, Kristian Skrede Gleditsch, and David E. Cunningham, "Explaining External Support for Insurgent Groups," *International Organization*, Vol. 65, No. 4, Fall 2011, pp. 709–744.

Sanny, Josephine Appiah-Nyamekye, and Edem Selormey, "Africans Regard China's Influence as Significant and Positive, but Slipping," Afrobarometer, Dispatch No. 407, November 17, 2020.

Saunders, Chris, "SWAPO's 'Eastern' Connections, 1966–1989," in Lena Dallywater, Chris Saunders, and Helder Adegar Fonseca, eds., *Southern African Liberation Movements and the Global Cold War "East": Transnational Activism 1960–1990*, Berlin: De Gruyter, 2019, pp. 57–76.

Schwartz, Stephen M., "The Way Forward for the United States in Somalia," Foreign Policy Research Institute, January 12, 2021.

Shalamov, G. G., "China's Presence in Africa: Lessons for Russia," *Russia and the Contemporary World*, Vol. 4, No. 101, 2018, pp. 112–128.

Sheehy, Tom, "U.S.'s 'Prosper Africa' Initiative Launches in Mozambique, Fighting Uphill Battle Against Corruption," *Foreign Policy News*, June 17, 2019.

Shekhovtsov, Anton, *Fake Election Observation as Russia's Tool of Election Interference: The Case of AFRIC*, Berlin: European Platform for Democratic Elections, April 2020.

Shi Hongyuan [时宏远], "The Modi Government's Indian Ocean Policy" ["莫迪政府的印度洋政策"], China Institute of International Studies [中国国际问题研究院], January 22, 2018.

Shinn, David, "China-Africa Ties in Historical Context," in Arkebe Oqubay and Justin Yifu Lin, eds., *China-Africa and an Economic Transformation*, Oxford, United Kingdom: Oxford University Press, 2019, pp. 61–83.

————, "China in Africa," testimony before the U.S.-China Economic and Security Review Commission, Washington, D.C., May 8, 2020.

Ship Traffic, "Mozambique Channel Ships Marine Traffic Live Map," webpage, undated. As of May 21, 2022:
http://www.shiptraffic.net/marine-traffic/canals/Mozambique_Channel

Shurkin, Michael, "The Good and Bad of the Trump Administration's New Africa Strategy," *The Hill*, December 20, 2018.

Shurkin, Michael, and Aneliese Bernard, "Ten Things the United State Should Do to Combat Terrorism in the Sahel," *War on the Rocks*, August 30, 2021.

Shurkin, Michael, Alexander Noyes, and Mary Kate Adgie, *The COVID-19 Pandemic in Sub-Saharan Africa: An Opportunity to Rethink Strategic Competition on the Continent*, Santa Monica, Calif.: RAND Corporation, PE-A1055-1, July 2021. As of May 19, 2022: https://www.rand.org/pubs/perspectivcs/PEA1055-1.html

Sicurelli, Daniela, "Italian Cooperation with Mozambique: Explaining the Emergence and Consolidation of a Normative Power," *Italian Political Science Review*, Vol. 50, No. 2, 2020, pp. 254–270.

Siegle, Joseph, "Russia's Strategic Goals in Africa," Africa Center for Strategic Studies, May 6, 2021.

SIPRI—*See* Stockholm International Peace Research Institute.

Smith, Patrick, "US/China/France: Africa's Security Woes Complicated by Foreign Boots," Africa Report, May 10, 2021.

SNG.Today, "Voyennii Expert Obyasnil, Kak Bazoi V Sudane PF Ochertit Nacionalniye Interesi V Afrike" ["Military Expert Explained How the Base in Sudan Will Help Russia Outline Its National Interests in Africa"], May 14, 2021.

"South Africa Sends 1,500 Troops to Mozambique to Fight Jihadists," Africanews, July 29, 2021.

"South African Military Deploys Troops to Pemba, Northern Mozambique," Africanews, August 5, 2021.

"Southern Africa: Mozambique Will Coordinate SADC Standby Force," *All Africa*, July 24, 2021.

"Statement of H.E. Mr. Moussa Faki Mahamat, Chairperson of the African Union Commission, on the Terrorist Attacks in Mozambique," African Union, March 31, 2021.

Statista, "Direct Investment Position of the United States in Africa from 2000 to 2020," August 4, 2021.

Stewart, Phil, and Aidan Lewis, "Exclusive: U.S. Says Drone Shot Down by Russian Air Defenses Near Libyan Capital," Reuters, December 7, 2019.

Stockholm International Peace Research Institute, Arms Transfers Database, web tool, undated-a. As of June 8, 2021: https://www.sipri.org/databases/armstransfers

———, "SIPRI Arms Transfers Database—Methodology," webpage, undated-b. As of May 9, 2022: https://www.sipri.org/databases/armstransfers/background

Su Xiaohui [苏晓晖] and Zhu Zhongbo [朱中博], "Summary of the 2015 International Situation and Chinese Diplomacy Forum" ["2015年国际形势与中国外交研讨会纪要"], China Institute of International Studies [中国国际问题研究院], January 15, 2016.

Sui Xinmin [随新民], "India's Strategic Culture and Patterns of Foreign Policy" ["印度的战略文化与国际行为模式"], China Institute of Strategic Studies [中国国际问题研究员], January 20, 2014.

Sukhankin, Sergey, "Russia Prepared a Foothold in Mozambique; Risks and Opportunities," *Eurasia Daily Monitor*, Vol. 16, No. 142, October 15, 2019.

———, "The 'Hybrid' Role of Russian Mercenaries, PMCs and Irregulars in Moscow's Scramble for Africa," Jamestown Foundation, January 10, 2020a.

———, "Russian Inroads into Central Africa (Part Two)," *Eurasia Daily Monitor*, Vol. 17, No. 59, April 29, 2020b.

———, "Chinese Private Security Contractors: New Trends and Future Prospects," *China Brief*, Vol. 20, No. 9, May 15, 2020c.

———, "Russian Private Military Contractors in Sub-Saharan Africa," *Russie.Nei.Visions*, No. 120, September 2020d.

Sun Yi [孙奕], "Xi Jinping Meets Mozambican President Nyusi" ["习近平会见莫桑比克总统纽西"], China Military Net [中国军网], September 1, 2018.

Sunday, Odita, "Nigeria Signs Military-Technical Cooperation Treaty with Russia," *The Guardian*, August 26, 2021.

Swedish Armed Forces Headquarters, "Swedish Senior Position in Task Force Takuba," September 16, 2021.

Sysoeva, Anna, and Ilya Kabanov, "Kak Rossii I EAES Obezpecit Svoyi Interesi V Afrike Odnim Klikom" ["How Russia and the EAEU Secure Their Interests in Africa with One Click"], Russian International Affairs Council, August 29, 2019.

Tareke, Gebru, "The Ethiopia-Somalia War of 1977 Revisited," *International Journal of African Historical Studies*, Vol. 33, No. 3, 2000, pp. 635–667.

Taylor, Ian, "Taylor on Chau, 'Exploiting Africa: The Influence of Maoist China in Algeria, Ghana, and Tanzania,'" *H-Asia*, April 2015.

Teil, Peter E., "United States Africa Command Posture and Requirements and IPL Overview," U.S. Africa Command, 2018.

Tham, Engen, Ben Blanchard, and Wang Jing, "Chinese Warships Enter East Indian Ocean amid Maldives Tensions," Reuters, February 20, 2018.

Thomson, David, "The Slow Decline of French Influence in Africa," France 24, February 15, 2010.

Tierney, Dominic, "The Future of Sino-US Proxy War," *Texas National Security Review*, Vol. 4, No. 2, Spring 2021, pp. 49–73.

Tiezzi, Shannon, "Chinese Nationals Evacuate Yemen on PLA Navy Frigate," *The Diplomat*, March 30, 2015.

———, "FOCAC Turns 20: Deborah Brautigam on China-Africa Relations," *The Diplomat*, December 2, 2020.

Torreon, Barbara Salazar, and Sofia Plagakis, *Instances of Use of United States Armed Forces Abroad, 1798–2021*, Washington, D.C.: Congressional Research Service, R42738, September 8, 2021.

Townsend, Stephen J., general, U.S. Army, "A Secure and Stable Africa Is an Enduring American Interest," statement before the U.S. Senate Armed Services Committee, Washington, D.C., January 30, 2020.

———, general, U.S. Army, "Africa: Securing U.S. Interests, Preserving Strategic Options," statement before the U.S. Senate Armed Services Committee, Washington, D.C., April 20, 2021.

Toyana, Mfuneko, "European Union Agrees to Help Mozambique Tackle Insurgency: Statement," Reuters, October 14, 2020.

"Twitter's Decision to Base in Ghana Raises Questions About Nigeria's Role as West Africa's Tech Hub," 14 North, April 26, 2021.

Ugbem, Erima Comfort, Ayokunle Olumuyiwa Omobowale, and Akinpelu Olanrewaju Olutayo, "Racial Politics and Hausa-Fulani Dominant Identity in Colonial and Post-Colonial Northern Nigeria," *Nigerian Journal of Sociology and Anthropology*, Vol. 17, No. 1, June 2019, pp. 87–102.

United Nations Children's Fund, "Civilian Joint Task Force in Northeast Nigeria Signs Action Plan to End Recruitment of Children," press release, September 15, 2017.

United Nations Department of Economic and Social Affairs, "International Migrant Stock: The 2017 Revision," webpage, undated. As of July 7, 2021: https://www.un.org/en/development/desa/population/migration/data/estimates2/estimates17.asp

United Nations Human Rights Council, "CAR: Experts Alarmed by Government's Use of 'Russian Trainers,' Close Contacts with UN Peacekeepers," press release, March 31, 2021.

United Nations Office of the High Commissioner for Human Rights, *Public Report on Violation of Human Rights and International Humanitarian Law in the Central African Republic During the Electoral Period, July 2020–June 2021*, Geneva, August 4, 2021.

"UPDATE 1-Mozambique Seeks Targeted Foreign Support to Help Tackle Insurgency—President," Reuters, April 7, 2021.

Uppsala Conflict Data Program, web tool, Uppsala University Department of Peace and Conflict Research, undated. As of April 14, 2022: https://ucdp.uu.se

Uppsala University Department of Peace and Conflict Research, "Independent Variables," webpage, undated. As of September 4, 2021: https://www.pcr.uu.se/research/views/methodology/about_the_data/independent-variables

———, "About ViEWS," webpage, last modified April 25, 2022. As of April 27, 2022: https://www.pcr.uu.se/research/views/about-views/

"US Accuses China of Pointing Lasers at Pilots from Djibouti Base," BBC News, May 4, 2018.

U.S. Africa Command, "State Partnership Program," webpage, undated. As of August 30, 2021: https://www.africom.mil/what-we-do/security-cooperation/state-partnership-program

———, "Russia, Wagner Group Continue Military Involvement in Libya," press release, July 24, 2020.

U.S. Africa Command Public Affairs, "AFRICOM Commander Conducts Visit to Manda Bay," U.S. Africa Command, January 17, 2021.

U.S. Agency for Global Media, "Middle East Broadcasting Networks," webpage, undated. As of December 13, 2021: https://www.usagm.gov/networks/mbn

———, *FY 2020 Performance and Accountability Report*, Washington, D.C., November 16, 2020.

U.S. Agency for International Development, "U.S. Overseas Loans and Grants: Obligations and Loan Authorizations, July 1, 1945–September 30, 2019," webpage, February 24, 2021a. As of April 9, 2022: https://foreignassistance.gov/reports

———, "U.S. Delivers Humanitarian Relief Supplies in Response to Insecurity in Mozambique," press release, May 6, 2021b.

USAID—*See* U.S. Agency for International Development.

U.S. Air Force, "C-17 Globemaster III," webpage, undated-a. As of December 13, 2021:
https://www.af.mil/About-Us/Fact-Sheets/Display/Article/1529726/c-17-globemaster-iii

———, "HH-60G Pave Hawk," webpage, undated-b. As of December 13, 2021:
https://www.af.mil/About-Us/Fact-Sheets/Display/Article/104508/hh-60g-pave-hawk

———, "MQ-9 Reaper," webpage, March 2021. As of May 20, 2022:
https://www.af.mil/About-Us/Fact-Sheets/Display/Article/104470/mq-9-reaper

U.S. Air Forces in Europe and Air Forces Africa, "U.S. Air Force MQ-9 Seychelles Crash," press release, December 13, 2011.

U.S. Army Special Operations Command Historian, "3rd Special Forces Group History," December 7, 2018.

U.S. Bureau of Economic Analysis, "U.S. Direct Investment Position Abroad on a Historical-Cost Basis," 2019.

U.S. Census Bureau, "U.S. Trade in Goods by Country," webpage, undated. As of August 28, 2021:
https://www.census.gov/foreign-trade/balance/index.html

———, "Trade in Goods with Africa," webpage, last updated 2021a. As of August 31, 2021:
https://www.census.gov/foreign-trade/balance/c0013.html

———, "Trade in Goods with Nigeria," webpage, last updated 2021b. As of August 31, 2021:
https://www.census.gov/foreign-trade/balance/c7530.html

U.S.-China Economic and Security Review Commission, *2019 Report to Congress*, Washington, D.C.: U.S. Government Publishing Office, November 2019.

———, "China's Strategic Aims in Africa," hearing, Washington, D.C., May 8, 2020a.

———, *2020 Report to Congress*, Washington, D.C.: U.S. Government Printing Office, December 2020b.

U.S. Department of Defense, "Releases," webpage, undated. As of May 21, 2022:
https://www.defense.gov/News/Releases

———, *Summary of the 2018 National Defense Strategy of the United States of America: Sharpening the American Military's Competitive Edge*, Washington, D.C., 2018a.

———, *Assessment on U.S. Defense Implications of China's Expanding Global Access*, Washington, D.C., December 2018b.

U.S. Department of Defense and U.S. Department of State, *Foreign Military Training Report, Fiscal Years 2018 and 2019, Joint Report to Congress: Volume I*, Washington, D.C., March 13, 2019.

U.S. Department of Defense Inspector General, *Evaluation of Niger Air Base 201 Military Construction*, Washington, D.C.: U.S. Department of Defense, DODIG-2020-077, March 31, 2020.

U.S. Department of State, "Websites of U.S. Embassies, Consulates, and Diplomatic Missions," webpage, undated. As of April 14, 2022:
https://www.usembassy.gov

———, "State Department Terrorist Designations of ISIS Affiliates and Leaders in the Democratic Republic of the Congo and Mozambique," Office of the Spokesperson, March 10, 2021.

U.S. Department of the Treasury, "Countering America's Adversaries Through Sanctions Act–Related Sanctions," August 2, 2017.

U.S. Embassy and Consulate in Nigeria, "U.S. Government Supports Nigeria in Fight Against Cybercrime and Financial Fraud," May 24, 2017.

U.S. Embassy in Mozambique, "Sections & Offices," webpage, undated. As of June 16, 2021:
https://mz.usembassy.gov/embassy/maputo/sections-offices

———, "U.S. Embassy Donates Boarding Team Equipment to Mozambican Navy," press release, August 24, 2019.

———, "U.S. Government Provides Military Training to Mozambican Marines," press release, March 15, 2021a.

———, "U.S. Embassy and Ministry of Defense Commemorate Security Cooperation at Closing Ceremony of JCET training exercise," press release, May 5, 2021b.

———, "U.S. Government Launches Third Military Exercise with Mozambican Armed Forces," press release, February 2, 2022.

U.S. Energy Information Administration, "Total Energy Production 2019," webpage, 2019. As of August 27, 2021:
https://www.eia.gov/international/rankings/
world?pa=12&u=0&f=A&v=none&y=01%2F01%2F2019

———, "Mozambique," webpage, July 2020. As of July 7, 2021:
https://www.eia.gov/international/analysis/country/MOZ

———, "U.S. Total Crude Oil and Products Imports," webpage, last updated June 2021. As of August 1, 2021:
http://www.eia.gov/dnav/pet/pet_move_impcus_a2_nus_ep00_im0_mbbl_m.htm

U.S. Government Accountability Office, *Military Equipment: Observations on the Transfer of Excess Humvees to Foreign Governments*, Washington, D.C., GAO-20-189, February 2020.

"V Afrike Obyavilis Noviye Naemniki Vmesto CHVK Vagnera" ["New Mercenaries Have Appeared in Africa Instead of OMC Wagner"], Lenta.ru, April 10, 2020.

"V Kremle Opovergli Prisustviye Rossiiskih Voyennih V Mozambike" ["The Kremlin Denied the Presence of Russian Military in Mozambique"], Interfax, October 8, 2019.

Van Hooft, Paul, "Don't Knock Yourself Out: How America Can Turn the Tables on China by Giving Up the Fight for Command of the Seas," *War on the Rocks*, February 23, 2021.

Van Sickle, Jan, and John A. Dutton, "The Control Segment," Penn State College of Earth and Mineral Sciences, 2020. As of May 28, 2021:
https://www.e-education.psu.edu/geog862/node/1718

Vandiver, John, "U.S. Special Operations Forces Train Mozambique Troops to Counter ISIS Threat," *Stars and Stripes*, March 16, 2021.

ViEWS: The Violence Early-Warning System, web tool, Uppsala University Department of Peace and Conflict Research, undated. As of June 16, 2022:
https://viewsforecasting.org

Vines, Alex, "Why the Insurgency in Northern Mozambique Has Got Worse," Chatham House, April 1, 2020a.

———, "China's Southern Africa Debt Deals Reveal a Wider Plan," Chatham House, December 10, 2020b.

————, "Violence, Peacebuilding, and Elite Bargains in Mozambique Since Independence," in Terence McNamee and Monde Muyangwa, eds., *The State of Peacebuilding in Africa: Lessons Learned for Policymakers and Practitioners*, Cham, Switzerland: Palgrave Macmillan, 2021, pp. 321–342.

Voice of America, "Programs," webpage, undated. As of August 10, 2021: https://www.voanews.com/programs/radio

Voice of America Afrique, homepage, undated. As of May 20, 2022: https://www.voaafrique.com/AVA

von Uexkull, Nina, and Therése Pettersson, "Issues and Actors in African Nonstate Conflicts: A New Data Set," *International Interactions*, Vol. 44, No. 5, 2018, pp. 953–968.

Waldhauser, Thomas D., general, U.S. Marine Corps, "A Secure, Stable, and Prosperous Africa Is an Enduring American Interest," statement before the U.S. Senate Committee on Armed Services, Washington, D.C., February 7, 2019.

Wan Lingying [万玲英], "Changes and Prospects of Africa's International Position" ["非洲国际地位的变化及前景"], China Institute of International Studies [中国国际问题研究院], June 4, 2013.

Wang Hongyi [王洪一], "The Influence of New Security Challenges in Africa on Sino-African Cooperation" ["非洲安全新挑战及其对中非合作的影响"], China Institute of International Studies [中国国际问题研究院], July 25, 2018.

————, "Sino African Industrial Parks: Progress, Problems, and Solutions" ["中非共建产业园:历程、问题与解决思路"], Chinese Institute of International Studies [中国国际问题研究院], March 5, 2019.

Warner, Michael, "Central Intelligence: Origin and Evolution—Historical Perspective," in Central Intelligence Agency, *The Creation of the Intelligence Community: Founding Documents*, Washington, D.C.: U.S. Government Printing Office, 2009, pp. 5–18.

Wasserman, Herman, and Dani Madrid-Morales, "How Influential Are Chinese Media in Africa? An Audience Analysis in Kenya and South Africa," *International Journal of Communication*, Vol. 12, May 14, 2018, pp. 2212–2231.

Watts, Stephen, Bryan Frederick, Nathan Chandler, Mark Toukan, Christian Curriden, Erik E. Mueller, Edward Geist, Ariane M. Tabatabai, Sara Plana, Brandon Corbin, and Jeffrey Martini, *Proxy Warfare in Strategic Competition: Overarching Findings and Recommendations*, Santa Monica, Calif.: RAND Corporation, RR-A307-1, 2023. As of March 24, 2023: https://www.rand.org/pubs/research_reports/RRA307-1.html

Wehrey, Frederic, "'Our Hearts Are Dead.' After 9 Years of Civil War, Libyans Are Tired of Being Pawns in a Geopolitical Game of Chess," *Time*, February 12, 2020.

Wei Hong [韦红] and Li Ciyuan [李次园], "The Development of the Indian Ocean Rim Alliance and China's Strategies for Engagement" ["环印度洋联盟的发展及中国的合作策略"], China Institute of International Studies [中国国际问题研究院], March 16, 2018.

Weiner, Tim, *Legacy of Ashes: The History of the CIA*, New York: Anchor Books, 2007.

Westad, Odd Arne, *The Global Cold War: Third World Interventions and the Making of Our Times*, New York: Cambridge University Press, 2005.

Wezeman, Pieter D., Alexandra Kuimova, and Siemon T. Wezeman, *Trends in International Arms Transfers, 2020*, Stockholm: Stockholm International Peace Research Institute, March 2021.

Whitlock, Craig, "U.S. Expands Secret Intelligence Operations in Africa," *Washington Post*, June 13, 2012.

Wiesmann, Gerrit, "Joseph Odindo on China's Influence on African Media," Mercator Institute for China Studies, January 29, 2021.

Wilkins, Sam, "Does America Need an Africa Strategy?" *War on the Rocks*, April 2, 2020.

Williams, Katie Bo, "AFRICOM Adds Logistics Hub in West Africa, Hinting at an Enduring US Presence," *Defense One*, February 20, 2019.

Windrem, Robert, and Jim Miklaszewski, "Why U.S. Drones Aren't Flying over Nigeria (And What They Could Do If They Were)," NBC News, May 9, 2014.

World Bank, "GDP (Current US$)," webpage, undated-a. As of September 1, 2021:
https://data.worldbank.org/indicator/NY.GDP.MKTP.CD

———, "GDP Per Capita (Current US$)—Mozambique," webpage, undated-b. As of May 20, 2022:
https://data.worldbank.org/indicator/
NY.GDP.PCAP.CD?locations=MZ&most_recent_value_desc=false

———, "Worldwide Governance Indicators," webpage, undated-c. As of May 20, 2022:
http://info.worldbank.org/governance/wgi

World Integrated Trade Solution, web tool, undated-a. As of August 27, 2021:
https://wits.worldbank.org/

———, "Russia Trade," webpage, undated-b. As of August 30, 2021:
https://wits.worldbank.org/countrysnapshot/en/RUSSIA

———, "United States Minerals Imports by Country and Region in US$ Thousand 2019," webpage, undated-c. As of August 30, 2021:
https://wits.worldbank.org/CountryProfile/en/Country/USA/Year/2019/TradeFlow/Import/
Partner/all/Product/25-26_Minerals#

World Population Review, "Nigeria Population 2021 (Live)," webpage, last updated 2021. As of August 10, 2021:
https://worldpopulationreview.com/countries/nigeria-population

Xing Jianqiao, "China, Senegal Continue to Deepen Comprehensive Strategic Cooperative Partnership in 2019," Xinhua, December 27, 2019.

Xinhua, "Backgrounder: China's Major Overseas Evacuations in Recent Years," *China Daily*, March 30, 2015.

Yellinek, Roie, and Elizabeth Chen, "The '22 vs. 50' Diplomatic Split Between the West and China over Xinjiang and Human Rights," *China Brief*, Vol. 19, No. 22, December 31, 2019.

Yiqin Fu, "UNView: United Nations General Assembly Voting Patterns (1946–2019)," webpage, undated. As of May 20, 2022:
https://dataviz.yiqinfu.com/unview/

Yun Sun, "American Companies and Chinese Belt and Road in Africa," Brookings Institution, July 11, 2018.

Zamfir, Ionel, "Security Situation in Mozambique," European Parliamentary Research Service, July 2021.

Zeng Aiping [曾爱平], "China and Africa Explore Exchanges on Governance Experience" ["中国非洲治国理政经验交流初探"], China Institute of International Studies [中国国际问题研究院], October 31, 2016.

Zhang Ying [张颖], "China's Africa Diplomacy: Concepts and Practice" ["中国对非洲外交: 理念与实践"], China Institute of International Studies [中国国际问题研究院], January 22, 2018.

Zhao Chenguang [赵晨光], "America's 'New Africa Policy:' Changes and Holdovers" ["美国'新非洲战略': 变与不变"], China Institute of International Studies [中国国际问题研究院], November 7, 2019.

Zhou, Jiayi, Karl Hallding, and Guoyi Han, "The Trouble with China's 'One Belt One Road' Strategy," *The Diplomat*, June 26, 2015.